The Butterfly Route

MICHELLE LAMPHERE

Mark,
Wishing you safe
and happy adventures!
Michelle

ISBN: 0-9967911-1-6
ISBN-13: 978-0-9967911-1-3
E-book ISBN: 978-0-9967911-2-0

Editor: Michelle Lamphere

Set in Garamond
Printed and bound in the United States

Photo by Brian Clarke
Cover design by Sonakshi Botham

Gumbo Lily Press
P.O. Box 9776
Rapid City, SD 57709
GumboLilyPress.com

For my mother.

Ladies first, Dad. The next one will be for you.

What is life?
It is the flash of a firefly in the night.
It is the breath of a buffalo in the winter time.
It is the little shadow which runs across the grass
and loses itself in the sunset.
Crowfoot, Blackfoot warrior and Chief

CONTENTS

Prologue - Oh, my God. What have I done?

As the dust clears, I sit up and try to gather my wits about me. Well, that sucked. Sort of a steel horse version of a rodeo that ended with me getting dumped on my butt.

Brian's silhouette shrinks into the distance as I tug at my chin strap and take my helmet off. I feel strange. My heart is racing, which is to be expected after just coming off my motorcycle in the middle of nowhere. But something's not right.

Am I okay? I hope I am.

I take a deep breath and try to calm myself. Betty is on her side in the middle of the gravel road ahead of me. I put my hands on the ground to brace myself as I move to stand. I gather my legs up underneath me, or try to, but it doesn't happen. My right leg bends at the knee, but my left leg just lays there.

Uh oh. Houston, we have a problem.

I try again, to make my leg react in a way I have thousands of times before, to contract my thigh muscles and pull my left leg toward me, bending it at the knee and moving it from an outstretched position to one that will allow me to stand. I'm really concentrating. But still nothing.

As I move my muscles I can feel the bones in my lower left leg grind against each other and I look down to see my foot lying awkwardly flatly against the ground. Houston?

Brian disappears over the next hill and suddenly I feel very helpless. And very alone. There goes my heart again, racing even faster. I see the yellow plastic case of the satellite phone stuffed under the black mesh cargo net stretched across Betty's backside. But it's small comfort to me from even just ten feet away.

Dozens of thoughts flood my mind in an instant. Am I really hurt? Is it just my leg or could it be something more that I don't feel yet? Am I going to be okay? Do I wait for Brian to come back? Or do I drag myself over to the phone? How will we get help way out here? And how long will it take?

Why did I decide to be unemployed and homeless only to end up here? What about Brian's visa expiration?

Oh, my God. What have I done? What about the rest of my trip?

What's that noise? Was that a bear?!

Oh, my God.

1 WHEN IT'S TIME TO MOVE ON

I wish I could show you when you are lonely or in darkness the astonishing light of your own being.

-Hafez

Nearly two years before…

As the other girls finish dressing for dinner in our hotel room, my phone buzzes to life with an incoming text. Giggles soften into the background as I focus on the message. It's my bosses, downstairs at a lobby bar asking me to come down before my team joins us for dinner. "On my way" is my reply as I slip on my heels and head to the elevator.

The past few days of meetings and interaction with other people in our industry has been fantastic, reinvigorating. This has been an incredibly tough year, but tonight, I feel like we've turned an invisible corner.

They're sitting at a cocktail table. As I sit down, one of them pulls out a gift bag and places it on the table. Inside is a handwritten message thanking me for all I've done for their family the past few months, along with a new iPad. It's uncharacteristically thoughtful of them and I'm choked up.

For a moment, it occurs to me that their father might have been very proud of them, and that the gesture is something he might have done. I wish he could be here with us tonight. It would erase the crushing grief of the recent past.

Two months ago, he reportedly committed suicide. His boys understandably haven't been in the office much since his death, which means I've had to make some big decisions without them. Our multi-million-dollar hotel remodel project is my responsibility. I'm especially motivated to make sure this renovation is a success because, as the owners have told me the past few years, a small part of the renovated hotel will be mine. I want them to be happy with the end result and their input could help ensure that, but I know they've had more important family issues to deal with.

A couple of years ago, their dad drew up a contract to transfer a small share of ownership to me. For the last two years, we openly discussed my upcoming ownership at our corporate meetings, and it remained an item on our weekly agendas. But in the months since their father's death, something has been different. His sons, now my bosses, seem to be stalling on transferring ownership to me. I have an uneasy feeling they may be backing out of giving me an ownership share.

But maybe I've been reading things wrong. I thank them both and slide the gift back into the pastel bag. It's almost time for dinner. As our team members arrive I rise to greet them. This is going to be a good night.

Six weeks later…

My paycheck doesn't look quite right. At first I think the Christmas bonuses must not have come through yet. My paystub shows $1000 was added, the same amount I've gotten as a bonus the past few years, but there's a deduction I don't understand. At over $700, it's roughly my entire Christmas bonus, after taxes, going right back out.

I walk over to our corporate accountant's office and peek in. "Hey, quick question. Can you tell me what this deduction is for?"

"Sure," she replies as she types on her keyboard, pulling up the detail. "That's the deduction for the iPad the owners gave you."

"Um...but they told me it was a gift."

"Not according to the note they gave me telling me to take it out of your paycheck," says the accountant.

"Oh, okay. Thank you." Out I go. Had I misunderstood?

I go home later that night and re-read the card they gave me with the iPad, having kept it out of sentimentality. I hadn't read it wrong.

The weeks after Las Vegas fly by. The manager at the remodel hotel gives his notice not long after the convention, so I make plans to move across the state to manage the property. The owners want to hold off on hiring someone, forcing me to cover two full-time jobs. In early December, I gather my things and my 12-year-old Weimaraner, True, and head to the project hotel to plunge into 65-hour work weeks.

Almost every employee at the hotel and an assistant from my office steps up to help however they can. After three months, we are making good progress on the remodel. I decide to go home for the weekend to get a break from my 24/7 responsibilities for a couple of days. True and I make the 5-hour trip across South Dakota on icy roads.

Late one evening I stop by the corporate office to go through my mail. As I drop a note on the office manager's desk, I see an envelope addressed to me. I pick it up and tear it open, hoping I've not missed anything important while I was out of town. Inside is a letter that catches me off guard. It's from the attorney of the estate of the deceased father of the boys, listing me as a creditor and requiring me to file a claim for any interest I have against his estate. If I don't, I could lose it.

The corporate accounting office has my personal mailing address on file. So why would anyone mail this letter to an office I'm not working at? It looks to me as though the boys had the letter mailed to their office, knowing I am working out of town and will likely never see it. Maybe they hope I won't get an estate claim filed in time and will lose my rights to any interest in the hotel. I'm stunned.

As a precaution, I consult with an attorney friend who suggests I file a claim against the estate regardless of what my bosses say. Otherwise, I risk losing any rights I have to my share. It puts me in an uncomfortable and awkward position. I'm afraid if I file a claim it will only deteriorate our working relationship and that they might be vindictive toward me. But I don't trust that they'll honor their promise if I don't. The first twelve years that I worked for their father, our company didn't have a retirement plan and he told me the share of ownership was to help make up for that. I don't trust them enough to risk my future. Their father's wishes and their own promises to me seem to mean nothing.

Not even a six-figure-a-year salary is worth staying in what I see as an unhappy environment that lacks trust and integrity. With only two days left, I decide to handwrite a claim against the estate and fax it to the courthouse myself.

When the boys find out, I feel like I'm in the doghouse. Their attorney disputes the claim, saying the brothers never knew about their father's promise. It's a tough realization, after nearly twenty years working for their family, to see they likely had no intention of honoring their promise. It's time for Plan B.

Two summers before, I'd met an Englishman who was traveling through South Dakota on his motorcycle. Brian had shipped his bike from England to Buenos Aires, ridden it south to Ushuaia, at the southern tip of Argentina, and then turned north and headed for Alaska. His stories and photos from that journey were incredible I remember wishing I could take off on an adventure like his, and mentally put it on my "someday" list. While I'd always loved to travel, and had ridden motorcycles for years, it never occurred to me to combine travel with my motorcycle.

He and I rode from South Dakota to Ontario to attend a Horizons Unlimited event where I had the great fortune to attend a "women only" class. Two of the loveliest Australian women, were there too, and offered sage, hard-earned advice from many years of traveling with their husbands by motorcycle. Carol-Ann Duval and her husband, Ken, had been traveling for many years all over the world. Shirley Hardy-Rix and her husband, Brian, had done the same, and had stories about the beautiful people of Iran that I found particularly interesting. Another women at the meeting gave me her email address and offered to connect me with some of her friends if I ever decided to ride through Mexico. I was surprised by their generosity and support, something I was only beginning to experience from other travelers.

On the way back to South Dakota, I told Brian that if the owners didn't give me the ownership that was promised to me, I planned to resign and take some time to travel. Now that possibility could become a reality.

I start a countdown. With patience, I hope to stay with the company until spring. I want to leave the employees prepared for a good year so they aren't affected by a transition. I spend the next few months preparing – put my house on the market, put my belongings in storage, etc.

My father agrees to take True, which gives me peace of mind. Out of everything, leaving her will be the hardest part. If all goes well, I will resign in May and hit the road in June.

Reading blogs and books fills my spare time as I try to prepare for what most people must think is a crazy idea. Boxes of gear fill my living room while I test equipment, clothing and shelter options. I sell my Harley and buy a Kawasaki KLR650, a bike good both for highway and off-road travel. I assign a power of attorney to a friend and write out a will. I practice Spanish, and review maps and routes. I'm not sure which is outpacing the other, my excitement or my fear. The reality of my impending untethering is setting in and I'm terrified about the risks ahead, mostly because everything is unfamiliar.

Slowly, I liquidate my assets, both to save money on storage and to convert some of my possessions to money for the trip. I sell jewelry and other things on eBay. I give away furniture and hold a rummage sale. I donate boxes of books to the local library, and boxes of who-knows-what to local charities. A friend once told me that a person spends the first half of his life trying to accumulate things and the second half trying to get rid of them. While I pack up my accumulations, I think to myself that I must have entered the last half of my life.

For months, I steadily prepare for my freedom. Even though we've been together for nearly two years, I wonder where Brian and I stand and force myself to think about whether or not I would take this trip without him. I run through scenarios in my head about us splitting up on the road and me continuing on my own. I'm not deterred. I want this trip for me, no matter how it turns out.

Finally, around Memorial Day I sit down with the owners and tender my resignation. I'm relieved it's over. Maybe someday I will thank the boys for giving me the courage to finally leave that unhealthy environment. After all, what I see as a breaking of their promise was the catalyst that motivated me to leave. Even if I never get a penny, I will think of it as the price I'm willing to pay to be healthy and whole again, to have my life back.

As I walk out of the corporate office for the last time after almost 21 years, I feel like I'm leaving a sinking ship and climbing into a life raft that I built for myself.

After my last day of work, I go home and start chipping away at my enormous list of preparations. I spend the afternoons with True snuggling with her on the couch while she naps. It's a luxury, even if I don't know it yet. She's been sleeping more than usual the past several months. Somehow, seemingly overnight, my 8-week-old girl has grown into an old dog with a gray muzzle and cloudy eyes. Twelve years have gone by in a flash.

She was diagnosed with hip dysplasia at age 6 which I treat with arthritis meds and supplements. At the time of her diagnosis, her veterinarian said he hoped to keep her comfortable for a couple of years, and somehow, we've managed six. Despite having moved to the basement to provide her one-level living, True's health is still deteriorating.

A couple of weeks before I resigned from my job I took her to the vet for a checkup before I planned to leave her with my dad. I was struggling with the idea because I knew she had limited time left, and I didn't want to miss a single day. Dr. Stonecipher and I had a heart-to-heart. True had been having bad days, more frequently than in the past. While I had always kept careful watch over her, wanting to be sure she still had more good days than bad, the count was starting to even up.

Everything was on the table as far as my plans, and I put him in the unenviable position of being completely honest about what was best for True. He said he couldn't be sure, but that he thought we could keep her comfortable for the summer.

"But...," he went further, "if she were my dog I wouldn't put her through another winter."

I was crushed. My unrealistic dream of having her waiting for me when I come home from the trip evaporated. I'd had her whole life to see this coming and six long years of managing her pain to come to terms with what needed to be done, but I still wasn't prepared. I took her home and decided to live in the moment.

Three days after I finish work, True has an exceptionally bad day. To take it a step further than her normal bad day, she decides not to eat. That's new, and not in a good way. One thing that's always been the litmus test for my girl is whether or not she'll eat. Appetite has never been a problem for her. She knows the words "cookie" and "treat" better than her own name. Now I know exactly how bad she feels.

I've researched online about where to draw the line between a dog having good quality of life and prolonging suffering. Let me save you the mystery - it's not black and white, and it's not easy. It's a horrible thing to worry over. A friend of mine who spent her life working with dogs offered this succinct insight, "When it comes to a life of pain, I would rather end a dog's life too early than too late."

My informal plan was to keep True going as long as she had more good days than bad, but the pendulum may have just swung the other way. Less than a week later, I make the agonizing decision. I call the vet and ask him to come to my house on a Friday to euthanize True. Brian and I keep packing, but I'm in a daze. I put my body on auto-pilot to keep doing the physical work and let my mind go somewhere else to cope.

The next day her appetite picks up again and I consider canceling the vet, but I don't. I know this good day should be treated as the blessing it is and not something I can count on. Treats have been limited as her metabolism slowed in recent years because any extra pounds are hard on her joints. But now that rule is forgotten.

Thursday dawns to an early morning walk in the backyard, but True doesn't have the strength to lift her back legs over a few small stones to get to the lawn. Her back feet knuckle over worse than ever before. She comes back to the house and goes straight to her bed and collapses. She hurts. But thankfully, she's hungry. I run out and buy her a package of hamburger and a block of cheese. She gets little dollops of ice cream delivered to her bed on a spoon.

On Friday, she wakes with her usual need to go outside. She's slow-moving and squinty-eyed. She stumbles over blades of grass and it takes her ages to squat at a painful-looking angle before she finally goes to the bathroom. She slowly makes her way back into the house and over to my bed, and looks up longingly. She lifts her front legs slightly to show me where she wants to be. I lift her up to the bed, and we snuggle together and go back to sleep.

A while later I awaken to sunlight shining through my bedroom window telling me the day is progressing. Only hours left with her now. I'm afraid to look at my watch to know how little time there is. True and I have spent nearly every minute together for the past few years, and I've barely left her side the past week. I debate about canceling the vet, selfishly hoping for a few more days. But in my heart, I know she's in pain and I force myself to remember that and to be strong for her.

She sleeps nearly all day, only waking long enough to get treats and lick my hand now and then. In the afternoon, I carry her bed to the back lawn and lay down with her for a while in the sun as it warms her bones. She groans in contentment while I rub her ears and back. A lilac butterfly flitters around her nose for a moment and then wings away.

Late in the day, I give her a teaspoon of cream cheese laced with Valium from the vet. I'm not prepared for how hard it is to push the pills into the cheese and carry the spoon downstairs to True, knowing what's coming. I have to remind myself that this is likely the only way that keeps her from experiencing a drawn-out and painful death. I can end it quickly and comfortably for her, and be here with her to the very end.

As she licks and nibbles the big dollop, I start to cry. I'm about to lose my best friend.

Sometimes life works out how it's meant to, without our knowing or having any control over any of it. I haven't had time to think about anything. Things are moving too quickly to allow me to have time to think. All I can do is hope that it's all working out as it should.

In the span of six weeks, I pack up and move my belongings to storage, pack my bike for a year-long international adventure, sell both my house and a rental property, come to terms with the end of my 21-year executive career and the loss of the retirement I'd been promised. Hardest of all, I had to bring to a close 12 years of companionship with my beloved dog.

True has been gone just over a week, and I can still barely get through a few hours without getting teary-eyed. My packing and organizing have at least kept my body moving, but my mind is still curled up with her taking a nap. Brian has been my rock. His presence alone is comforting and he's tried his best to ease my pain, if only by sharing it with me. In the last two years of her life,

True loved him as much as she loved me. What is it they say about pain shared being halved and love shared being doubled? I'm grateful to have him.

My best friend, Heather, flew in to see me off. She keeps me going. She's my cheerleader, even when I don't know I need cheering on. Most of my furniture is gone and dozens of boxes are already gathering a fine layer of dust in a storage unit. True is already back with me again, and I will keep her ashes in a box of my belongings. I'm broken-hearted when I think that she will be waiting for me when I come home, but not in the way I had hoped. It's amazing how much there has been to do, and yet, somehow, I'm getting it done. We plan to leave in 2-3 days.

We haven't made much of a game plan, or even looked at a map, strangely. Brian has been talking about riding north and east across the U.S. toward Canada. Somewhere he heard about the Trans-Labrador Highway, the TLH, and has recently put it in our route. Unfortunately, adding it to the itinerary puts us under some serious time pressure from the start. Brian's visa for the U.S. runs out 90 days after he arrived, in late July. It's already nearing the end of June. That means we have to cross into Canada, complete the TLH, get back into the U.S., and ride to the Mexico border in less than three weeks. Hard work by anyone's standards. Right or wrong, I'm just going with the flow. We'll give it our best effort and figure it out as we go. But I'm nervous.

The TLH spooks me a little. There isn't a lot of information online about it, but what I do find confirms that it's remote and daunting. Just the sheer number of miles we have to cover gives me pause, not to mention what comes after.

Crossing into Mexico terrifies me. I've had friends and relatives ask if I plan to take a gun with me. Mexico has a bad reputation and puts fear in the heart of many Americans. People get "disappeared" there, and I don't want to be one of them. The countries south of Mexico sound even worse from the little I've read about them. Sometimes being informed isn't a good thing. It causes more worry and dread than the colossal mountain of fear I already carry around about this trip. It's overwhelming.

I stop reading Department of State warnings, and decide to trust that since so many people ride safely through these countries each year, I should be okay. I file away my fear of mugging, robbery, rape and kidnapping. I feel strong enough and prepared enough to avoid or survive most anything. As long as I don't have a bad wreck in the middle of nowhere I should be okay.

The night before we leave, Brian, Heather and I have dinner with friends. They present me with a surprise going-away present. As I peel back the tissue paper I find a picture frame. In it is a photo of my mother from nearly 40 years ago, with a relaxed smile on her face. Perched on her lap is the "me" of a lifetime ago. It is an especially touching gift.

Strangely, my friends have never met my mother and I have no idea how they've just presented me with a photo of my mother and little-girl me. It turns out, a friend of theirs and my mother were friends nearly 40 years back. I'd met their friend at a party some time ago, but she never knew my last name.

About a week ago, she saw a post in the business section of the local paper about my leaving the hotel company. It showed my last name which caused her to recognize me as the daughter of her friend from all those years before. She had no way of knowing that the little blonde girl in one of her photographs from decades ago was connected to her through mutual friends.

She sorted through her photo albums and found the old picture that she took of my mother and me, framed it, and gave it to our friends to pass along to me on the eve of my departure. What an incredibly small world. What a thoughtful and serendipitous gift.

The next morning is the 25th of June. From the moment I climb up from my blanket bed on the floor of my now empty house, my heart is racing and I feel sick. I'm terrified, of today and every day that will come after it before I'm safely back home. I want to stay home, go back to bed, and stay safe. I want my friends and family and a familiar life. But I want this adventure just a little bit more.

It's too daunting to think of making a 20,000-mile journey to Ushuaia, across two continents. Instead I do as Brian suggests, I think of each day separately. Today I will ride 300 miles. Tomorrow I will ride another 300 miles, and so on. In small pieces, the journey doesn't seem so surreal or overwhelming.

As much as I have prepared, I'm not sure that I will ever really be ready to go. Life is like that. There is very rarely a perfect time, or a perfect set of conditions. Maybe all we can do is to prepare the best we can and take a leap of faith, and then do the best we can as we go along. As I stand here on the precipice of this enormous journey, it's a plan that I hope will work for me.

I load last-minute things onto my bike late in the morning, and finally, there is nothing left in the house but my riding gear. I take some pills for a headache and cold I have coming on. I dress and put on my boots, grab my tank bag and close the house, locking its front door. I carry my helmet out to the drive where my bike warms up. Out of habit, stash my house key in an inner pocket in my tank bag, absent-mindedly thinking I need to keep it safe so I still have it when I get back. It won't occur to me for another 14 months that I'm carrying a key to a home I no longer own.

I throw my right leg over the bike and stand it up, pushing my kickstand back. As I adjust my mirrors with shaking hands and check the balance of my bike and its heavy luggage, a small yellow butterfly flutters around my helmet and then wanders off to the lilac bush on the side of the driveway.

I look at Brian through my right-side mirror and see him nod, my sign that he is ready to go. I pull in the clutch, put the bike in gear, take a quick last look at the home and life I'm leaving behind and then release the clutch and roll out of the drive.

2 ADVENTURE BEGINS

A journey of a thousand miles must begin with a single step.
-Lao Tzu

These first few weeks will be a whirlwind, thousands of miles have to be covered quickly. On the first day, we ride 350 miles, all on South Dakota highways, crossing to the other side of the state. We meet friends for celebratory beers after my first official day of a six-month to one-year adventure.

Our second day takes us south, still on interstates, which helps us hurry our way across the U.S. toward Canada and the Trans-Labrador Highway. I-29 leads me to my first state line crossing of the trip, into Iowa. Not knowing why, I blow a kiss to South Dakota from my helmet as I leave.

We hit stopped traffic near Sioux City and shut off the bikes, sandwiched between trucks and cars. I'm baking in the sun in my heavy black riding gear. My cold is getting worse and the dust and heat aren't helping. Brian parked in the shade of a semi-trailer and isn't taking the brunt of the sun, but there isn't room for both of us in the shadow. Each minute we sit feels like ten, and I grow impatient and bitchy. I tweet on my new account a mini tirade about the place feeling like hell. Later in the day a friend comments about my negativity, giving me a sharp reality check. Liz is a writer and spiritualist, and fellow female rider. I respect her immensely. Her words weigh heavy on my mind and help set the tone for my perspective for the rest of the trip. It's hot. Get over it. Get used to it. It's part of the journey. Besides, many people would give anything to be where I am. I chose to be here. I will try to appreciate every detail of this experience in some way.

After half an hour, we finally move, and make our way to Des Moines to stay with friends. While passing dozens of giant tri-bladed, white windmills I quickly learn to associate them with unpredictable, gusty winds crossing our path. For the rest of my trip, I will dread seeing them looming in the distance.

My friends make us a fabulous pasta dinner and welcome us into their home. It's wonderful to have a few hours with them. One of the luxuries of this trip is the chance it gives me to spend a little time with friends and family along the way. They even have two dogs to give me canine company.

We carry on the following day to Chicago. My cold is in my chest now and I rattle slightly when I breathe. Another day gets us to Vermilion, Ohio, and the day after to Syracuse, New York, after passing through my first really heavy thunderstorm.

At a fuel stop at an interstate travel plaza I see the storm ahead in the distance. I dread the thought of riding into an enormous dark cloud and silently hope it will keep moving away from us. But this too is another lesson for me. I'd been a fair-weather rider before this trip, a luxury most people can enjoy under the clear blue skies of South Dakota. I need to get comfortable with changing weather conditions. While I would likely sit and wait it out, Brian herds me out of the café and back onto the bikes to keep pushing on.

Dozens of rapid-fire random thoughts pop into my head all day, and I make a mental note to start a blog about my "Helmet Thoughts". Ridiculous, strange things…

- I ride like a girl, and I'm good with that.

- If football is a game of inches, adventure motorcycle travel is a game of ounces. You have to pack light. Very light.
- Those pink piggy noses sticking out of the truck passing me are so cute. Oh, but wait. It's sad to think of them being crammed into that smelly trailer. Worse still to think of where they're going. Poor pink piggies.
- Something smells amazing along the road. I think it's sweet grass and clover.
- Something smells horrible along the road. I think it's a feedlot or a pig farm. Or is it road kill?
- If there is such a thing as a lead foot, can I have a lead hand?
- When the grass on the prairies of the Midwest blows in the wind, it looks exactly like the surface of the ocean, complete with waves and ripples, and birds surfing along above the whitecaps of western wheatgrass and foxtails.
- Even though I know we have to hurry to get through Canada and back into the U.S., I don't want the miles to go too fast because it means I'm moving further from my home, and my friends and family.
- No matter where I go, I will always see the world through South Dakota-colored glasses of honesty, trust and hope.
- Led Zeppelin lyrics are hard to get out of your helmet.
- If a bicycle is called a bike, and a tricycle is called a trike, why isn't a motorcycle called a mike? Wait, then people would go for a mike ride and that would be weird.

Stop daydreaming, girl, and pay attention to the road. Just like that, I'm back in the present moment.

After a night in Syracuse, we stop in Watertown to fill up on America's cheap fuel before we cross the border into Canada by way of Thousand Islands National Park. An arching bridge carries us over the St. Lawrence Seaway while I catch glimpses of the tiny islets that give this area its name. Sailboats drift at a snail's pace on the glass calm water. Beautiful homes line the shores. I wonder if the salad dressing came from here.

Since leaving home I've been looking for a rear tire, but I haven't had any luck yet. Everything will be closed tomorrow for Canada Day but I'm hopeful I can get one in Montreal the day after so I can break it in before we get to the Trans Lab Highway. There are fires on the TLH so we may not even be able to get through, but it might be possible to build a piecemeal back up route from the sounds of it. I know Brian is going to push for the TLH since it's his first choice.

In places, the highway sinks into the rocky landscape, giving the impression of driving through the world's shallowest canyon that is only four to eight feet deep. Stone inukshuks perched along the top edges of the shallow walls at random places along the highway make me feel like small stone guardians watch over us as we pass. Wildflowers cover everything. Miniature yellow and white daises mixed with purple rockets and yellow Queen Anne's Lace decorate miles of roadway. I spy a red-colored doe on the right side of the road and her head looks like a periscope breaking the surface of a sea of tall grass.

We ride into Ottawa, happen onto a wonderful parkway and stop for a break at a park. A man feeds Canadian geese along the riverfront, and they all seem to be enjoying it. Downy babies gather too and he makes the adults share nicely, correcting any bad behavior. A father, mother and kids riding bicycles along the river's edge stop to spark up a conversation with us. He asks about our bikes. He suggests we follow the river through the city for a lovely ride and says there are rapids further up the river. If we continue up the parkway, we will ride through downtown, the best part of the city. Just before we go, he warns us of the famous potholes of Montreal since we are headed there.

We ride through the center of town and past the Parliament buildings, past embassies and a national museum. It's beautiful. Giant red and white maple-leaf flags are everywhere, hanging from apartment balconies, businesses, and all along the streets. At an overlook, we stop for a photo of the river. It's a popular place, and crossing traffic to get into the parking lot is like playing a live game of Frogger. A sweet couple approaches us and asks about our license plates. She is Polish and her husband is Hungarian. She's heard of South Dakota and of the Polish man who carved Crazy Horse Memorial and has always wanted to see it.

They give us directions to the highway, which sound very confusing, and then wish us well and go. Brian turns out of the parking lot. As I wait for a car to go by, the couple turns around and comes back. He rolls down his window and says they're going our way and will lead us back to the Trans-Canada Highway, so we pull over and let them pass. They lead us through several turns and lots of traffic before waving and honking their horn as they turn off. We do the same as a sign of our thanks, and turn onto the eastbound highway. It's very kind of them.

Canada is lovely and spacious. As we cross into Quebec, I find myself hypnotized by the blur of trees reflected in my visor. We stop for a map and fuel, which is painfully expensive - $42 to fill two bikes. On the last stretch to Montreal, Brian finds the right exit, but misses the fork in the road for east vs. west and incorrectly leads us up the wrong ramp. We stop on the left side of the highway and paddle backwards a good distance along the shoulder to backtrack to our ramp rather than riding a few extra miles in the wrong direction. My legs are tired when we get moving again in the correct lane.

Signs lead us toward the city center and our hotel. We're tired and hungry, and opt for a quick bite in Chinatown. The next day will be our first day off since leaving home almost a week ago, a splurge both of time and money. After dinner, we walk back to the hotel and along the way a beggar asks Brian for money. Brian tells the beggar that he probably has more money than Brian does and the man says, "You know that's not true".

But I think to myself that it might actually be. Brian and I are both homeless and unemployed.

Montreal is a gorgeous mix of modern and old worlds. Plazas, parks, statues and lovely French-style architecture decorate the beautiful city. We climb Mont Royal for a view from the chateau terrace before descending for a greasy gut-bomb lunch of poutine, and a walk through a riverfront festival in the old part of the city.

We ride east to Quebec City the following day, and take an hour-long detour through construction to get to a motorcycle shop in hopes they have a tire for my bike. The stop and start traffic in the heat is unbearable. Smoke from forest fires in northern Quebec burns my nose and already inflamed sinuses.

The shop has a new tire in stock and a nice pair of gloves too, which will be more comfortable than my sweat-soaked leather gloves. I strap the tire onto the back rack of my bike and cinch my gear bag down on top off it for the ride to the hotel. My left thumb has been completely numb the past few days. While I don't think it has anything to do with my gloves, the extra attention I've been paying to my hand has reminded me that I need something tougher for the road ahead.

Brian and I have an arrangement. His twenty-plus years of mechanic experience have earned him a place as our team mechanic. My love of food has given me the position of team chef. So as part of my responsibilities, I round up cold drinks while he changes our tires in the parking lot.

A chatty older Quebecois salesman having a cigarette under the shade of the hotel carport sparks up a conversation. He used to ride motorcycles and asks a lot of questions about our trip. When it's time to inflate each tire with my bicycle hand pump, Brian pumps it dozens of pumps, then I take a turn.

"Here, gimme that," says the Quebecois man as his cigarette dangles dryly against his lower lip. He grabs the tire pump and begins to work it furiously without so much as a single inhale. After pumping away for half a minute, he stands up to exhale his long-held lungful of smoke and take another deep drag. We chat while we do a couple of rotations, the three of us, until the tire is filled. His help makes shorter work of it.

We carry on to Baie-Comeau and cross the Saguenay River to

Tadoussac on the first ferry ride of our trip. My rusty high school French skills get dusted off at a local information center where I try to inquire about places to eat and camp. Four student volunteers praise my accent and speech, overly generously, and I renew my vow to always make an effort to learn the local language when I travel.

They tell us the TLH is closed but can't offer any details. Brian and I look at each other and shrug our shoulders, resolved to worry about it later. We camp in lush new sod at a campground and enjoy a fire while having cold beers.

The next day brings the end of the pavement, and the beginning of the wilderness. We pack up and head out, bound for the Manic 5 Dam, hoping to make Relais Gabriel for the night. Brian found a ride report of the TLH and hopes we can follow the same pace and use the camp spots the blogger used. The paved highway leads us out of town and over the series of dams along the Manicouagan River, 1 through 5, until we reach the fifth, the Daniel-Johnson Dam, named for the 20th Premier of Quebec who was responsible for the creation of this dam project. Satellite images of the area reveal an enormous round impact crater from a meteor which now, by aide of this dam, forms the world's fifth-largest reservoir.

Hydro-Quebec offers tours of the dam, and we arrive just in time to catch the afternoon bus. We secure our riding gear and stash our tank bags and jackets at the office. Taking my coat off for even a few moments is refreshing. I'm drenched with sweat and self-conscious of how I must smell to other visitors. I spend the entire tour trying to stay away from my fellow passengers just in case.

There's a last stop before the end of the pavement, near the dam, where we stock up on fuel and water, and one last reprieve from the heat. As we carry on north toward the gravel we pass a Superman-style phone booth marked with a red "S.O.S." sign. I feel a small cringe of fear as it occurs to me these must be here for a reason.

Just past the dam, I see the end of the pavement and a rising cloud of dust from a truck that climbs up out of the canal to the road above. We have 65 miles of gravel to ride before we camp for the night. I'm excited…and terrified, and decide I have terra-noia.

This is the longest stretch of gravel I've ever faced, which doesn't take much since I've only ridden only a handful of miles in the Black Hills. That's more like little league gravel, whereas this is world class. The gravel is deeply spread across the road and it takes me a few minutes to adjust to the feeling of swimming along. Enormous double-trailered trucks rush toward us every few miles, not even budging slightly from their center-of-the-road track, and shower us with mushroom clouds of dust and stinging stone shrapnel. I'm glad I remembered to wet down my buff and cover my nose, which helps me breathe a little easier. My visor and glasses are coated inside and out with a fine layer of road. We push on for ten miles before Brian pulls over to check with me. I'm doing fine, at least I think so, except for being slow.

After nearly two hours, we finally arrive at the roadside collection of sheds that is Relais Gabriel. We fill up at the old-fashioned fuel tanks out front and stop at the store for a cold drink. I've stocked up my bike pantry for a few days of camping, as long as we find water as we ride. Just below the store is a small lake. A sandy road leads down to a flat spot that looks like a turnaround. We ride down and decide to camp here, out of sight of most of the traffic, and in sight of nearly every black fly and mosquito ever hatched.

I note in my journal that this place feels nearly biblical with its plagues. The smoke from northern Quebec's fires has steadily thickened as we've ridden the past few days, and the haze nearly blocks out the setting sun except for an eerie red glow cast over everything. Heat, which has been ever-present for the past week, somehow seems worse up here, no doubt hampering the fire control progress. Small black flies cover every inch of exposed flesh the very instant it is bared. In fact, they do that even before you bare your skin. As I park on the sandy roundabout, and step off my bike, tiny pests crawl between my high motorcycle jacket collar and my helmet base to burrow into my hair and scalp, biting at my ears and neck. Then there's the gravel, the trucks, and the bears…and the series of plagues is complete.

My camp stove needs fuel so I syphon gas from my freshly filled bike tank. We warm cans of soup and enjoy it quickly with fresh bread, before hurriedly setting up our two tents. Gear goes in one, and Brian and I in the other. After dinner, I wash our dishes in the lake while loons call out over the water in the twilight. It's too hot to sleep, and I'm sticky, dirty and uncomfortable. But the biting flies are annoying and aggressive, so I take cover in the tent.

In the morning, we both dress completely in our heavy bike gear before sticking so much as a toe outside the tent into the cloud of Parana-like flies. My nose and sinuses are completely blocked and I'm achy. The smoke is irritating my throat and my lungs burn. I should be nearly ready for antibiotics by now, but I decide against starting my stash of Cipro, saving them for an inevitably worse illness somewhere ahead. When I blow my nose something hard, about the size of an almond, comes out of my right sinus and I gag at the feeling and sight of it. I'd probably be appalled to know how much dirt and exhaust I inhale each day. No wonder I'm stuffed up.

We pack quickly and ride out, hoping to make Labrador City for the night. We still don't know if or when the TLH may open but are continuing on in hopes we can get through without much delay. The ever-present visa deadline looms over us.

Miles and miles of rolling hills covered with scrubby, skinny evergreens stretch out before me. The gravel changes all the time, sometimes it's deep and swishy and other times more sparsely strewn. A stretch of ten random miles of paved road pops up in what must be literally the middle of nowhere. Halfway along, I see why it's here. We've stumbled upon the ghost town of Gagnon, a former mining town which packed up in 1985 when the mine no longer turned a profit. All that is left of the community is an airport runway and a few miles of pavement. Concrete foundations scattered around a clearing belie the town's former layout. It's mildly creepy, but a good place for a break.

We carry on to Fire Lake and long straight stretches of road give way to a hilly plateau and a stretch of winding curves that intertwines with more than half a dozen badly-angled railroad crossings. The highway runs along the lakeside quarry of an iron ore mine while smokestacks puff away at the far end. Less than an hour ahead we pull over at the provincial border marking our arrival at Newfoundland Labrador. Just a few miles ahead, is the town of Labrador City. A woman at the visitor center explains that the TLH remains closed, and a visit to the road block at the far edge of town confirms it will be closed the rest of today. A few convoys have been allowed to go through in the past week, and they hope to release another tomorrow.

With nowhere to go today, we decide to shop at Canadian Tire for supplies, including oil and mosquito coils, which turn out to be completely pointless. We need a place for tonight, or longer, and a policeman at the blockade points us in the direction of the only hotel with a room. Local campgrounds are closed due to the proximity of the fires. At $150 for the night, it's painful, but it's our only choice, so we park by the front door and settle into a room just as it starts to rain. I'm hopeful this rain will dampen the local fires enough to open the road tomorrow.

I find I'm so happy to be indoors again that I feel a little spoiled. Apparently, my camping limit maxes out at two consecutive nights and needs to be followed by a hot shower. My daily bird bath of three baby wipes is not enough to keep me happy. When I inspect the damage before my shower, the tally from my recent bouts with the small midges stands at 46 bites. Dried blood is crusted inside and behind my ears and on my neck. Each bite itches badly.

By the end of my scalding hot shower, I find I've shed more than just a few pounds of dirt. I've started to relax into my exhaustion enough to realize the madness of the past few weeks is finally weighing on me. More than anything, I miss True.

I open a small gift that my sister and friends sent with me. Knowing that space is at a premium on my bike, they converted a plastic pill box into 7-day happiness kit, to be opened as needed. I've been saving it…until now. Each little pocket, it turns out, holds a few skittles and a small fortune-cookie-like slip of paper with a quote, a message or memory from each of them. While Brian is outside changing a headlight bulb on my bike, I bask in a few minutes of happiness in the room.

In the morning, we pack up, ride out to the blockade and line up behind dozens of cars and trucks. We shut off our bikes and stand and chat, wondering aloud how long it will be before we know anything. The overcast skies gently open up. A family parked ahead offers us seats in their car, out of the rain, but we politely pass. Our gear is waterproof and as long as we keep our gloves and helmets on, we will stay dry inside them. Then the couple parked behind us brings us folding camping chairs from the back of their van so Brian and I can have a seat while the minutes pass, rather than stay straddled on our bikes. Everyone is so nice.

After two hours of waiting, the blockade opens for a single convoy. Four dozen pickups and cars slowly start moving out of town and the domino affect approaches our bikes. We start them up and ride out. This is the start of the Trans-Labrador Highway.

I'm nervous about keeping up with the convoy if the road is gravel, because I'm still slow on it. But we only go a mile or two before the conga line stops, waiting for everyone to get into place before proceeding. People get out of their cars. I watch as a man crawls out of pickup truck and saunters off into the woods for a bathroom break and returns with a flower in his hand for the girl riding with him.

Ten minutes later, we start moving again. It's still raining. We go maybe 20 miles and then come upon a fire crew and helicopter parked on the side of the road as they take a much-needed break. The smoke thickens, and as we crest a hill I catch a glimpse of burned forest on the left side of the road. Not far ahead it is burned on both sides. Around a bend, dark slender evergreens give way to a blackened and smoldering landscape that resembles the back of an angry porcupine with only blackened quills of tree trunks left on the land. We are escorted just over 30 miles. At the end of the bridge crossing the Ashuanipi River the escort pulls over and parks with flashing lights, releasing us to the road ahead. We ride for another 100 miles or more before running out of gravel and stop at a roadside workshop so I can go to the bathroom. It's a good place to rest and eat the sandwiches we bought this morning.

When we first pull into the gravel lot we are swarmed with hornets of some kind. I ran into one just up the road and see its remains dangling from my helmet. I wonder if the smell or sight of him will upset his cousins and cause them to sting me. I turn and ride 30 feet away from the buildings but they follow. I ride to the back of the buildings in the lot, and they still follow. We stop, shut our bikes off and wait to see what will happen. We have helmets on, but without opening a visor for fear of letting a bee in, we won't be able to eat, let alone breathe.

I'm reminded of the time I rode my Harley into Joshua Tree National Park. Rangers at the entry gate had warned me about the aggressive African bees that were hanging out at trash cans and near bathrooms. There was a severe draught going on, and they were desperately seeking any moisture they could find. Not a concern really, they said, except that noise and vibrations make them angry. Not a good thing considering I was riding a Harley.

I finally have to tinkle so badly I'm willing to risk a sting or two, so I ditch my coat and drop my suspenders and pants, and go. A few bees fly around me but they don't bother me. I get dressed and go back to the bike, my fear subsiding now as their perceived aggression dissolves into perceived curiosity. Like the local people, they must not get many strangers in these parts.

Brian has a saying that "hunger makes the best sauce", which I'm sure is doubly true today. For whatever reason, my sandwich tastes especially good. As we eat, we see a pair of bikes ride by and are disappointed that our distance from the road has caused us to miss them. A few minutes later a single rider goes by – all in the opposite direction of us. These three came from the other end, and I hate missing the chance to get road condition reports and useful information. Occasionally, a motorcyclist is killed on the TLH when he rides off a steep banked edge or goes down on the deep gravel. My level of respect for this road is high for a reason.

After lunch and a cool drink from my Camelbak, we get back on the road. We cross what seems like the largest reservoir I've ever seen, but is actually a series of lakes. This is wilderness.

Finally, we reach a sign for the Churchill River which carries us over a single lane bridge. The metal grid surface of the bridge pulls my tires by the tread and gives me the uncomfortable feeling of being out of control. A sailboat-like tacking strategy seems to help. We stop at the far end of the bridge for a photo, but don't see the falls themselves. There's hardly more than a trickle in the riverbed below. I wonder if the river dried up in the heat.

When we reach the town of Churchill Falls, we go straight to the only gas station, fuel up and ask for an update on the road. We've decided to stop at the Midway Travel Inn for an emergency satellite phone which Brian read about in a blog about the TLH. Free satellite phones are available for the upcoming desolate stretches of road and can be picked up and dropped off at a few places along the way. I provide an imprint of my credit card as insurance that I will return the phone at the other end, or I will have to pay for it. As we strap the phone on my bike, a man tells us the road out of Churchill Falls to Happy Valley-Goose Bay, has been closed due to yet another fire. We are surrounded. Both the road into, and the road out of town are now closed.

We go back to the hotel to see if they can call ahead to Happy Valley-Goose Bay and ask for information on the status of the fire and the road block. The desk clerk says the road has been closed for a couple of days, and only opens intermittently. Not that it would have made any difference but I wished I'd known that before leaving Labrador City. We can't afford several days of delays and now are sandwiched between fire blockades which will cost us more time.

An overnight in Churchill Falls is added to the itinerary. We grab a handful of things at the grocery store to get us through. When we check in the clerk tells us the town is now also out of gas. Because of all the fire blockades the fuel trucks haven't been able to get in, and who knows when the next one will get here. Can't say that I'd want to drive a semi-load of fuel through a forest fire either. It's a good thing we got the last few gallons when we first hit town because they must've been the last.

Up and ready at 7:00am. The desk clerk says the road is open. We load our bikes and for the first time since leaving home it feels chilly out. I add my jacket liner to my jacket but wear a short-sleeved shirt under it. I'm still learning the system of adjusting to weather and temperatures by changing layers and using my gear vents. We head east out of Churchill Falls and pass an enormous electrical plant at the edge of town. The hotel staff solved the mystery of the missing Churchill River for me last night. Hydro-Quebec has diverted the river underground through a dam to create electricity. Turns out the rocky canyon riverbed and the skinny trickle that I rode over on the way into town is all that is left of the mighty falls.

We ride 70 miles of gravel and don't see another vehicle except for a few wrecked cars in ditches. These are the rusted remains of cars and trucks that no one bothered to recover. I stop for a break by one wreck and take a photo and a deep breath. I wonder aloud how many wrecks there are on this road each year. Was it speed? Was it the gravel?

All along the wide road there are crate-like boxes built around the bases of the telephone poles made of 4X4 posts stacked up in a Lincoln Log-like pattern and filled with big rocks. Later I find out they support the poles which settle and shift in the thawed bog that the land becomes in summertime. Dark clouds hang overhead today, with gaps of blue sky peeking through here and there. The clouds move quickly, but, thankfully, don't rain on us. A porcupine crosses the road.

At yet another break, Brian tests his newly purchased bear horn while I climb up a bank to take a photo of our bikes on the road. On a whim, I decide to take off my boot and get a photo of my pedicured pink toes on the gravel road.

More random helmet thoughts:

- It occurs to me I really love dogs and this province is named for two dogs, Newfoundlanders and Labradors, or more likely the dogs are named for them. I think I love it here.
- Despite my lifelong love for South Dakota and my eternal devotion to her, I've decided to have an affair with Canada, wild mistress of the north.
- I want to see a bear.
- I don't want to see a bear.
- I have funny, fearful thoughts about bears and camping and decide I've developed bearanoia as well as terranoia.
- The funny clumps of moss perched on top of scraggly spruces looks like lime-green Donald Trump comb-over pompadours.
- There's no roadkill in Canada. Are they really good at cleaning it up? Or is the food chain just that efficient?
- What would be a good name for my bike? I've been singing Black Betty in my helmet today…maybe that would work? She's black. Maybe she's also Betty.

We finally reach the tarmac west of Happy Valley-Goose Bay, and drop over a hill into a valley with dramatically different scenery, tall spruces like those on the west coast mix with silver birch adding softer shades of green to the hillsides. The smell of spruce is light and fresh. A large sweeping hill deposits us into a wide river basin, the remains of the Churchill's drainage path.

In Happy Valley-Goose Bay we break for lunch, buy water and fuel, and head out, hoping to cover half of the 240-mile uninhabited section of the road ahead before we camp for the night. The fires of the western part of the province haven't reached here, so camping is an option again. Until just a couple of years ago, the TLH ended at Happy Valley-Goose Bay. Cars and riders had to take a ferry to Cartwright to start the next section of road, which is the Labrador Coastal Drive.

After getting supplies we double back to the western edge of town and turn south, taking note of the sign warning that there is no fuel for 400 kilometers. This is the new road, that runs through land which hasn't been settled in even the slightest way. There are no houses or services until we reach the coast.

We cross over the Churchill River on a large metal-grid decked bridge, and ride out into the wilderness. The road ahead stretches out like a ribbon across the treed tundra with its ever-changing shades of gray and beige gravel looking like spliced knitting yarn. There's nothing out here. Nothing but miles of gravel and trees, and the occasional bridge over the occasional creek. Somehow, it's stunning.

I'm relaxed and comfortable, and the miles pass quickly. We don't see any cars, and it occurs to me that perhaps it's quiet because it's Sunday. Then I remember the waitress in town saying it's rare to see cars on this road.

We've worked out a system where I am free to stop for a photo or bathroom break whenever I like as long as I hurry. Brian leads and watches in his mirror to be sure he doesn't lose sight of me for more than a few minutes before stopping or turning back to make sure I'm okay.

We hit a nice long stretch of road and Brian speeds up a little while I gawk at a fox disappearing into the brush. The road rises slightly across the low flatness of the land until it finally reaches a high point. When I top the hill and start down the other side, my front wheel feels strange. It's smeary, and hard to control. Something isn't right. My front tire is going flat, and fast. When the weight shifted onto the front wheel as I topped the hill, it became harder to control. I ride the bike to a stop, careful not to apply my front brake.

I climb off to find my front tire completely flat. Perfect. Oh well, what's an adventure without actual adventure? I empty the contents of my left pannier to find my bicycle hand pump, and make a mental note to buy a small compressor when we get back to civilization. I evaluate my tire as a white pickup pulls up from the other direction.

"Ma'am, are you ok?" he asks.

"Yeah, thanks. It's just a flat."

"Well, this isn't exactly a good place to have a flat tire."

"I didn't think there was any good place to have a flat tire," I reply, with frustration in my voice.

"Well, we just saw a big bear over the next rise. So, I really don't think this is a good place to be." Message received, loud and clear. "Do you want us to help?"

"I'm not sure. I think the tube needs patched. My boyfriend was just ahead and if you don't mind waiting with me until he comes back, I'd feel safer."

"No problem," he replies.

They wait with me. Brian rides up a few minutes later and sets to work on my tire while the truck drives away.

I stand watch over the road with wide eyes while Brian works hurriedly to slip the tube out between the side of the loosened tire and the rim, without taking it off the bike. He swears by Grant Johnson's (from Horizons Unlimited) tire repair classes and now has the chance to show off his skills. He finds the small hole and sticks a patch on it, but it doesn't hold, so he starts over. On the second try it seals. He puts the tube back into the tire and we take turns pumping it up.

It doesn't take me long to rethink camping out here tonight, especially after finding the excuse that we were outpacing our water rations anyway. We decide to double back the 42 miles to Happy Valley-Goose Bay and camp there for the night. We'll get a fresh start tomorrow.

3 DETOUR

Life is either a great adventure or nothing.
-Helen Keller

The next morning, I find I've lost my voice but I start to creak again after twenty minutes. Brian notices his right pannier is crooked and inspects it to see what's wrong. A closer look reveals that the rough road battering we've taken has worn out and broken a lock on his case. He's lucky the box didn't fall off while he was riding yesterday. We stop at a hardware store on the way out of town for straps, one for each pannier, which Brian puts on in the parking lot. I buy two large bottles of water so we have enough for the day.

We hope to cover the entire 240 miles of gravel to Port Hope Simpson in one long day. The recent delays have put us behind schedule.

Heading out of Happy Valley-Goose Bay for the second time, we pass the place where I had a flat yesterday and keep moving, happy to put miles behind us. About 70 miles into the day, I see something fly off Brian's bike as he tops a low rise, and pull over to see what it is. It's one half of our freshly purchased water supply. The skid across the road has scraped small holes into the plastic bottle turning it into a colander. I have just enough time to save a liter of it in a collapsible bottle before it runs dry. I strap it to my bike and get moving again. Twenty miles later, I pass a road grader and ride over a foot-high ridge of gravel he pushed up in the center of the road to pass him. Ten miles past that, I come to a wide section of the road which is meant to be a rest area. I see a black blur run off into the trees and think it's a fox.

The day is still cool, like yesterday, but the clouds are thicker and there's a gusty wind blowing. Brian read somewhere that a rider described this road as having seven unique kinds of gravel on it, each worse than the last. It's ever changing in size, color and depth. Lines across the outstretched road, changing from red gravel to gray, and then to beige, reveal the many quarries used for this road. The dark gray rock is the worst. Jagged and sharp, it wedges momentarily into my tire treads before shooting off into the ditch.

I'm tired. I wanted a shower this morning, but we didn't have time. Once in a while I feel like the bike is swimming. It feels like my front tire is going flat again, and I stop twice to check it. Brian put a new tube in it last night at camp, and turned the tire so it's rolling in the opposite direction of the arrow that tells you how it's supposed to rotate. My tire has been wearing in a strange lumpy way. He thinks reversing it will help me get more life out of it. There's no choice. We won't find tires again until Newfoundland.

I'm uncomfortable all day. Then it gets worse. I get the feeling like the bike really is swimming. More than usual, almost like it's trying to crawl out from under me. At 102 miles into the day I get hit by a strong cross wind that pushes me sideways across the road. After the first couple gusts caught me off guard, I'd slowed down to about 40 mph. This gust comes out of nowhere, and then drops off immediately. When I correct for the wind and it dies, I find I've overcorrected.

It happens so suddenly it causes me to fishtail, and my bars weave back and forth a few times without my being able to control them. Each arching swing becomes more dramatic and deep. I feel like I'm watching this on a movie screen instead of through my visor. I don't apply my brakes, but instead try to control the steering, which I swear makes it worse. Really, I'm just trying to hold on. I can see this isn't going to end well and I think to myself, "here I go," knowing that my bike is going down.

As the bars jerk to the left once more…it happens. Like a top that has lost its centrifugal motion, the bike drops over onto my left leg, causing me to slide feet and tires first down the road. I land on my left side, not on my wrist or arm, but onto my elbow which jams into my ribs and knocks the wind out of me, and onto my left leg with the full weight of the bike. Dust flies everywhere, a cloud of it, and I worry that anyone behind me won't see me in its midst and might run into me.

I slide to a stop on my back with my legs stretched out in front of me pointing down the road while the bike slide a little further. My immediate reaction is to stand up so that I can take a deep breath and get my wind back.

As the dust clears, I sit up and try to gather my wits about me. Well, that sucked. Sort of a steel horse version of a rodeo that ended with me getting dumped on my butt.

Brian's silhouette shrinks into the distance as I tug at my chin strap and take my helmet off. I feel strange. My heart is racing, which is to be expected after just coming off my motorcycle in the middle of nowhere. But something's not right.

Am I okay? I hope I am.

I take a deep breath and try to calm myself. Betty is on her side in the middle of the gravel road ahead of me. I put my hands on the ground to brace myself as I move to stand. I gather my legs up underneath me, or try to, but it doesn't happen. My right leg bends at the knee, but my left leg just lays there.

Uh oh. Houston, we have a problem.

I try again, to make my leg react in a way I have thousands of times before, to contract my thigh muscles and pull my left leg toward me, bending it at the knee and moving it from an outstretched position to one that will allow me to stand. I'm really concentrating. But still nothing.

As I move my muscles I can feel the bones in my lower left leg grind against each other and I look down to see my foot lying awkwardly flatly against the ground. Houston?

Brian disappears over the next hill and suddenly I feel very helpless. And very alone. There goes my heart again, racing even faster. I see the yellow plastic case of the satellite phone stuffed under the black mesh cargo net stretched across Betty's backside. But it's small comfort to me from even just ten feet away.

Dozens of thoughts flood my mind in an instant. Am I really hurt? Is it just my leg or could it be something more that I don't feel yet? Am I going to be okay? Do I wait for Brian to come back? Or do I drag myself over to the phone? How will we get help way out here? And how long will it take?

Why did I decide to be unemployed and homeless only to end up here? What about Brian's visa expiration?

Oh, my God. What have I done? What about the rest of my trip?

What's that noise? Was that a bear?!

Oh, my God.

Dust still lingers in the air. That's how quickly this has all happened. Then, seemingly out of nowhere, a man walks up from behind and asks, "Ma'am, are you ok?".

I turn to look over my shoulder as he comes into my periphery and the relief I feel is instantaneous. He isn't just anyone, he's an RCMP officer. I think I'm gonna cry. Just to know another human being is here with me is unbelievably comforting. Add to that his being RCMP, and he's now my lifeline.

Officer Dykes asks if I'm okay. I tell him that I think my leg is broken, but that otherwise I think I'm fine. He runs back to his car to call dispatch for an ambulance. He gathers up a couple of emergency blankets to put over me. Even though it's a hot day, the strong wind gusts are enough to chill me, although that may be shock setting in.

He asks me to describe how I feel and why I think my leg is

broken. He wants to know if I can feel blood coming from my injured leg or if I hurt anywhere else. I don't feel warmth or wetness, so I think the break is a simple fracture. He asks if I need a helicopter or if I can wait for an ambulance to drive out from Happy Valley-Goose Bay, which means a 2-hour wait followed by a bumpy 2-hour ride back to the town's small clinic. I pause for a moment to be sure I'm not just being naively strong, but I genuinely think I'm in no immediate danger. I tell him I can wait. He goes to the car to update the dispatcher. I lie back onto the road, and start to shiver, my nerves starting to come apart now that my reality is sinking in.

I look up and see a plume of dust above the road ahead and am grateful that it's likely Brian coming back to see what's holding me up. But as I watch it get closer I see it's a van. As it nears me, it slows, its progress blocked by my motorcycle lying across the road. The cargo van parks and its driver walks over to see what's happening. The officer, driver and I converse a moment and they decide to move my bike to the side of the road. As the van driver leans down to pick it up, for whatever reason, it occurs to me that I want a picture of this. I dig into my jacket pocket for my small camera and snap a picture while my bike is still on her side.

As they park the bike on its kickstand, Brian rides up. I can see his wide eyes through his helmet. He walks over and asks me what happened. I tell him I think I've broken my leg and I can see his face fall. He's worried, and I'd guess having the same mental dialogue I had just a minute before.

The driver of the van comes to check on me and explains he is an EMT. How lucky can I get? He and the officer ask more questions about how I'm feeling. They aren't convinced my leg is broken since I seem to be doing so well. I haven't cried, and am trying to be upbeat, even making jokes, which throws them off. I'm surprised I'm not really in much pain. But I'm worried about the long delay in getting to a hospital leaving plenty of time for me to hurt. The officer confirms that an ambulance is on its way from Happy Valley-Goose Bay, just over 100 miles back up this long empty stretch of the TLH.

Another truck arrives. Two Fisheries and Oceans officers walk over to see if they can help. I'm getting cold, so they set to work building a windbreak around me with their spare tires and tarps, and then layer their jackets over the emergency blankets the officer had put over me. One of them is married to a nurse who is on duty at the hospital and he messages her to see if there is anything they should do for me.

Brian talks with the driver of the van and it turns out he has room in the van for my bike, so they load it while we wait for the ambulance. The van driver lives in Happy Valley-Goose Bay and has agreed to keep my bike secure for as long as I need. Brian comes over to fill me in and we talk quietly about what to do. I know things will move quickly once I leave here and I'm not sure what will happen, especially with his visa expiring soon. We had no room for errors, and I've just made a big one. I have him get my tank bag and give him all the cash I have for whatever he might need to do on my behalf. I ask him to get everyone's names and a photo or two.

My heroes stand in a circle around me and chat, trying to pass the time. After an hour on the road I start to shiver uncontrollably. I half-jokingly ask if it's too late to change my mind and get the helicopter. The second hour moves at a snail's pace. We talk about cod tongues (which I'd seen for sale in Labrador City), the Quebec fire and never-ending smoke, and black flies. I tell them I'm shaking partly because I have to pee, to which they say "go for it" and that it might warm me up. We all laugh. If it weren't for the thought of lying in cold wet pants for an unknown amount of time, I might consider it. They comment that the one good thing about the strong wind today is that there are no flies around, and for the first time in over a week I realize I'm enjoying the luxury of a few bite-free hours.

Not long before the ambulance arrives, Brian suggests that he ride ahead to town to meet me at the hospital. I worry about him riding back alone after all of this, but he's right. He gathers up a few essentials for me, including my wallet, cell phone and the SPOT beacon, and puts them on his bike. We steal a kiss, and he takes off.

A car comes over the ridge making us think the ambulance is here, but it's a false alarm. Finally, it arrives. It passes me, and backs in toward my feet and parks. Two techs, Buzz and Jill, start to uncover me to get a better look. Jill asks me questions to assess me and see how I'm holding up. I tell her I think my leg is broken. She goes to the rig to get her kit and comes back, accidentally bumping my foot with her toe, the worst pain I've felt since the wreck. When I tell Brian later, he says he almost did that too, and had thought about putting something around my leg to protect it.

The female tech cuts my left pant leg from the hem to the crotch and lays it open. I wonder when I last shaved my legs. My femur lays in its correct position, but my lower leg is twisted so that the left side of my foot is lying flat against the ground on the boot buckles, making it impossible to remove without moving my leg. Jill thinks she can cut through the boot and take it off without turning my shattered leg, but I don't think so. She gives it a try and starts cutting down the leather boot shaft toward my ankle. She says her scissors can cut a coin in half, but when she gets to the reinforced area by the heel, her scissors prove useless. In the end, she concedes there is no way to remove my boot but to straighten my leg and do it the normal way.

I've done well so far, but all bets are off now. As she gently takes my left leg and starts the 90-degree turn to align my foot with my knee so she can get to the boot buckles, my bones start to audibly grate against each other. It's absolute agony. I spout a stream of profanity and start to cry. The Fisheries and Oceans guys squat on each side of me and hold my hands while she sets about her gruesome task. I tell her I'm fine and to keep going. I apologize for swearing.

I think I would have preferred just laying still on the road forever rather than moving my leg. The enormity of my situation finally sinks in as I tell her I can feel bones grinding. Then we each hear clicks and pops, to which I blurt out "Gross!," which makes us all laugh and stops my tears.

She gets my boot off and moves quickly after that. I'm loaded onto a stretcher, moved into the ambulance and strapped down for the two-hour ride back to Happy Valley-Goose Bay. Jill splints my leg but I can still feel the shattered pieces of it moving around as we go over each bump. There's a fine line between hurrying back to the hospital and getting an airborne ride. I'm not sure if I want to go slow to avoid the bumps or to go fast and get the ride over with.

More than halfway to town we pass Brian. I 'd asked the EMT if she could watch for him, and feel a wave of relief when she sees him.

Jill and I laugh a lot on the way. I tell her several times how badly I have to pee but that holding it somehow keeps my mind on my bladder instead of my leg. When we get to the hospital Buzz, the driver, opens the back door and asks "What's all the laughing about?"

"I almost peed my pants," I reply.

"That makes two of us", he says and winks.

At the hospital, I'm moved quickly into the Emergency Room. A doctor comes to check on me and says he has ordered x-rays. It's been nearly five hours since my wreck and I still haven't had any medication or even a sip of water.

First things first, I need a bedpan. I'm wheeled into a curtained bay in the ER and tell the nurse. She smiles and runs for a bedpan while another nurse takes my vitals and starts an IV. Amazingly, I'm not hurting too badly at the moment and having ridden in the ambulance covered in blankets I'm starting to warm up a little. I'm dying for a drink but am not allowed anything if there is any chance I will have surgery tonight.

Brian arrives, giving me instant relief, both that he is ok and that he's here. After a brief reunion, I'm wheeled off to another room for x-rays.

Two nurses try to move me from the gurney to a table and ask a doctor for help, but he refuses, saying that he will just watch. I sit up and scold him, "Are you kidding? Get over here", so he comes to help.

I move myself from the ambulance gurney to the hospital gurney and then to the x-ray table and back. As long as someone holds my leg up, I'm fairly mobile and strong. Afterward, I'm rolled back to the ER bay to await the results. A few minutes later another doctor comes to give me the news. It's official. I shattered both the tibia and fibula in my left leg. Although the doctor has seen many tib-fib breaks in his years of practice, he says he has no idea how they will fix mine. He consulted with an orthopedic specialist who has no idea either. I will be flown to St. John's, Newfoundland for a complicated surgery that cannot be done in this small town's hospital. There isn't a flight available today, so I will be kept here overnight and flown out as soon as an air ambulance can retrieve me tomorrow.

My nurse returns and offers to run and get me anything I want to eat, now that I can, even something from Tim Horton's across the street. No doubt Canadians see Timmy's as a cure-all. It's very kind of her and I'm grateful, but it doesn't interest me. She comments on the gray-green pallor of Brian's face. I know hospitals are not his favorite and I feel bad for landing us here. She gets him some toast and juice while he lies on the floor for a few minutes.

The doctor orders a "back slab" cast which forms a plaster tray under my leg and up the sides to keep it mobilized without completely encasing it. I ask Brian to leave while they do it. I'm back to joking with the nurses and doctor and find it strange that this turns is my way of coping. But I'm grateful for anything that helps me deal with this. Brian isn't laughing, and I can't blame him. He's the one with a visa deadline coming and he may have to go on without me.

Perhaps the best news of the afternoon is that I can finally have some morphine...nearly seven hours after my wreck. My leg is swelling, and starting to ache and throb.

My team moves me to the maternity ward where I hear a woman in labor crying out. Brian watches baseball on TV, mostly to drown out the noise of the woman in delivery. We make a few plans. He will email my dad if he can get wi-fi at the campground where we stayed last night. We discuss his choice of words and decide he will tell my dad I've had a low-speed accident so my dad understands my injuries are limited and that I will be fine. Brian will try to figure out how to store and ship my bike down to St. John's so I can get back on it when I'm able. We discuss him posting something on an online forum to get advice and help.

I feel terrible that he has to deal with my mess and carry on alone for a few days to catch up to me. He looks really worried. I tell him I'm fine and that he should go get some rest. He gives me a kiss and heads out. I get another dose of morphine and an accompanying anti-nausea medicine, just in time for loud birthing mother number two. This one keeps up her wailing halfway through the night. When she finally has her baby, it cries all the rest of the night. I think they should put the poor thing back in so we can all get some sleep.

Brian arrives early the next morning and we continue planning between my bouts of drug-induced narcolepsy. I've asked when I can get on the bike and am told 8-10 weeks. But no one knows for sure. It will be up to the surgeon and depends on the method he uses to rebuild my leg. The nurses tell me that I should get an hour or two's notice before I'm taken to the airport, but there's still no time set for my flight. My nurse comes in to tell me I need to bathe before I go. Brian leaves so I can.

Just as I'm starting my bed-bound bath someone peeks in to say the plane is ready and I will be going to the ambulance in 15 minutes, so there's no time to wash my hair. Not the notice I was expecting and now Brian is gone. I hope he will come back before I go, but he doesn't. I ask the nurse to tell him I love him, to be careful on his way to St. John's and to come find me at St. Clare's Hospital which is where they say I'm going. It's strange to leave this way, without a goodbye. I express my gratitude to the nurse and ask her to pass along my thanks to everyone who helped me.

I wonder if I need to pre-authorize any of this with my insurance company. What will a private air ambulance to St. John's cost? It would have been another 1000 miles by road, so I'm guessing it will be expensive.

The crew of two women ambulance drivers and two female techs loads me into the ambulance at the ER entrance. One of the techs is my flight nurse. She takes out my IV and gives me a dose of morphine before I leave the hospital. I ask one of the ambulance women to take my camera and get a photo of me and the plane. I'm not sure with all the morphine that I'll remember it clearly without photos. More than anything, I want to remember their names so I can thank them properly someday.

My flight nurse carries a black trash bag that holds my jacket, boots, wallet and shredded pants. The pilot and co-pilot go through pre-flight checks on the jet in preparation for my 1 hour 17-minute trip to Newfoundland. They wiggle my gurney through the narrow door and onto the plane, clearing a place so the nurse can get situated. She hangs my new IV from the ceiling with two bags, saline and morphine. She inserts each into a mesh bag that she pumps up with a blood pressure cuff, squeezing the fluid-filled bags to the point of nearly popping. She says the air pressure changes in flight and the fluids won't flow well without pressure. I drift in and out of consciousness, and catch glimpses of the Labrador coast and Newfoundland before succumbing to the morphine darkness.

At the St. John's airport we wait for the ambulance from St. Clare's Hospital. As the two pilots unload me, they wish me well. I'm transferred to the ambulance, with its two hilarious drivers, for a bumpy 10-minute drive to the hospital. One driver leaves an invoice on my gurney, tucked under my good leg, before leaving me at the ER. $425. So begins my accrual of debt.

I'm told my IV is too small for surgery so they pull it out and give me yet another, larger one. My attending physician tells me they have to run some tests to be sure I'm cleared for surgery, which, if all goes well, will take place tonight. My EKG looks good.

I'm taken by a "porter" down a maze of hallways to radiology, to wait in the hallway by myself. The fluorescent lights flicker overhead in the gray cinder block hallway. This place is straight out of a horror movie. Finally, a tech comes out and wheels me in. They take a frontal x-ray of my chest and then reposition me to take a side view.

The four techs all look like young students. Within seconds of taking the images I can hear one say, "Whoa!"

Another tech runs back to the booth to look. After a long minute of whispered discussion, the lead youngster comes out and asks me if I have ever had heart surgery. It occurs to me that they've seen my heart patch, which I'd told all the doctors about at the hospitals so far, but had forgotten to tell these techs about. As I confirm the intentional presence of a PFO-closure device in the center of my heart, I can see the kid is visibly relieved.

"I bet it looked like a spider with eight titanium legs," I say, and he confirms that it did. "I'm glad to know it's still there." He laughs.

A porter comes to escort me back to my point of origin and asks me where that should be. But I'm too high to remember, so he parks me and goes to ask someone.

Eventually, I'm moved to a room and try to greet my elderly roommate but she can't understand my slurring. Sleep catches me for a few minutes before another nurse comes to take me to the operating room. As she starts to move my bed another nurse comes running in to make sure someone removed the Barbie pink nail polish from my toes. She runs to get some acetone and sets to work on my left foot while I sit up and take care of my right foot myself. Apparently, the doctor can better judge the circulation to my toes if he can see my toenails. Makes sense to me even in my morphine stupor. A resident comes to see what is taking so long and my nurse says she's trying to be gentle. I tell her she doesn't need to be gentle because I can't feel that leg anyway.

Dr. Stone greets me in the OR and explains he will insert a tibial nail into my lower leg, which will run the length of my tibia, and attach it to my knee and ankle with screws. These titanium pieces will stay in my leg for the rest of my life unless I have problems with them. The fibula will not be treated and will need to heal on its own. The anesthesiologist who I spoke with in the ER about my medical history and heart issues is waiting for me along with several nurses. I take one long last look around the white room as I'm moved to another bed and start to go to sleep.

I wake in recovery with two nurses hovering over me, saying that they've been waiting for me. They take me back to my room. Through the fog, I remember I have a roommate and whisper goodnight in case she can hear me. Sleep and morphine drag me under, only allowing me to surface during occasional vitals checks. In one brief waking, I think to myself that I wish my mother was here.

In the morning, I drift out of sleep and into a haze of exhaustion and medication. I'm quiet for a few minutes and try to wake up enough to get my bearings before pushing the button for a nurse. At some point, I'm told that my blood pressure is very low – 80/40, way below my normal range. For several hours during the night and through most of the first day after surgery it seems to keep everyone on their toes. All my other vitals are good – oxygen, heart rate, temp, etc. The tech last night had a hard time finding a place for my new IV because my veins were "so low".

Dad calls the next night and again the following morning to see how I'm doing and the nurse's station lets me know. As I start to drift more from sleep to consciousness I hear a woman talking to my roommate behind the curtain around my bed. Her voice is soothing and calm. At lunchtime, my curtain is pulled back and I finally greet my roommate and her companion for the first time with some sort of clarity.

During the day, I ask for water. They bring me small cup of ice water and I slurp it down and want more. Since it's been nearly two days since I ate my ER toast in Labrador, I'm hungry. Luckily, I'm not nauseous. My morphine drip gets exchanged for pain pills. My IV site starts to swell in the afternoon and it hurts. I tell my nurse who then takes it out. No physio for me today, my blood pressure is still too low.

My roommate is a 90-year-old sprite of a woman whose smile is contagious. Lily is reserved and quiet, but has a twinkle in her eyes. I catch a glimpse of her only occasionally the when staff moves the curtains between our beds. Neither of us feels much like talking but I hope she can sense that I'm wishing her well from my side of the room.

Lily was in her garden last Thursday with two of her great-grandsons who love to play soccer. They were playing around and kicked a soccer ball to her and she kicked it back. Once. Twice. On the third time, she tried to kick the ball it wedged under her foot causing her to lose her balance. She toppled over and broke her hip. After a short stay in a local hospital Lily was brought St. John's for hip-replacement surgery and is now recovering while earning a reputation around the hospital as the soccer playing grandma. She lives in a small house next to Sylvia, her daughter, who owns a book and bible store. Lily, it turns out, is nearly deaf without her hearing aids, which explains why she hasn't replied to my scattered hellos and good nights.

Many family members come to visit her, children and grandchildren, to which she responds with subtle glee. I find out from another of her daughters that Lily's late husband worked on the penstocks at the Churchill Falls Dam project, in the dried river bed I'd crossed.

Sylvia takes me under her motherly wing, without my knowing it at first. She overhears my difficulty in getting a phone installed because I don't have a Canadian telephone account. She hands me her cell phone and instructs me to ignore the cost and let my family know I'm okay. With my vulnerable physical and emotional state, it moves me nearly to tears.

Dad doesn't answer, but at least I can leave him a voicemail telling him I'm alright. It's all I can do to not cry on the phone, even without him on the other end. As I dissolve into quiet tears after hanging up I see that Sylvia is choked up too. She tells me everything is going to be okay. This handful of kind words from a stranger gives me comfort.

An occupational therapist comes to discuss my "exit plan" for leaving the hospital. She wants to know about my home and things like wheelchair access, stairs, etc. I tell her I don't have a home, which I don't have the energy to explain. She says they won't release me until Brian is here because I have to have a caregiver for the next few days. She wants to know if I will fly home to recover, but I haven't even begun to think about what to do next.

Dr. Stone tells me I can't put any weight on my leg for six weeks. I'm not allowed to travel for two weeks because of the high risk of developing clots. My ribs hurt when I sit up and I wonder if it's from the wreck or if it has to do with my not being out of bed since my surgery. I feel a lot of irregular heartbeats, my arrhythmia acting up. It would normally make me nervous, but the pain meds turn it into merely a passing thought.

The nurses call Lily and I things like "my love" or "my darling" and later I find out these are turns of phrase in Newfoundland. It's endearing. I notice the gauze on my left leg wraps it entirely up like a mummy, terminating at my foot in a small gift-like bow, which makes me smile. Lily and I sleep at alternating times during the day. Sylvia waits patiently to pick up each of the conversations she has going with us wherever we left off.

Somewhere after my evening pain pills I drift into a ragged sleep. My pain wakes me again for another round during the night but only worsens until I'm also given a shot of morphine since I don't have the IV anymore.

By morning, my low blood pressure is finally starting to improve. I'm worried about Brian. When my dad calls again, I ask the nursing staff to tell him I'm being a smart-ass and joking so that he'll know I'm okay.

A doctor on rounds says my bones were broken in too many pieces for any repair other than a tibial nail, so that's what they used. She says my surgery went perfectly and the x-rays look great. By midday my blood pressure is within a safe range for me to get up and moving. Staff comes by before lunch to have me stand with a walker and make my way ten feet to the bathroom.

Unused to the walker, and without any strength, I teeter on the edge of the toilet but lose my balance. Luckily, I land on the seat while my walker slides up against the wall. Not bad placement except that I've trapped my physical therapist in the corner between me and the toilet and I'm already going to the bathroom. Poor Ashley has to wait for me to finish before I can get back up and move myself out of her way. She laughs politely.

Just ten feet of walker use wears me out. I'm dizzy. Ashley ushers me back to the edge of my bed for a few minutes. When I'm feeling a little better she has me use the walker to move to a chair to sit up for 30-40 minutes with my leg down. The lower my limb, the worse the pain, and the more purple my foot becomes.

Sylvia brings her mother strawberries and grapes, and a chocolate pastry. She is kindness itself, and made sure to bring along enough for me. She says things with a slightly Irish lilt – "ice" as "oice", "why" as "whoy", and "that's right" as "dat's roight". She uses lovely phrases too, asking Lily if she would like a "drop of milk" or a "drop of soup". We joke about the curtains between Lily's bed and mine being like the Canadian and U.S. Border and that the nurses are playing "border patrol" when they come to close the curtain.

A motorcyclist woman learns to live with various versions of helmet hair and lowered expectations with regard to hairstyling. Although the hospital has a policy that supports nurses assisting with bathing, it doesn't support the staff helping you wash your hair from bed. If you're bedridden or can't get in the shower because of incisions, you have to bathe in a small basin or with disposable wipes.

One afternoon, a nurse comes to help me with a bath. I work up enough desperation to ask her if she could find a way to help me wash my hair. She explains that they don't have the supplies to do it unless I'm able to get into a shower. Since I barely made it to the toilet, that won't happen today. I understand. About an hour later though, after finishing her rounds, she comes back. She's rounded up baby shampoo from the nursery downstairs, a big bowl from the staff breakroom and a clean bed urinal to use as a pitcher. She's here to wash my hair.

She props me up gently and goes to work on my tangled and dirty mop. She pours a bit of warm water on my head over the bowl and adds some shampoo. As she does so, I begin to cry. She massages my scalp softly and slowly, and thoroughly washes and rinses my hair as best she can. She doesn't say anything but continues to tenderly care for me, making sure the water is warm, but not too warm. When she's finished, she wraps me up with a towel and pats my hair to dry it out as much as she can. She apologizes for not having any conditioner or combs. She loans me a pen cap I can use to untangle my hair, one strand at a time. Her name is Amanda, the same as my sister who is studying to be a nurse. She gives me more than cleaner hair. She gives me her time and caring effort, and she gives me some of my dignity back.

There have been so many generous people helping me the past week, that it's changing my idea of the balance needed between giving and receiving. Flying in the face of what we've all been told about it being better to give than to receive, I'm starting to disagree. I think they are equally important. This isn't meant in any way to lessen the importance I place on giving, because it's always been important to me.

In the past, I haven't been a person who asks for help. I've been independent and self-contained. I've never wanted to need things from others or to be a burden to others. I'm not good at taking help, even when it's offered, and I'm downright bad at asking for help. But I'm learning something here in my lumpy hospital bed. Until you desperately need help, receive it, and are truly grateful for and overwhelmed by it, I don't think you completely understand the true weight and importance of the giving you do. They are intertwined – giving and receiving.

Finally, a phone is installed in my room and my father and I get a chance to speak. He's been following Brian's check-ins on the SPOT and reports that Brian finished the bad stretch of road, and is on the coast making his way to Newfoundland. My uncle and sister each call too. While I'm so happy to talk to them, I already feel like I'm ready to have the phone taken out so I can go back to sleep. I consider calling my grandmother to let her know what happened but I don't think I sound well enough yet. I will only worry her. I don't want her to hear about it from anyone else, so I need to call her soon.

My pillow is covered with handfuls of my hair which is starting to fall out, a side effect of the anesthesia. There's no air conditioning in this old building and with the unusual heat wave going on, I sweated and stuck to the sheets all night.

I try crutches with the physical therapist this morning. I make it out of the room to start a 75-foot walk up the hall when I feel dizzy, break out in a full sweat, and have to go back to bed. At this rate, I will never get out of here. While I'm silently frustrated with my weakness, Lily asks me why she can't be up and walking like I am, which changes my perspective entirely. I tell her I think she'll be up and around soon, and silently hope I'm right.

Dr. Stone stops in to check on his surgical handiwork. "Good morning, sunshine", he calls out. I think I'm in love. That's one of my favorite phrases. With that and the gauze bow he tied on my foot…a girl swoons. He wants me to come to his clinic next week to get my staples out. I'm not to touch my leg until then. No bathing. No re-wrapping it. He'll put me in a walking boot which will be lighter than the backslab and easier for getting around.

The therapist comes back and I get a little further on my second attempt at crutches. I crutch my way as far as the bathroom late in the day. The social worker comes in after lunch to see if anyone has arrived to help me yet. Brian isn't here, but may arrive today. I've been thinking about things. Even though I have no idea what he plans to do, I've made some decisions for myself. I'd like to find a small apartment for a couple of months to recover, whether Brian stays or not. I don't see the point of flying home for a few weeks only to come back to get my bike later. It's too expensive to ship home from here. But most of all, I want to finish my trip.

Brian arrives and shows me photos from the 200 miles of

Labrador I missed, including a small iceberg at Red Bay. Amazing, an iceberg in July. He ran into horrible crosswinds on the coast of Newfoundland and looks exhausted from his three days hard riding. I'm happy he's safe.

My leg swells badly tonight, likely because of the heat, but possibly because I twisted it while learning to walk again. A male nurse comes in to help Lily tonight. He's wearing a long-sleeve gray tee under black scrubs and comments on the heat. Sylvia wisecracks "Well, if you're too hot, you can always take off your shirt", and turns to wink at me.

I add, "You must be cooking."

To which Sylvia replies, "He'll soon be ready to eat,". We giggle.

Saturday morning brings a final test from the physio team to be sure I can walk 75 feet. At the end, they tell me I also have to climb stairs with the crutches. Not likely. I have to climb up and down a set of three steps for them to approve me for release. While it looks like Mount Everest from my wheelchair, I'm motivated to get out, so I give it my best.

"Good go up and bad go down" is the trick they give me to remember which leg steps first on stairs. My good leg goes first when climbing and my weak goes first when descending. I need to rest at the top. Three steps and I'm spent. This is ridiculous. The tech says I'm pale. She puts a belt on me and stands behind me, holding me as I descend. Thankfully, I make it. I passed my test.

Back in our room, I tell Lily that I'm going to miss our slumber parties. In a way, it will be like leaving family when I go. As the staff finishes my paperwork, I lay back in my bed and wait. Sylvia is sitting on Lily's bed humming a hymn and reading the weekend paper. Lily is in her chair quietly working on a puzzle while a fan blows a gentle breeze around our overly warm room. I can smell the lotion that Sylvia has put on Lily's feet after her morning bath and the flowers sent from well-wishers. It's like a lazy afternoon weekend at home with my own family, relaxing and peaceful. For a moment, I'm completely whole. I drift off to sleep.

Brian arrives to escort me to a Holiday Inn in a cab. He brought me a pair of shorts and a right shoe so I can dress to go. When it's time, I ask the nurse to pull back the curtain so I can wave goodbye to Lily from my wheelchair. She blows me a kiss that warms my heart. This experience, all of it, has been a gift, and I will be forever grateful.

4 RECOVERY

The real voyage of discovery consists not in seeking new landscapes, but in having new eyes.

-Marcel Proust

The haze lifts, slowly but surely, as anesthesia and trauma recede into my past. By my second day out of the hospital, I opt for Tylenol instead of Percocet, choosing to come out of the cloud and get busy with healing. Sleep is now my favorite pastime, and I only get up to go to the bathroom and take my twice daily stroll down the hall. I could never have imagined how weak I would be after walking only 60 feet with crutches.

Brian helps me with everything at first, but then I start to build strength and do more on my own. The physical therapists insisted I get moving as soon as possible.

I look online for a place to rent, but most listings want tenants for longer than three months. Brian's decided to stay in Canada with me and will figure out his visa later. He went to the grocery store to get supplies for the week and made sure to get calcium-rich milk in hopes of getting a head start on re-building my leg.

His post on ADVRider.com triggers an outpouring of support,

which he shares with me in my scattered moments of consciousness. A forum member, Ski Bum, stops by to see how he can help. We chat for a bit and he shows me a tattoo on his lower leg of two broken bones, shattered tib-fib just like mine. We are welcome to stay at his house which is two hours away, but he knows a local woman who might have a room in town instead. Another named Murph messages offering to help. He calls our room one day, and his baritone voice catches me off guard, "Well, hello there, young lady? Are you the miss with the broken leg?"

I giggle and confirm that I'm the bum-legged girl before handing the phone over to Brian. I wonder if his voice is actually that deep or if it was a lingering effect of morphine. Murph and his girlfriend, Danielle, were in a motorcycle accident in January and she's still recovering from a leg injury. He suggests that Brian and he prop up the "injured girls" in a coffee shop while they go riding.

Brian emailed Scott, the driver of the cargo van who has my bike, and says it's safe and secure. A shipping company quoted $600-$1000 to transport my bike to St. John's, which seems expensive. Another forum messenger, Lee, messages and offers an alternative. He and his fiancée will drive from Happy Valley-Goose Bay to St. John's in a couple of weeks and he plans to bring his own motorcycle with him. He generously offers to make room for my bike too, hauling it more than 1000 miles in exchange for "a bite and a beer". What is it with the people of Newfoundland Labrador? I wish the world had more of them.

Ski Bum forwards an email address for Tammy who is part of the local motorcycling community. Her daughter has just moved out leaving a spare room that we can rent for the rest of the summer. She offers to pick me up, so that we can move out of the hotel. She doesn't want any rent, but says we pitch in for utilities. Her generosity moves me to tears. Not that it takes much to do that these days. I'm not sure if it's my exhaustion or the lingering drugs, but I'm an emotional, sentimental mess. I cry at even the slightest hint of a happy, sappy or sad moment.

Murph stops by the hotel and introduces himself, a giant teddy bear of a man. He offers to store my bike at his place when Lee brings it to St. John's. The chain of people I'm grateful to continues to grow. Brian and he go for a ride while I work up the nerve to call my grandmother and tell her about my accident.

One day I crutch my way down to the hotel lobby and hail a cab to the hospital. I'm scheduled for a follow-up appointment with Dr. Stone. The only clothes I can get on over my cast is a pair of track shorts. I pair them with a down jacket and a single tennis shoe. The rainy day, and subsequently wet sidewalks, make me nervous while my shoe and crutches slip on the wet surfaces.

X-rays provide my first look at my new mechanical leg. It's intense. After I'm shown to an exam room, a tech comes to remove my bandages and half cast. He cuts the gauze, exposing my leg all the way to my toes. The entire front of my leg is yellow and swollen. I don't see much bruising, but I'm afraid to look too closely.

Cam spreads the bandages wider and uses my big toe as a handle to lift my leg out of the tray-like cast. There's dried blood around my incisions. My knee was disassembled and used as the entry point for hammering the 13-inch titanium rod down through the center of my tibia to my ankle. At my ankle and knee there are incisions where screws were inserted to hold the rod in place.

Dr. Stone reports that my x-rays are good, and tells Cam to pull all 22 staples and book a follow-up appointment in five weeks. One of the staples placed too close to my ankle bone is bent and mangled. Healing skin has grown around it and Cam has to tear it out. I'm told to wait another week before getting my leg wet since the incision sites are still open. As Cam maneuvers my leg to do his work, I catch sight of the back of my lower leg and my breath catches in my throat.

It's as black as any bruise I've ever seen. I was once kicked by a horse which left a grapefruit-sized black lump on my thigh for more than a month, but this bruising is worse. I feel sick. From my mid-thigh to my ankle, my leg is a collage of various shades of purple, black and green and it's oh, so dark.

Dr. Stone says he thinks I could be back on my bike 12 weeks post-surgery, but that I won't be completely healed by then. He thinks I'll be able to handle having my leg down for longer periods of time without much pain, but that I won't have much strength and will have a limp for a long time. I can rest my leg on the ground now but can't put any weight on it for five weeks. I'm supposed to start working on ankle and knee range of motion.

Cam washes my leg and wraps it in fresh bandages. He fits me with a boot and says I'm good to go. I have to wear it 24-hours a day including while I sleep. I'm exhausted after my outing, but in good spirits. There's enough summer left for me to heal, get back on the bike and continue my trip before winter arrives.

At the weekend, Tammy picks me up to move me to her house. Our trip goes quickly and we talk the entire way. Before I know it, we arrive at her house and I begin the long journey across her short driveway and up the four daunting steps to her front porch.

I spend my first few days blogging, reading and resting. After a day or two I get the urge to cook a meal, which makes me feel useful and normal. I spend afternoons on the deck listening to birds and watching three chubby spiders weave webs under the grill. We spend evenings learning about Newfoundland, its music and history. Sad to think we would have rushed our way across, if it weren't for my accident. Maybe that's the silver lining.

Lee and his fiancée, arrive two weeks after my surgery, and meet us at Murph's house to deliver my bike. They're incredibly nice. We dine together on moose burgers, cod and chips, and cod cheeks at a local pub. Lee suffered a tib-fib break in a wreck a few years back. It took him a while to get back on a bike, but eventually he did. Later he had another wreck which broke his femur and laid him up for six months. His story makes me feel lucky. My accident could have been much worse.

I thank him for helping me, and wish them both a lifetime of happiness after their upcoming wedding. It's early but I need to go home. I'm exhausted.

It's finally time to take a real bath, all by myself. I work my way into the bathroom, run a bath, and start to unwrap my leg. It's hard to find a way to maneuver into the slippery tub, with my lack of upper body strength and only one leg to brace myself. Eventually I do, and submerge my injured leg for the first time in weeks.

My skin is thick and scaly, with a strange texture. Hairs have grown long and seem abnormally dark against my pale skin. My toenails are long and yellow. My poor leg is repulsive. As I sit and soak for a minute, I feel completely vulnerable. I don't want to bump or hurt my leg, but I have to stop babying it. I soak for a few minutes before beginning small movements with my ankle and knee in the warm water, trying to gain millimeters of flexibility.

Tammy invites Brian for a motorcycle ride. As I prepare for yet another nap, Murph calls to invite me for a drive along the coast with him and Danielle. I excitedly accept and hurry to get ready, forgetting my camera's memory card in my rush. They collect me in Danielle's SUV since Murph only owns motorcycles. Danielle is lovely and sweet and her beautiful peaches and cream complexion frames a radiant, kind smile. I'd forgotten about her injured leg until I catch a hint of her limp as we get into the car. They make me feel instantly comfortable.

We head out on the Irish Loop past rocky highlands dotted with scrubby spruce trees and small ponds. Just outside the city the rugged land opens up as we head south to Witless Bay. Small dead-end arms that branch off the highway lead to villages on the sea, each with its own protected harbor and fleet of fishing boats. Crab pots, casting nets and lobster traps are stacked near homes and harbor shanties waiting for their seasons.

At St. Michael's we park and walk down to the dock and where I see white clouds floating under the surface of the water. A closer look reveals these are fish heads and attached vertebrae slowly swaying in the drift. Danielle says that back in the day fish heads were used in stew so nothing went to waste, but now the fishermen strip the fish of the fillets and discard the rest.

We stop in Fermeuse where they treat me to the best fish and chips I've ever had. Afterwards, Danielle drives us to Port Kirwan to a hidden camping spot high on a rocky cliff overlooking the sea. The land is covered with evergreens, lush grass and wildflowers. Sea birds nest along the cliff faces and ride the winds over the dark blue ocean. I make a silent promise to myself to come back again someday when I can more fully enjoy the incredible beauty of Newfoundland. It's like no place I've ever seen.

Murph is like an encyclopedia of Newfoundland, aka "The Rock". He entertains me for hours with his knowledge of the language, history and culture, the sea, the cod industry and nearly any other topic.

He tells me about the shortest conversation in the world: Two fisherman are rowing, one coming in from the sea and one rowing out of their small bay. They have their backs to each other as they row, and meet without having known about the other until their boats cross. The outgoing cries "Arn?" (as in "are there (any fish)?") and the incoming replies "Narn." (as in "there are none").

In the old days, the men of Newfoundland rowed all the way out of the coves each morning, fished all day and then rowed back to deliver their day's catch to the women before a few hours' sleep and then starting all over again the next morning.

While Danielle drives us in and out of coves, Murph points out rocky islets just off the coast covered in puffin nests. Icebergs are common here and the most southerly herd of caribou in the world is grazing nearby. Murph has hosted countless riders from around the world and is an open, warm and genuine host. I can only imagine how many people he has shared this beautiful place with.

After a thoroughly enjoyable day, they drive through Petty Harbor, one of the prettiest villages so far. Its narrow inlet leads to a rocky cleft which is peppered with candy-colored hillside homes. We drive to Cape Spear, the easternmost point in North America, and through the center of St. John's so I can see the Battery, a neighborhood of century-old cliff-side homes.

St. John's is a working port located in a large bowl-shaped harbor, and its mix of industrial and Victorian-era homes is lovely. We stop at the railway station to admire the lovely copper-roofed building which was home to the Newfie Bullet, a steam train that had to stop every several miles to restock wood for its stove and water for steam, and therefore took ages to cross The Rock. Leave it Newfoundlanders' good sense of humor to give it the sarcastic name.

Danielle drives us to Quidi Vidi, nestled just inside a narrow crack of rock from the sea, only wide enough for a single small fishing boat at a time. Finally, we head for home. At Tammy's, Murph helps me up the steps after I thank them for the incredible day. It's 8:30 p.m. Unbelievably, it's the longest stretch of wakefulness I've had since my accident. I go straight to bed.

Tammy's ex-husband, Ian, offers us a family cabin for a week while Tammy has visitors. I haven't even met Ian, which makes his offer that much more generous. Newfoundlanders, as I am learning, are a tight-knit community who support each other and strangers equally, in any way possible. Tammy drives me to Brigus and helps me settle into the cutest little coastal cabin I've ever seen. Its hillside lot overlooks a tiny village and the small bay of fishing boats. Wildflowers and heavily laden blueberry and raspberry bushes surround the cabin on all sides, and will later keep me busy with their offerings.

Notwithstanding its seaside location, the cabin itself is a small paradise. There is a wood stove in the central room. Tiny rooms radiate out from each of the living room's four sides - a kitchen to the south with hand-carved wooden cabinets, a bathroom to the west, a bedroom to the north and a sunroom to the east which overlooks the sea. The walls are covered with planks, varnished to seal in their golden hue. The sunroom is filled with books, record albums, games and binoculars to provide hours of entertainment. I prop my leg up on a floral chintz ottoman and droop into the matching chair.

One morning, I take a shower and hobble my way to the bedroom to dress. In the three weeks since surgery, I've gained flexibility and can bend my leg more, offering my first good peek at the damage.

While my incision sites are healing fairly well, they are lumpy and starting to build thick scar tissue. My bruising must be working its way loose now, as the color of the back of my leg has darkened further to a purplish black from the top of my thigh to the bottom of my foot. My leg is sore, and my skin stings as though it had been burned. As I run my hand lightly down my leg, I can feel a large lump of hard knotted tissue in my calf. It feels like someone shoved a piece of lumber under the skin, as big as a paperback book.

Areas of sickly yellow and sour green have started to creep out from the blackness into the previously healthy looking skin surrounding the bruise, leaking around the sides of my leg. Spider-web-like hairline streaks of blood radiate out in all directions like microscopic lightning bolts stretching out from the blackest of storm clouds. My leg is swollen, nearly all the time, and as I hold my foot for a moment to feel its heat, my hand leaves a 1-inch deep impression in the blister-like bubble that covers the top of it. A New England expression pops into my head: my leg looks "wicked bad".

I crutch myself out to the small back porch one afternoon and sit down in the warm sun, armed with a quilt in case of a chill. I try to wander out ten or twenty feet from the cabin, but my crutch tips get tangled in the long, uncut grass. I'm afraid of toppling over so opt for the safety of the porch. Tiny blue butterflies take pity on me and momentarily leave their flowers to flutter by.

Lovely variations of grass grow here, some with fluffy foxtail plumes and others with crested herringbone patterned wheatgrass tops, and bear grass that I've only ever seen in flower shops back home. For something to do, I braid grasses together, and bundle small bouquets of wildflowers that I gather from the safety of an arms-length of the porch.

One afternoon, Murph and Danielle bring a buffet of treats from Bidgoods, including moose pie and seal flipper pie. They've brought homemade bread, muffins and a partridgeberry pie. Danielle warms the meat pies in the oven while we sit and Murph inspects my leg. He used to be a nurse.

Danielle and Murph start the buffet with cod au gratin, a delicious homemade casserole, made with some of her family's catch. Next up is moose pie, which is like a pot pie covered in golden crust. Larges cubes of meat are mixed with potatoes and carrots, and covered in a rich brown gravy. It's delicious.

On to seal flipper pie. I ask if the pie really is what the name implies, and they confirm that it is. I hesitate for a moment as I envision a baby fur seal looking imploringly to me, but put the image out of my mind and take a bite. It too is like a pot pie. The flavor reminds me of beef liver, which is one of my least favorite dishes, so I pass it to Brian.

As the men do the dishes, I look out the small window of the kitchen to the sea, and watch the fog roll in. I feel whole and healed, even if only temporarily. Danielle and Murph feel like they've always been a part of my life, like family.

They warm dessert up while Brian dries the dishes. Partridgeberries are exactly as Danielle described, like tiny cranberries. She suggests that a pie filled with them is much better with whipped cream to sweeten them up a bit.

Finally, Murph announces that it's "moose thirty", meaning the roads are becoming more hazardous with the combination of the softening twilight of the day and the increased moose activity brought on by dusk. Before they go, Danielle mentions a work trip that she will take in a few weeks, to the Burin Peninsula. They invite us to go with them. We quickly accept.

Our days at the cabin fly past. I watch whales as they cruise along the coast giving away their position only now and then by a momentary breach or spray from their blowholes. One particular day the sea looks extra sparkly, like an ocean of glitter. The sun shimmers off the ripples, better than any sequined Oscar dress.

I'm getting restless, which must mean I'm getting stronger. One morning, I lie awake staring up at a lovely melon-colored glow on the bedroom ceiling, and sit up to see the sunrise coming in through the window at the foot of the bed. There's a beautiful sky of red, orange, and pink. I get up and wander out to get my camera. I take a couple of shots and go back to bed.

My second shower is highlighted by my having to ask Brian to help me clean something from my injured foot. I thought it was a slippery handful of shampoo or softened soap, but I can't figure out how anything would have gotten on the bottom of my foot. I've been so careful to not put it down because I'm still not allowed to put any weight on it. As I lay back onto the bed and raise my left leg in the air, Brian inspects the white sludge plastered to the bottom of my foot. He thinks it may be soap too and goes to get paper towels to remove it.

When he wipes off the bottom of my foot, I can feel something slide off and my foot cool immediately and start to itch. Then it hits Brian, and a moment later hits me. The stench. What he wiped away isn't soap at all, but nearly half an inch of thick slimy dead skin. My poor foot has been rotting away in its boot without my knowing it. It's hilarious, embarrassing and disgusting all in one breath, literally. I laugh, then start to cry, then laugh again. After he cleans me up I rip the boot liner out of the boot and see the inside spotted with moisture which must be perspiration. My numb leg has been a traitor hiding this putrid secret from me.

After we return to Tammy's, Danielle calls to invite us on a last-minute trip to another part of the island, where she has a short work assignment. We gratefully accept. She drives me while the men ride their motorcycles. I like Danielle. There's no end to our conversations and giggles.

She tells me about a time when she and Murph rode up a narrow lane lined with trees when suddenly they came into a small clearing. At first, they weren't sure what they were seeing. It took her a moment to realize they had stumbled into a migrating colony of Monarch butterflies, thousands of them. She says it was the most magical thing she'd ever seen.

While she works during the days, the men go for rides to explore the area. One evening we all drive to Burgoyne's Cove to see a motorcycle friend of Murph's. Glass calm waters and colorful fishing boats list in the tiny inlets of this idyllic coast. I wait in the car while the others go into the friend's shop to talk motorcycles and sample some of his homemade iceberg beer. Apparently, that's a thing around here. You can tow your very own "bergie bit" in from the sea and capture the centuries-old pristine water that melts from it to use in making beer.

On the way to the apartment that evening, we pass a movie theater, and I catch myself fantasizing about what a luxury it would be to simply walk into a theater again. Things I've taken for granted for years, now seem like liberties. While I'm definitely making progress, I still have a long road ahead. My leg aches and throbs if it's not elevated for more than two hours. By then my leg has also turned from a slightly purplish tint, to grayish purple, indicating that my circulation still isn't working right.

Danielle's job takes us further up the coast to the Bonavista Peninsula. Caravanning suits me, I think to myself, as I feel a wave of gratitude for Danielle and Murph supporting my still ravenous case of wanderlust. We drive up the eastern side of the peninsula to the village of Bonavista, and out to the cape and lighthouse where she stops to take in the view. There's an enormous dark storm cloud passing Bonavista Bay which makes me grateful for my mode of transportation today. I hobble over as far as I dare to look down the sixty-foot cliff to the sapphire water. We carry on to Dungeon Provincial Park before we make a hasty retreat to the hotel as the storm hits us.

We enjoy the evening with a group dinner in the hotel restaurant, including iceberg beer and partridgeberry cheesecake. After dinner, we drive to Elliston, the root cellar capitol of the world, which is much more impressive than I thought it would be.

Dozens of cellar entrances made with dry stack stone (making them look like hobbit holes) dot the landscape. A sign as we come into town says "road is bad for…", and where it should say how many kilometers someone has spray painted "ever" which seems more appropriate as we bounce along.

We drive to Maberly to see if we can catch a glimpse of the puffins which have inadvertently created a local business by their choice of residence. Tours are offered everywhere along this coast which is littered with lots of small islets just offshore. While I see tons of birds from the mainland, I don't see any puffins.

After a single night in Bonavista, we make our way back to Clarenville late in the day. It's been a month since my surgery and I feel stronger each day.

Danielle and I meander along the coast, popping in and out of villages for each new spectacular view, as we make our way to the western side of the peninsula for the return journey. All the while the bikes circle like satellites that can't escape the orbit of the SUV.

The road turns inland. Several miles in, we meet a car that flashes its headlights at us. Murph puts his splayed hand up to his helmet imitating antlers, signifying that he thinks the car was warning us of moose near the road ahead. I get my camera ready. Half a mile ahead I see them, a bull and cow, on the left side of the road up on a bank. Dani backs up for me to take a photo but the moose are already gone, having ducked into the trees only feet from where they'd been grazing.

At dinner, Murph tells us about a rider from Maine, a woman named Molly, who rode up to St. John's on her way to the Trans-Labrador two years previously on her TW 200. While she was inside a shop in town her bike was stolen. Murph says locals wouldn't have done it, but that the influx of people from all over the country for oil industry work has changed things. Molly's story was shared on a local radio station, which spurred locals to donate gear and money so she could finish her trip. Murph says locals found her bike chained to a fence at a house, so Molly got her bike back too.

Back in St. John's we settle into quiet life again. I catch up on my journal and Brian tinkers on the bikes, working to get mine hammered back into shape. My left pannier took the brunt of the wreck, and needs work to get it back into a useable shape.

A side effect of the surgery and stress of the accident is that I'm still losing my hair by the handful. I spend more than one afternoon hobbling around the house while sweeping up my shed. I'm amazed I'm not bald yet.

Little did I know how strange and painful it would be to start to put some weight on my injured leg. I can't believe how hesitant I am to even try. One morning, as I prepare breakfast in the kitchen I spin around to catch the refrigerator door and come straight down on my leg. A lightning bolt of pain blasts right up through me to the top of my head. It's so sharp and strong that I think I might pass out, but then it passes. At least now I know how it feels and that I can get through it. I have less than six weeks until I want to be back on the bike. I'd better get busy.

We take another trip with Murph and Danielle. Our plans include a detour to St. Pierre, an island just off the coast which is legally part of France. It's a lovely day trip. Just a few miles off shore from Canada lies this tiny French oasis, complete with patisseries and boulangeries.

We pass through immigration on either side of the ferry ride, which means processing our passports and new entry stamps for Canada. It occurs to Brian that his new six-month entry permit into Canada may help with his visa trouble for the U.S.

That night Danielle prepares a Jiggs Dinner, a traditional Newfoundlander meal, made of boiled vegetables, salted beef and a bag of Pease pudding all boiled in a large pot. The hours of delicious smells torture us while it stews.

Before I know it, the middle of September is upon us, and I nervously count down to the day I will have to be strong enough to get back on the bike. I sort through gear and start to prepare for traveling again.

Brian and I rent a car and spend a week driving to the top of Newfoundland via Gros Morne National Park and the western coast. I want to see some of the things that I missed on the 1000 miles of road that my accident cost me. We see caribou and black fox, and even a strange new species, a Coywolf, half wolf and half coyote, which I recently read about in a local paper. We take the ferry to Labrador, visit Twillingate and take a ferry to Fogo Island. We visit Burgeo, Cornerbrook, Lark Harbour and Trout River on our way back to St. John's. Each stop holds me in a trance with its postcard-worthy quaint fishing villages. I hobble around docks, and to and from our campsites, getting stronger each day.

Brian tells me that a friend of his is coming to Newfoundland in a few days and he wants to go meet him. This will be the end of Nevil's round-the-world motorcycle ride. He crossed Europe and Asia and then rode from western Canada to his home in Canmore, before finishing this last stretch of his ride, which will bring him to Cape Spear.

Brian organizes an informal welcome party at the finish line. He reaches out to local riders and invites a half dozen people to meet Nevil. Brian offers me a space on the back of his bike if I'm able. I've just started going without crutches occasionally, and decide to give it a try.

A local man has done a bang-up job of Franken-stitching my boot back together after the EMT's attempt to cut it off me the day of my wreck. I wear jeans, since I have no riding pants, and my riding jacket. I grab my helmet and gloves and hobble out toward Brian as he warms up his bike. I'm terrified. But I don't allow myself to stop even for a second to think about it. If I do, I might not go. Not just to Cape Spear, but anywhere. Ever again.

I'm not even sure how to get on his bike. My left leg would normally be placed on the back peg and used to lift my entire body up onto the bike as I swing my right leg over to the other side. But my left leg is less than three weeks into bearing any weight at all, much less all of me in a maneuver like that. Instead, I try the reverse from the right side and awkwardly climb aboard. Before I know it, I nod to Brian and we are off. This is it. The first time I've been on a motorcycle since my accident.

As he rolls out of Tammy's driveway and toward the main road, I grab Brian tightly. Having ridden my own bike for so long, I'm not a good passenger. But today, I'm even worse. I try to relax and breathe deeply. He turns onto the main road and heads through the suburbs of St. John's toward the center of the city.

I'm fearful of traffic. I dread bumps. I'm uncomfortable in turns and at stops. I feel out of sorts and disconnected. But I'm here, and I'm doing my best. We ride for 10 minutes or so before I realize that I'm shaking. And not just a little. Both my legs are uncontrollably and visibly shaking on the pegs. It spooks me that I can't make it stop. It's a little chilly, but it's not the cold that's causing it. Five more minutes into the ride, and I start to get overwhelmed. I want off the bike.

I'm dreading every mile we have ahead of us and I don't think I can do it. I'm so uncomfortable and panicked that I'm about to nudge Brian and have him drop me off somewhere. I never imagined what it would be like to get back on the bike. I had no idea I would hate it this badly or be so scared. It's not the thought of a wreck. I trust Brian more than myself. I have no idea what it is, but I feel completely vulnerable and exposed, and I hate it. I want off this fucking bike.

My chest starts to squeeze and I feel like I can't breathe. My throat closes. How is it that at 43-years-old my instinct is still to want my mother? I'd want my Dad, but he would tell me to toughen up, and right now I feel like a good dose of sympathy. We still have miles to go. I tell myself if I can make it just one more mile I will allow myself to tell Brian I've had enough and to let me off. It's all I can do to finish that mile. When I do, I decide to hold on for just one more mile. I keep this up until I reach a tipping point, where I know we have more miles behind us than ahead of us, and I start to think I might be able to make it.

After roughly 45 minutes, we finally make it to the Cape Spear parking lot and see our friends. I've never been a hotter mess of emotions all at once – fear, frustration, relief, pride, anger, and panic. I practically leap off the bike, happy to leave it behind me.

We watch the entrance of the parking lot and spot a rider coming in who parks next to our group and dismounts, pulling off his helmet to introduce himself. He is Allan from Vancouver, a solo rider just finishing his post-retirement cross-Canada ride, and jokes he thought our welcoming committee might be for him.

A half-hour wait produces two more bikes. There's no mistaking the look of a true adventure bike, and these are. They aim straight for us and we cheer as they pull up. Nevil lowers his kickstand as I notice the red maple leaf at the base that holds his bike up. His friend Jim accompanied him for this last leg and both men smile broadly as they catch their breath.

It's an incredible moment to witness, and it makes my nerve-wracking first ride on the bike worth it. After photos and stories, we ride off for food and beers. Later that night a group of us go downtown to get Screeched in at a local bar. Several of us even kiss the cod.

On Sunday, Ian has us over for a Jiggs dinner which is fantastic. A friend of Ian's, Michelle, is there too and offers Brian and I the use of her cabin on Prince Edward Island when she finds out we plan to ride there in a couple of weeks. Will the generosity of people, of Canadians, never end? I hope not.

Allan suggests we keep in touch with him and let him know when we plan to cross into Mexico. He and his wife have a home in Tucson and he's ridden into Mexico several times. He might ride with us into Baja.

I spend my last weeks on the Rock trying to get my mind and

body ready to get back on the bike. I practice the small ankle movements I know I will need. It'll be hard for me to get my toe under the shift lever with the limited flexibility I have in my ankle. After sitting on the bike and practicing the movement without it running, I finally decide it's time to take go for my first ride. I don my Franken-boots and borrowed camo dirt bike pants, go out, and start my bike.

I climb on from the right side. Brian helps me lift Betty upright, since my left leg isn't strong enough. But once she's upright, I can hold her in place. I pull in the clutch, drop her into first gear and slowly pull out of the grassy drive and onto the paved dead-end lane of Tammy's house. It doesn't amount to much of a first ride, but it's successful.

About a week before we catch the mainland ferry I take my first ride in real traffic. We ride north to the next town. Evening traffic provides lots of practice with stops and starts, and having to balance the full weight of my bike with my bad leg. Even with both legs on the ground I'm unsteady. My leg is just too weak. But it will have to work. I'm worried about stopping on slopes or angled road surfaces where my leg will really have to bear a lot of weight. I will have to become very selective about intersections, and where I stop.

Before we know it, it's time to go. Murph rides my bike to the ferry, not so much because I don't think I can do it, but because I worry it will take everything I have just to get across the peninsula and I want to save something for the miles I have to cover on the other side. Danielle gives me a lift in her Jeep, just like old times. Tammy and her friend Dave ride along too, a small going away party of sorts. Murph rides my bike the last few miles to the ferry port guard shack. Danielle and I chatter our way through the last mile as we follow.

I get the last of my riding kit on, just to cross the quarter-mile long dock to the loading ramp. Before I put my helmet on, I give and receive a round of hugs. My hug with Danielle brings us both to tears. I feel like I'm leaving my sister behind but I hope to return someday.

With shaking hands, I grip my bars and wave one last goodbye before riding my bike through the gates to the lineup. After a short wait, we are waved onto the deck and directed to the side to park and tie down our bikes. I'm surprised to see two other riders. We tend to the bikes and make our way upstairs, finding a place on the lounge deck and settle in for the night crossing to Sydney, Nova Scotia.

Hours pass while we take turns sleeping. Our tank bags and jackets serve as pillows. My leg is elevated while I journal. We watch a movie, and watch the show of human life as it unfolds before us in the form of bearded truck drivers at the snack bar and weary travelers who walk over to the windows occasionally to see if they can spot land yet.

Eventually we hear the ship's call notifying us we're nearing port. After a short wait, we are allowed to go to the lower decks to unstrap the bikes and get ready to ride onto the mainland. The thought of maneuvering my heavily loaded bike on the wet metal deck fills me with fear. I have hardly any footing on dry surface as it is, much less on slippery decking. We gear up, turn the bikes around in the empty hold and wait for the deck crew to wave us out the open door.

When we are called forward, Brian rides up first. I watch where he chooses his line and follow him up the ramp to the concrete slope and onto the road to Sydney.

Well, I guess this is it. I'm back on the road.

5 A NEW BEGINNING

Let me recommend the best medicine in the world: a long journey, at a mild season, through a pleasant country, in easy stages.

-James Madison

As luck would have it, this season is perfect for riding in New England. Having experienced its autumnal foliage years ago, I'd hoped to witness nature's brilliant autumn show once more. But at the outset of our trip I knew we wouldn't be riding through the northeastern United States and Canada at the right time of year to see it. My accident changed that timeline completely.

The Cabot Trail is one of a dozen roads I've heard about the past few years while talking with other riders about their favorite highways. Fortuitously, the ferry drops us onto the mainland less than hour from it. After a good night's sleep, it seems the perfect way to re-start my trip.

Meandering along the coastline around Cape Breton in northern Nova Scotia, the Cabot Trail darts in and out of quaint villages and offers picturesque views. I'm told it's beautiful any time of year, but being here when the leaves are turning from green to shades of orange and red, make it especially lovely.

Leaving Sydney, we head for Saint Ann's on the southeast corner of the loop. I'm feeling well rested, and look forward to the 200-plus miles of scenery today. Just after Saint Ann's we hit a section of construction and a few miles of milled asphalt, which makes my front wheel wander a bit, giving me the feeling that my bike is out of control. My heart races.

We stop on a hillside to wait for a pilot car. It takes effort to maneuver my bad leg to get the kickstand down for the wait. And again, to raise it when it's time to go. But soon enough we are on our way. I haven't covered this many miles in a single day for more than three months, and I'm worried about my energy level. I pay close attention to how I feel and take frequent breaks. My endurance isn't a fraction of what it was before my accident. I get worn out on a short walk these days.

The road leads up a hill and through the forest, which is accented with autumn colors, until it comes out again at the coast. It's the last day of September, and the colors won't peak for another week or two but it's gorgeous. I'm tentative with my riding, each pothole, breeze and slick spot spooks me. Deep shadows on the road blind me and I have a hard time concentrating. The road twists and turns in places but it's an easy enough ride and offers me a chance to enjoy the view.

We pull in for gas at Wreck Cove, and then carry on through Ingonish, along the eastern shore of the peninsula, reaching Cape Smokey for a break in a small park. I stretch my leg and eat a banana I have stashed in my tank bag.

A short ride up the road we reach a turn at Neil's Harbour to head over the highlands to the western shore. We've been riding in and out of Cape Breton Highlands National Park. Each of the communities is excluded, but the forested stretches are all park land. At Pleasant Bay, there is a lovely spot I want to stop, but I already know we are short on daylight, so we keep going. Just beyond, we wind up a hill and stop at a scenic overlook to take in the view of the town and sea. A Ducati and a Triumph Tiger stop to chat for a few minutes before they blast off ahead of us.

The western coast road is the loveliest part yet. As we wind in and out of the coastal turns, I look out at the apex of each outer curve and see miles of serpentine roadway laid out ahead decorated in fall colors. I watch a bald eagle flying overhead, drifting on the breeze.

I love that in one day I've traveled from a part of Canada that seems like it was transplanted from Ireland, to this part which was settled by the French and has names like Cheticamp, La Prairie and Belle-Marche. At Margaree Forks, we turn back toward Sydney. The tradeoff for lovely fall colors, is shorter riding days, and the sun is getting ahead of us. My bike is running well and I stayed upright for over 250 miles. All in all, a good day.

After another good night's sleep, we ride around the south edge of Bras D'or Lake on our way to Halifax. Near Irish Cove it starts to rain, and I'm amazed how quickly I get cold. By Port Hawkesbury I'm frozen and exhausted. We duck into a Tim Horton's for a hot drink. My leg hurts much worse in the cold, making me limp badly. Most of the time I can hide it, but today I look like an old pirate with a peg-leg stride.

Tammy's donated riding pants aren't waterproof. So Murph generously donated a pair of his riding pant liners, to serve as rain pants until I can get to the U.S. and buy new riding gear. They require a Jethro-style rope belt to keep them up. I can just imagine Murph getting a look at me and bellowing "Lard, thunderin' Jeezus". But in this downpour, I'm grateful to be fairly dry.

Nova Scotia is gorgeous. Rolling hills and vivid green meadows give way to spruce and pine covered forests. Red barns and small white farmhouses dot the fields of this "Ann of Green Gables" fantasy land. Lovely lakeshores and rocky coasts combine to make it the perfect mix of beautiful landscapes. The rain clears by Antigonish, but only for a few miles. By Truro it's pouring again. Another Tim Horton's comes into view just in time. I'm shivering and miserable. My gloves are soaked and I expect my hands to be black from dye but they aren't. It's raining hard enough to rinse the dye out of them before my hands get stained.

Two sixty-something men, one big and one small, sit at the table next to us and strike up a conversation with me while Brian gets our tea. They run a security company and used to be prison guards. Brian chat with them while I'm in the bathroom and tells him about his ride up from Argentina and my breaking my leg. They're kind, and ask about our travels and inquire as to whether or not people cut the bikes off in traffic. We sit in the dry indoors for an hour, but the rain never lets up. Finally, it's time to just get it over with.

We gear up. I tuck my hair inside my jacket and pull my Buff over the top of it to hold it in place. Back into Murph's pants and my Jethro belt. Back into wet gloves. Back into the rain.

On the bike, we join in busy traffic which is now filled with freshly loaded school buses. We ride south to Halifax. The rain is heavy and steady but thankfully there's no wind. After several miles, I see a sign. Halifax is 40 miles away. At some point, we relinquish two-lane roads to the highway. The further south we go, the heavier the traffic and rain. At the northern edges of Halifax, we watch for signs for our exit. It's a relief when I see it. I'm happy to call it a day. This second consecutive day of 200-plus miles has left me tired and cold.

In our room, we hang gear over every possible surface to try and dry it out. Nothing like a couple of smelly vagabond gypsies in your local Holiday Inn. Brian hangs his gloves and socks over the heater which makes the room stink. We strip and get our swimsuits on and head to the pool. I look down and see my injured leg is a lavender gray color from thigh to toes, while my other leg is beet red.

When I slip into the warm water, I instantly stop the downward spiral of emotions that began take over this afternoon. I feel like a child, whiny, and on the verge of tears for nearly anything. I have to remind myself to be patient and that this is part of the healing process.

My boot has left a deep indentation the length of my calf and ankle. I can make out the knit pattern of my wool socks where they were pressed into my skin. Without being elevated today, my leg has swollen more than normal so I rub it to try and get some of the stiffness out of it. After 10-15 minutes, Brian decides to go back to the room, and asks if I want him to run a bath for me. I'm grateful for his thoughtfulness.

In the morning, I search for nearby UNESCO world heritage sites, and we gear up to ride out. We avoid the center of Halifax, and drop onto a twisty two-lane that rolls along the shore for miles. There's no wind today but plenty of sun. We ride along the water's edge past Shad Bay, Prospect Bay, and through West Dover. At a sign to Peggy's Cove we stop to take a photo before turning into the village. A sign explains that a passenger on a passing ship, Peggy, was headed to meet her fiancé in Halifax when the ship foundered. She was rescued from the sea, and when people came to visit her they called her "Peggy of the cove". Her name stuck to the cove where she was found.

The ground is solid granite. As we hike up to the lighthouse I stumble over the crevices and uneven terrain. I'm getting tired of my leg not cooperating. It doesn't exactly make me feel graceful or feminine, especially with my wonky gangster limp. But it still gets me around to see beautiful places like this, so I remind myself to keep my perspective.

Peggy's Cove is a popular place this time of year, as is the entire area. Gift shops are bustling; cafes are overflowing; and roads are lined with traffic. We chat with a local Harley rider for a few minutes after he asks where Brian's license plate is from. He thought the "GB" for Great Britain stood for Green Bay, which makes me laugh. My South Dakota license plate draws a little attention too, but not like Brian's bright yellow plate that doesn't reveal its home.

We carry on to Hackett's Cove for lunch. The coast road is beautiful as we continue west around the peninsula to the main part of the island. At some point, we pass a sign the Swissair Flight 111 Memorial, for the flight that crashed into the ocean just off Peggy's Cove in 1998.

The next day is filled with researching roads and places to visit, journaling, blogging, etc. It's amazing how much there is to do to maintain a life on the road. Brian constantly works on the bikes and I work to keep us fed and organized.

We find a note on our bikes one morning from a jealous rider - "FYYFF for getting to go ride long distance while I ride in a cage." (you're welcome to look the abbreviation up, but it's a tad vulgar). It makes us laugh. The reaction I get from most everyone is overwhelmingly positive, first, that I'm a female rider, and second, that I'm off on this big adventure. But once in a while I receive a little extra dose of encouragement from someone, an extra kind word, or a reminder that I'm living a dream, and it makes it all even more meaningful.

One afternoon we ride to the village of Lunenburg, one of the UNESCO sites on my list. I'm mesmerized by the beautiful red waterfront buildings in this British colonial settlement. There's a double-masted tall-ship tied to the pier flying an American flag on her stern. Two men work at the top of the rear mast while two women work on deck. I think for a moment about calling out to see if I can come aboard and take a closer look, but I don't. Later, I google the Unicorn and read she's owned by a New Jersey couple who partner with Sisters Under Sail, an organization that offers a sailing school to girls through a scholarship program. I wish I would have met them. Note to self - never miss an opportunity like that.

We walk up a side street from the port and find a café with a back patio overlooking the water. The breeze is a little strong which makes me second guess our choice of locations, but we stay. We each order a cider and a bowl of seafood chowder.

After lunch, we carry on along the coast to Mahone Bay where I see mannequins on the front lawns and porches of several of the Victorian houses. I wonder what they're for. We park on the side of the road and walk to a local gift shop to get the scoop. We've happened upon an annual autumn scarecrow festival which draws people from miles around. There's a tour of the cemetery tonight complete with pumpkin luminarias.

As we try to keep pace with the sun as it moves farther south each day in its autumnal drift, we ride for the northern coast to catch the ferry to Prince Edward Island at Pictou. A blog that I stumbled across suggested taking the ferry to the island and riding the bridge back to the mainland.

On our way out, we stop in Truro again, on the edge of the Salmon River to watch the tidal bore, the reversing of the flow of the river as the ocean tide rises higher than the level of the river. This unique event isn't something I've ever seen, and since it happens roughly every twelve hours, it's easy to catch. It looks like a 3-foot brown wave rolling gently up the river the wrong way. It passes and then it's gone.

The ferry crossing goes smoothly and we find ourselves on the quaint island riding across picturesque rolling hills of farms and pastures. We ride up a short dirt road to see the lighthouse at Point Prim before carrying on around the island to the small cabin that a friend generously offered us for the night. Dalvay Beach is our halfway-point, stunning with its high windswept dunes. PEI would be a paradise if it weren't so windy and chilly. But October isn't high season here, so I'm sure I'm not seeing the best weather of the year. The place is deserted.

We spend one night on the island and then pick up the pace. The 8-mile long Confederation Bridge takes us back to the mainland. We carry on toward Cap-Pele where we stop for fresh fried clams, Moncton where we detour to see the Hopewell Rocks at low tide, and Saint John where we are reminded of the difference in spelling between here and St. John's, which apparently is a big deal. This week is a series of one-night stands, so to speak, as we continue toward the U.S. border. Each day I get a little stronger.

I'm impressed by the miles and miles of chain link fence along the Trans-Canada Highway, intended to keep moose from wandering onto the road. Spruce trees and rock outcroppings fill my visor for a few days.

In early October, we reach the United States, three months later than expected, but at least we made it. I'm a little emotional when I arrive at my own country. Canada and her people have been kinder and more generous to me than I could have ever imagined, but there's still no place like home.

Brian and I rehearse our story at our last Tim Horton's stop. He's nervous about mentioning that we are a couple and would rather say we are travel companions. We aren't sure if he will be granted re-entry into the United States, and don't know what to do if he isn't. It's up to the border guards whose moods vary day by day.

We exit the TCH at Saint Stephen where Brian waves me ahead as we approach the border. I lead us through downtown and past the sign directing us to "USA/E-U" which confuses me momentarily until I remember my French. I pull into a lane to go through the Canadian checkpoint. We wait a few minutes, moving one car at a time, until we proceed through the Canada side and over the bridge to the United States. I go first and present my passport while Brian waits silently behind me. The officer asks how long we've been gone, where we are headed and how long Brian will be in the U.S. He seems nice, gives me back my passport and tells me that we need to go inside an office to apply for Brian's entry. We park and walk in.

Behind a long counter stand four large and intimidating U.S. Customs officers. I can feel Brian getting tense as we walk through the door. The officer from the booth walks in ahead of us and tells another officer what we need. Brian hands over his passport.

I'm a believer in breaking the ice with a smile and a laugh, to hopefully set a relaxed tone. Brian has a bad case of white coat syndrome at borders, so I try to take the happy offense (rather than defense) approach. The United States is operating under a federal government shutdown at the moment and I wonder how it will affect the officers' moods, but decide to dip a toe in the pool anyway. I smile and ask how they are, and the big guy of the bunch shoots some comment back about doing pretty well for not getting paid these days. That's all it takes.

The first officer hands Brian's passport on to another one that he refers to as "a straight shooter". I'm glad he's passed us off because he seems a little cocky. Not a good combination when mixed with Brian's tension.

There's an older officer sitting at a desk who says he's a "sugarcoater" when we ask who is the nicest of them to work with. I tell them it's a yin and yang thing since he complements the cocky one. A fourth officer working at a tall counter is quiet, not joking with us. Brian asks Straight Shooter if it's always this busy here and he says it is. Cocky guy says it's the sixth busiest port of entry to the U.S. and will be until he retires, whatever that means. Sugarcoater says they built a new complex of border offices up on the highway which has six lanes and it would've been faster for us to use it. I explain we are enjoying the coastal road and that from the looks of the long line behind us, everyone else must be too.

Straight Shooter asks Brian how long he will be in the U.S. Brian says we are headed to Mexico and plan to take 3-4 weeks to get there. Straight Shooter ask Brian for $6 for the application fee, but Brian doesn't have any U.S. dollars, so I run out to my bike to get my wallet. Silly me for having left it there anyway.

Just like that, Brian has a new three-month visa. We chat with them a few minutes more when they seem curious about the bikes and our travels. Cocky guy asks where we are headed and I say we're off to Acadia National Park. That national park has been on my bucket list for a while. Sugarcoater tells me it's closed because of the government shutdown. I'm crushed.

He says some people hiked into the park, despite the closure barricades, and that a few days ago, a woman who had done so fell and had to be evacuated. Now the handful of workers who are on site to manage the park have been authorized to arrest anyone caught hiking for federal trespassing. We ask for suggestions of places to camp and Silent guy points out a tourist office across the road. That's our cue to move along.

It's good to be home.

We ride out to Quoddy Head State Park, the easternmost point in the United States, and stop in Lubec for a Shepard's pie in a pub while we watch seals frolicking in the harbor. Late in the day we find a campsite just outside of town, happy to have the border behind us.

For all my hoping and wishing that Acadia will open before we get there, I'm rewarded with a bright orange blockade at the entrance. This national park will have to remain on my wish list. The road leads us on to Bar Harbor instead, for lunch and a view of sailboats and rock-studded shoreline. We meander the inland roads and coastal lanes for the next couple of days, and pass through a town named Ellsworth which reminds me now both of my home, where we have an Air Force Base with his name, and of Newfoundland, where the U.S. Air Force General (for which the South Dakota base is named) died in an airplane crash.

Wiscasset provides a lovely stop one day, with its views of the marshlands and the lovely buildings with their gray salt-air weathered shingle siding and white trim and shutters. We go on to Brunswick and Freeport.

As we pass a turn for Boothbay, I'm a tiny bit broken-hearted. Charles Kuralt's book, America, is one of my favorites. It recounts his first year of retirement during which he chose to spend each of those 12 months in his 12 favorite places in America. Boothbay Harbor, Maine was good enough to make his top 12, so it must be worth a look. But we're running out of time on this particular day. We've been invited to stay with Molly, the woman Murph told us about who had her bike stolen in St. John's, and need to make it to her place before dark.

There have been lots of caterpillars on the road the past few days, big fuzzy black ones, each with a copper band across their middles. When we meet Molly, she tells me that the width of the band is said to foretell the length of the upcoming winter. I avoid them once I figure out they aren't dried leaves. I comment to Brian on the thousands of them we have passed but he doesn't know what I'm talking about.

It's amazing how far we've come together and yet how insular we are, how individual our experiences are. We ride the same roads, pass the same things, etc., yet somehow can have completely different days. Cocooned in our own helmets for hours on end, we really don't spend any more time interacting with each other than couples who spend a couple of hours together each evening after their separate days.

Molly instructed us to watch for a road just before Cornish in Limington Township. She gave us directions for where to turn and said we should "follow the pavement until it ends and turn right at the fork", so I do. Or at least I think I do.

The road we take is rocky and narrow, just wide enough for a car if you don't stop to open any doors. We wind in a mile or two but never see even a single house. I finally stop and call her from my cell phone. She says I've missed a left turn early on in the road. We turn around, go back down the rocky hill and correct my error. We finally make our way up the lane, through our series of turnings, when I see a sign that says "donkey zone" letting me know we've arrived.

As we turn into an open meadow I see Molly walking toward us in trousers, a wool sailor cap and a large woolen men's quilted jacket. She has short salt-and-pepper hair, beautiful blue eyes, and an enormous warm smile.

Molly's family's farm is tucked into the woods on a back lane and is freckled with quirky cabins and critters. She feeds us a home-cooked dinner of roast chicken, and squash and vegetables from her farm. She introduces us to her family and her two burros, before starting a campfire outside the rustic artist's cabin across the meadow from the farmhouse. Her two sweet mutts, Booger and Badger follow us over. Molly lost Blue not that long ago and adopted Booger in hopes that Badger would perk up after having slept on Blue's grave for two days.

We have only just met this energetic and unique soul when she announces she's heading "down east" to the coast tomorrow to see her mother. But, she's quick to point out, we should stay as long as we like. She has some great rides to suggest. She's a generous woman.

Mid-October nights are chilly in Maine, so the fire pit is the perfect place to warm up, enjoy the outdoors and spend a couple of hours with Molly. She calls me "buddy". I like her instantly. In fact, I probably liked her long before I met her, from Murph's stories. She's a hoot. She regales us with tales from her Trans-Labrador motorcycle trip and the theft and return of her bike in Newfoundland. As she talks, we hear snapping twigs somewhere outside the ring of the fire's light and Molly says it's the orphaned raccoons she raised last year returning for a peek at the goings-on.

This land has been in Molly's husband's family for many years. She tells us they had to sell part of it a while back which she likens to losing a limb. Their two girls have been all over the world and have chosen to put down roots here. The girls have their own land and run their own farm-stand, having done so since they were kids. One of the girls wrote letters to the Diane Fossey/Jane Goodall counterpart who worked with orangutans in Borneo, and applied for a chance to go work there as a high school student. She was accepted and she and Molly went off to Borneo. Molly's been to Kenya, Madagascar, Nagaland and God only knows where else.

When their girls were little, Molly and John took a road trip for a couple months across the middle of the United States. They even visited South Dakota and Molly remembers John liking it because the land had good soil. Spoken like a true farmer.

Molly lost her dad recently to bone cancer and is mourning the loss. She's also missing her dog and the two orphaned raccoons she forced to go wild. Poor Molly.

She gives us a tour of her studio which has no electricity and is illuminated by candlelight. It's like touring a natural history museum with collections of bones, fossils, shells and seeds. Her father's paintings decorate the wood walls.

As it nears midnight, we retire to the cutest rustic cabin I've ever seen. It's small enough to make tiny homes look enormous and just big enough for a double mattress and the inward-swinging door.

In the morning, Molly draws us a map before she leaves. Her

husband, John, is heading out to go moose hunting with a friend so we have the place to ourselves. Molly's friend Jessica wants to buy us dinner at a bistro in town tonight. We've barely met Molly and have never even heard of Jessica. This kindness-of-strangers thing is overwhelming. I feel blessed nearly every day. We are supposed to stop at Krista's in Cornish this evening and ask for a gift certificate Jessica left for us at the counter.

Brian and I opt to travel light today and unload our gear into our small cabin. It's nice for a change, and makes the riding easier. Molly's hand-drawn map leads us onto dirt roads in rural Maine to a highway which will take us to Conway, just over the border in New Hampshire.

I'm headed to Whitehorse Gear for a new pair of riding pants. It turns out to be easy to find and a popular place. Riley, a blond shepherd collie mix, greets us at the door, and I know I've found my new favorite motorcycle gear shop.

A salesman named Jeff rode the Trans-Labrador Highway with a friend one summer and remembers his friend fishtailing up the road. He said he had to pour on the throttle to pull through the soft spots and straighten out. His buddy told him he did it because he didn't want to "break his leg". Hmm. Wish I'd known that before I went, although it's hard to imagine I would have had the courage to pour on the gas just before my wreck.

Jeff gives us the nickel tour before leaving me to shop. Trial and error leads me to new pants with removable liners. My camo pants will get one more day out before I donate them to Molly's local biker girlfriends, the Mechanical Donkeys.

Triumphs, Urals, Beemers and Harleys, with varied license plates, mingle in the parking lot. A woman from Whitehorse comes out to take our photo, a tradition with all long-distance visitors, and gives us a free copy of a book of great motorcycle rides in New England, compliments of the Whitehorse publishing division.

Molly's map leads us back across the Maine state line. Just before we cross, we stop for a slice of pizza. A local man asks where we are headed and confirms Molly's map is leading us to pure gold, literally. He says he's owned a motorcycle shop in the area for four decades, so he would probably know.

Highway 113 heads north to Evans Notch, one of the most beautiful day rides I've ever experienced. Trees are at their peak color at the moment, turning from chartreuse to bright gold. The road is freshly-sealed jet black, without so much as a single white stripe to ruin its perfect dark contrast against the golden canyon. Yellow leaves fall gently from above like a New Year's Eve cascade of balloons in Times Square. I lean back and forth, as the road winds up the notch, uninterrupted by any other traffic. For the first time since my wreck, my bike feels really good. It's absolute perfection. I will have to be sure to thank Molly for this beautiful day.

We stop at the Evans Notch sign for a moment to enjoy the silent stillness of this golden oasis. Behind a tree at the edge of the pullout, is a grave of a soldier who died in 1963. I think to myself it would be a lovely resting place. We ride further north and then turn to Bethel and Waterford. We stop at Melby's and go into the soda fountain to order a whoopee pie and a milk shake. Afterwards, we head back to Molly's to do some journaling before cleaning up and heading to Cornish for dinner. The farm is quiet and peaceful. Not a peep from anywhere except Booger who snuffles when he greets me.

Just before dusk we ride into Cornish and find the restaurant just past a few antique shops. There will be a wait unless we want to sit at lounge chairs in the cocktail area or take a table on the back deck which will be cool tonight. We opt for the deck.

A screened porch is canopied by small colorful paper lanterns while a stream rumbles somewhere below the wooden deck. There are only half a dozen tables, all of which are full except ours. To my surprise, Jessica is working tonight and will be our waitress. She comes over to welcome us, smiling brightly. She's sweet, slightly built, energetic and oh-so friendly. She keeps saying "yea!" which makes me giggle and feel at ease.

The menu is incredible and I'm genuinely impressed with this gem tucked away in rural Maine. We opt to split a steak dinner, but when it arrives, the plates are each served with steaks that look like full portions. It's pure heaven.

Jessica stops to say she won't let us go away hungry. As she walks away, I turn to make a comment to Brian about how amazing this is, but can't get a word out. Instead, it hits me, this overwhelming generosity-of-strangers thing, and I start to cry.

"What's wrong?" asks Brian, although he already knows the answer.

I can't even reply. But I don't have to. He asks if I am feeling grateful and I can only nod.

"Well, stop it. You're embarrassing me," he teases, trying to make me laugh and lighten the mood. It helps me get myself together. I wipe away a couple of tears and finish my dinner.

Over the next week, we make our way to New Hampshire to ride the Kancamagus Pass and see where the Old Man of the Mountain used to be. We ride through covered bridges and lush green valleys ringed with low mountain ridges. The valley floors are dotted with black and white dairy cows, while the hillsides are painted a bright mixture of autumn golds, greens, and crimsons. I find it strange that we ride over the Connecticut River to cross from New Hampshire to Vermont. My analysis of names continues as I think the names of the mountains, White and Green, really don't describe them well at this time of year. Still, it's postcard pretty.

Eventually, we make our way south to Boston and stop for a couple days' rest and sightseeing. Brian and I debate the politics of my forefathers rebelling against his at the Boston Tea Party over beers in Quincy Market. We take a tour around town to the Old North Church, Fenway Park and the Boston Harbor, among other places. This city is steeped in history. Our guide drops us near the Old State House, a short walk from a small graveyard where Mary Chilton is buried. Eric, the tour guide, says she was the first passenger to set foot on land from the Mayflower. It surprises me to hear her name after seeing it in my family tree album since I was a little girl.

Brian indulges me as I wander through the city later to find her grave. We pass the Old South Meeting House on the way, the site of the Boston Massacre. I find the church and graveyard, and go in to find her. Mary was my 11th great-grandmother.

We follow the inlaid-brick Freedom Trail along the sidewalk toward the Boston Common. On the way, we stop at the Granary Burying ground to see the graves of Sam Adams, Paul Revere, and John Hancock. While Brian walks the cemetery searching for recognizable names, I watch a handful of sparrows bathing in the talcum-soft dust around base of a fence post. They are adorable as they flutter busily and roll in it as if it was water. Each bird basks in droplets of sunlight that fall through the trees.

We ride south and duck into Plymouth to see where the Pilgrims, and Mary Chilton, came ashore centuries ago. We ride onto Cape Cod and stop to enjoy a short break on a rocky seashore before making our way inland again to ride alongside rows of mansions in Newport, Rhode Island.

Shades of autumn wax and wane as we ride across New England. Sometimes the colors are at their peak and sometimes we get ahead of the southward-rolling wave of changing foliage. Sometimes we get behind and only see bare trees. We make our way across Connecticut to New York, stopping to let the Big Apple abuse my leg with its miles of sidewalk for a day. I drag Brian through New Jersey and on to yet another city of the American Revolution, Philadelphia.

We cross into Delaware and Maryland before turning north to track down a Mason-Dixon line marker on a rural road, only to find it was stolen a couple of years before. We spend an afternoon at Gettysburg. Brian is being force-fed my beloved Americana, not that he seems to mind.

When I was a child my mother bought me an old set of encyclopedia to practice with while learning to read. I was in first grade and struggled with the big words, but those 15-year-old two dozen books stayed perched at the foot of my bed for many years, entertaining me and sparking my curiosity for nearly every subject known to man. Having the time and freedom now to visit so many of the places I read about – Boston, Gettysburg, Harpers Ferry, Washington, D.C. – is a luxury that I don't take for granted. Our national parks and monuments are places I treasure, and I hope to visit as many as I can.

My aunt and uncle welcome us into their lovely home near Washington, D.C., so we can tour the Capitol and enjoy a visit with them. They spoil us rotten the entire time. My uncle, a docent at the Air and Space Museum, gives Brian and I the best tour of the museum at Dulles that anyone has probably ever had. We spend six hours wandering the enormous hanger admiring the historic aircraft while Uncle Richard tells us interesting tidbits about each one. Brian and I are mesmerized and genuinely can't believe that many hours have passed until my growling stomach says differently.

Just an hour west of their home is the northern end of Skyline Drive, a 109-mile scenic road tracing the ridge of the Appalachians through Shenandoah National Park as it makes its way south through Virginia. Its views are spectacular.

The tide of changing foliage seems to be catching up to us. The trees are on fire, at least color-wise. We round a curve not far into the park and grab a handful of brake as we hit the back end of a line of stopped cars. Bear jam – cars stopped to watch a couple of cubs, not unusual in this part of the world.

Weather patterns favor us for the next several days as we stop at Charlotte to spend a day at Monticello and then carry on to North Carolina. Where Skyline Drive ends, the Blue Ridge Parkway begins. These two form only a portion of the hundreds of miles of a string of pearls that I've planned for the next week. We're heading to the Tail of the Dragon at the far end of the Blue Ridge Parkway and the Cherohala Skyway.

Shades of pumpkin and red edge the roads all along our route south, as we skim the Appalachian roofline. I spy copper-banded caterpillars on the roads again, and decide they must be the

Appalachian autumn mascot.

A night in Boone is followed by an early morning ride to Blowing Rock State Park where I climb onto a pier-like rock to gaze out over the colorful trees of the gorge below. These are the Smoky Mountains, and low clouds and haze make the name seem fitting. Our winding along the Blue Ridge ends in Asheville. It's been a few years since I was here, but it feels like a lifetime ago.

While serving a three-year term on a Holiday Inn board, I'd flown to Atlanta to attend a quarterly meeting and rented a car to take a side trip to Asheville and the Biltmore Estate. That trip, as most of mine were, was made up of executive meetings, suits and heels, lipstick and laptops. This trip is about washing out my two pairs of sock in the sink every other night and the never-ending battle to suppress my urge to buy souvenirs.

Cool mountain air fills my lungs as we stroll through the tree-lined rows of brick buildings in downtown in search of a curry and a pint. Just what I need to warm up. A man in a full black and white nun's habit rides past me on an old-fashioned hot pink bicycle with a horn on its bars. I love Asheville.

Thankfully, the next day dawns clear and dry. I'm happy to be taking the 318 turns of the eleven miles of the Tail of the Dragon on dry asphalt. It's a treat to ride Betty when she's unburdened and light, while my bags are stowed at the hotel.

West of Asheville we pass through a small town where I see pumpkins on several porches. I hadn't thought of it before, but today is Halloween. Such is the luxury of not living by a calendar. Eventually our turnings lead us back onto the Blue Ridge Parkway. We climb up and up, through the incredible fall colors. Winding back and forth, up and down, we turn onto yet another road and I see a visitor center.

We've entered Great Smoky Mountains National Park. My friend Megan took some of the most beautiful photos I've ever seen in this part of America one year. Much as I would love to try that too, we have far to go and slow riding today, so we press on. We have had good weather so far.

But I've jinxed myself. As we round a bend I see clouds settling in from every direction, moving quickly. The forecast calls for the wind to pick up just after lunch. Rain is possible, something I feared. The further west we ride, the worse it gets, as the storm comes in. I watch the surrounding hills become shrouded.

It starts to get cooler. My thin gloves had been enough so far but I start to get chilled and make a mental note to swap them for winter gloves at our next stop. I rethink that as I remember all the maneuvering I have ahead of me on Highway 129, preferring the light gloves for that.

The cloudy mist settles lower and as we ride I can feel the various pockets of air, some more dense than others, reminding me of turbulence on a plane. Haze turns into thick fog for a few miles, but finally, it lightens up again. I hope it won't be like this all day.

A broken branch blocks my entire lane so I ride into the oncoming lane to get around it, making me more grateful for the fairly empty roads. We pass Clingman's Dome, but don't bother to stop since there won't be a view today. As we reach the top of the ridge and drop over the other side, I notice the trees are bare, having been stripped of their colors by the wind. As I descend the back of the ridge it starts to warm up. By the bottom, it's comfortable again. And halfway down the ridge the leaves start showing up again.

Somewhere along the way we cross from North Carolina into Tennessee, indicating our nearness to the Tail of the Dragon which straddles the state line. Traffic picks up. We pull over for break and I text my dad to say I'm thinking of him. Yellow leaves rain down on me as I type.

As the sun sporadically breaks through the clouds, the fall colors along the Foothills Parkway change from bright and crisp, to muted, as though the landscape is a watercolor painting. At the far end of the parkway we turn onto the 129 and a moment later see signs warning trucks to turn around, due to the steep winding "hairpin" turns for the next 11 miles. Brian pulls over and calls out to see if I can check my phone to be sure that this is the Tail of the Dragon.

My app shows a spaghetti bowl of noodle-y curves ahead, which I assume is our road. Off we go.

After a few turns I spot a professional photographer kneeling on the edge of the road at a tight corner taking photos of riders and drivers. His SUV advertises his website. I'm caught off guard for a moment, processing this, and realize I'm not in my helmet and had better get there. The turns are tight, some amazingly so, and banked. For a moment, I worry about being slow, but I don't really care as long as I get through. After the first few times adjusting my feet and shifting my weight from peg to peg, gauging my speed, I start to enjoy myself. It's really, really fun.

I lean left, then right, speed up and slow down. I love rolling onto the throttle to pull out of a tight curve, while being mindful of leaves on the road. Adding to the intoxicating roller coaster of turns is the explosion of colors. It's like an amusement park for grownups. I feel a rush of adrenaline.

Brian and I leapfrog each other and ride ahead to quickly park and get off our bikes and get positioned to take photos of each other. My dismount is too slow to get a good head start and be ready for him. My first attempt results in shots of Brian's back.

I don't see any cars behind or ahead of us, such a luxury. It's perfectly still, not a breath of wind and dead silent. We couldn't have asked for a more beautiful day. After 11 gorgeous miles of smooth black asphalt curves and hairpins, we finally reach a sign marking the crossing from Tennessee back into North Carolina and the end of the Tail of the Dragon. I feel like a little kid who didn't want the ride to end. For a moment, I consider asking Brian if we can go back and do it again. But then I remember the storm.

We stop at Deal's Gap to buy stickers. I snap a photo of the chrome dragon out front. My adrenaline rush is over and I begin to relax, shaking off the tension in my arms and neck. Hard to believe I have the Tail of the Dragon behind me now, instead of ahead of me as it has been for so many years.

From Asheville, we ride to Raeford, a small town south of

Fayetteville, where my friend's husband is stationed at Fort Bragg. Even the thunderstorms and downpour around Charlotte can't dampen my spirits. I'm so excited to see Megan and her family. It seems like one of the longest riding days of the trip, no doubt distorted by my anticipation.

We spend nearly a week at Robert and Megan's, making time to work on the bikes, get gear sorted and play with my Godchildren. It's November and the weather is already changing. A new tent was waiting for me when we arrived, along with a new camera. The grit and rain of a life on the road have been too much for my last one.

I ride my bike to Durham to have it fitted with a new progressive shock. I'm absolutely amazed the difference I feel when the suspension has been adjusted for me and my heavily loaded bike.

Because I know it will be a while before I get to see my bestie again, we make the most of the time, as I always try to do. I'm sad to move on after only a week, but winter is coming and I have a lot of miles to cover.

An overcast day hovers over us as we ride to Oak Island and turn south along the Atlantic coast toward Myrtle Beach. The next few days take us through the moss-strewn live oak alleys of the Lowlands and eventually into Charleston.

Late afternoon rush hour traffic doesn't do anything to improve the ride on East Bay Street. An elderly woman stops and starts at an intersection, cutting off two cars and plowing into my lane, nearly pushing me into a parked car on my right side. Not realizing she had her window down, and forgetting that I'm not soundproofed, I let fly with a few swear words. She winces and locks up her brakes. I regret it for a second but then remember I'd watched her weave and stutter her way up the street for several blocks, endangering everyone in her path. She really is a hazard.

In Savannah, I search the lovely squares to find the bench made famous in the movie Forest Gump, but a local says it was moved. I got to see it a dozen years ago, when I came to Savannah with my friend Heather. I had just picked up 8-week-old True, and not having anyone to keep my new gun-metal-blue puppy, or the will to leave her behind, I brought her along in a carry-on bag. In the week that I was in Georgia, my little girl sprouted from a blue-eyed wobbler to a social butterfly who barely fit into her bag for the flight home.

One day as Heather and I strolled with her through Monterey Square, a couple stopped to admire my beautiful puppy. They wished me luck, with a slight sarcasm, and explained that they had a family member who owned a Weimaraner, and that the breed required lots of supervision. But they agreed she was stunningly beautiful and likely worth the risk.

I feel a pang of sadness as I recall that happy memory. It's strange to think her whole life has passed, from toddler to old girl and even to the grave while I have passed a dozen years arriving at my middle age.

From Savannah, the road leads southwest to Valdosta and eventually to a tiny part of the panhandle of Florida. Brian and I are ticking off states. I've visited 49 so far, and only have Alabama yet to visit. Cotton fields and swamps alternately line the roadway for miles. I stop for photos of the bowls of fluffy cotton somewhere in the Florida panhandle, just before the Alabama border. We have a fair amount of ground yet to cover tonight and plan to ride to Mississippi, having started in Georgia. That will make four states in a single day.

I follow a pickup and open horse trailer for half a mile and notice my bike makes the equine passenger nervous. I slow down to give it space. Finally, I decide to go around instead of torturing the poor animal by stalking it from behind. As I pass him, I see the black gelding pull back on his halter. In a moment, I'm out of his earshot and flying on toward Alabama.

I stop for a photo at the state line. It's my last of forty years of collecting states so I savor the moment. Alabama itself is a blur, as we try to make up time from our photo stops and reach my cousin's home in Columbus for the night. But there's one more stop I cannot pass up. A boiled peanut stand on the side of the highway, with a line of cars pulled over indicating it's a good one, beckons to me. A pound of Cajun boiled peanuts later, we ride off for the next gas station where we park and enjoy our treat. I haven't ever had them and am anxious to try them while they're hot. I can imagine what a sight we must be with windblown hair and black Stormtrooper gear while squatting on a curb shelling smelly boiled peanuts and swigging Cokes.

It's after dark when we get to the Air Force base outside Columbus and stop at the gate to call my cousin. Her family warmly welcomes us into their home. It's wonderful to share a meal with them and catch up.

The next day I'm bursting with excitement as we ride to the home of another friend, and my favorite person in all the world. Heather and I have been friends for ages, and she and her boyfriend, Bruce, will put us up for a few days. Bruce is an airplane mechanic and thankfully has tools and a garage where Brian can do more work on the bikes while I catch up with Heather and their two Bullmastiffs.

When we leave Memphis and ride north, we ride against the grain of the winter weather patterns, hoping to cross a small part of Kentucky before turning to Missouri. There we catch up with a friend Brian met while riding in Utah a couple of years ago. He just wed his high school sweetheart. They're lovely people.

Continuing west, we stop at a three-state marker at the junction of Oklahoma, Missouri and Kansas, giving Brian a few more of his missing states. We wake the next morning in Bentonville to find we've finally lost our head start on winter. It's a balmy 19 degrees outside. My bike is filled with 20/50 oil, which must be as thick as tar after the sub-zero night, and doesn't start before its battery gives up. We try a push start. My leg gets gimpier in the cold and as I try to push Brian and my bike across the level parking lot, it's all I can do to not collapse in fits of laughter at what I must look like with my lop-sided stumbling.

I'm disappointed to have to forego the Pig Trail in lieu of turning southward, as we try to get ahead of the ice storm. But even skipping that route, it's too late. We wake to ice again the next day in Hot Springs and have to lay up for two days.

When the weather breaks, we cross into Louisiana, bound for a holiday meetup with two Aussie friends in New Orleans. I spy a dead armadillo on the side of the road and remember I want to show Brian what they look like but decide to hold out for a live one. It rains off and on and there's a deeper chill each day. My leg aches all the time. I giggle in my helmet one day at the thought that I'm now like arthritic old-timers who can predict storms and witch wells with their achy bones.

Beignets and Cajun food make for a good Thanksgiving with friends, Craig and Sharon. Their company is wonderful and a couple of days off the bike leave my leg a little more rested. We take the bridge over to Metairie, and head west along the Outback Trail following the Delta coast toward the border with Texas. We pass bayou houses on stilts and fish camps, crayfish paddies and swampland, until finally the road comes out at a rocky shore. Oil rigs linger on the horizon of the Gulf of Mexico.

We take a ferry crossing at Monkey Island just east of Beaumont, Texas. As we wait for the ferry a kindly redneck hops out of his truck and strains his bib overalls while reaching into a cooler in the back of his pickup to retrieve a tub of freshly shucked oysters. He offers us each one as a cool treat in the surprisingly warm sun. He's funny and amiable.

At the border with Texas, Brian rides his bike up to the state entrance sign for a photo and spies a sticker put there by Tiffany Coates years before. I had the pleasure of meeting her at the Overland Expo a few years ago, where she gave an inspiring presentation on her ride through the "Stans".

Helmet thoughts of the day:

- When my grandmother and her sister were young college

students at a small university in South Dakota in the 1940s, they had the chance to attend a conference in Cuba. It was during Havana's heyday, before Fidel Castro, and required them to travel by train for several days across America before boarding a ship in Miami to make the voyage to Cuba. What an adventure that must have been for two farm girls who had never been anywhere before. Maybe I get my adventurousness from her.

- I miss my grandma, especially the way she beats me at Scrabble.
- I miss my whole family, my sisters, my stepmother, my niece and nephews, and especially my Dad.

Texas is big country. Three days riding might not be enough to cross it, but we are headed north anyway, so it will take us even longer. I want to visit a dear friend of my mothers' in Waxahachie, just south of Dallas. After a seafood dinner across the street from our hotel near Beaumont, I plot a route along the east side of the Lone Star State. Brian wants to find some parts in Dallas and I have a few things I'd like to do too.

My mother and I lived in Dallas for a few years when I was a child. I have a lot of memories of this place, some good, some bad, and am having mixed feelings about going back. But I'm hopeful that it will be a happy visit, and that I can turn a corner and make peace with the parts of my past that still linger in this part of the world.

It's time to go back and heal some old wounds.

6 THE LONG ROAD BACK TO DALLAS

There are dark shadows on the earth, but its lights are stronger in the contrast.

-Charles Dickens

Dallas and I have a torrid past. I've made lots of wonderful memories there, and the worst memories of my life were made there too. Talk about yin and yang. Dallas is that for me.

My mother moved to Dallas in the mid-1970s to start a new life as a single mother with a little blonde girl in tow. She eventually remarried and we lived a pretty happy life until one horrible morning in March more than 30 years ago.

She and my stepfather were having marital problems and she asked him for a divorce. My mom, very wise for her young age, and such a good mother, had made arrangements for me to stay at a friend's house for the weekend while she broke the news to my stepfather. She made sure I was safe, and far away from our house in case anything happened. I'd packed a weekend bag for what I thought was a sleepover...and I never went home again.

On a Saturday morning, while I watched cartoons in my pajamas, and giggled with my friend in her living room, my mother had been shot and killed by the man she was trying to leave. She was 32 years old.

The minister from our church drove to my friend's house and broke the news to me. I remember hating him for it, which makes me feel horrible now. It was the understandable reaction of a freshly-orphaned 12-year-old. Looking back, I can only imagine what my friend and her mother must have had to deal with. I'd just lost my mother to a violent death and didn't have another family member within a thousand miles. They cared for me for two days until my father came to take me back to South Dakota.

After that, I never saw my friends in Texas again, except one who came to visit me when I testified against my stepfather at his trial. I wrote letters to a couple of friends for a few years, but was a young, rudderless girl, in the days before the internet's easy social connections. Eventually, I lost touch with the friends of my youth and even with the dear friend and her mother who cared for me in those first days after my mother's death. It's so surreal, even now, to think about.

One night about a year ago, out of the blue, I received a friend request on Facebook from Paulette, the friend who came to see me during my stepfather's trial. I couldn't believe my eyes when her name popped up. I was overjoyed. I hoped if I was going to be close to Dallas during my trip, I might get a chance to see Paulette again, after more than 30 years.

Once we made it to Louisiana and knew that winter was still not quite here, I'd planned to spend some time with my mother's best friend, Billie, near Dallas, which would put me nearly in Paulette's back yard. Billie, and I have loved each other for 35 years and have kept the ties that my mother made for us all those years ago. Seeing her will be a highlight of my trip. I already know this, even with barely having started it. She is a source of peace and comfort for me, surrounding me with happy memories of my mom, and of our own, made in the years since my mother's death.

As Brian and I cover the two days of riding to Billie's, the weather turns colder. Each mile is filled with another memory.

I remember picking peaches in our back yard and my mom canning them for us to eat over ice cream during winter. She sewed clothes for me and matching outfits for my Barbie dolls. She read excerpts from an encyclopedia to me every night. We planted a garden together each summer and watched fireflies. She taught me to bake, to cook and to sew.

While I sometimes disliked being an only child, if only for the loneliness I bore alone after her death, it meant that all the time I had with her was mine alone. I never had to share her time or attention. She showered me with enough love in our 12 years together to make me feel her presence in my life.

Near Athens, I drift mentally down another road. As I ride across Texas, I'm more than ten years older than my mother ever got to be. So tragic, and so unfair. But I know how lucky I am to have so many wonderful memories of her and to have had her shape my life for however long she could. Her life, and its brevity, inspire my desire to not take time for granted and my love of life.

She is with me always, even now, as I ride back to Dallas.

We arrive in Waxahachie at mid-day and spend the night with Billie. She and I stay up late chatting. In the morning, Brian and I ride downtown to visit the Book Depository at Dealey Plaza, site of the assassination of JFK. While Brian visits the museum, I walk across the street to meet Paulette.

I'm nervous as I wait on the corner of Elm and South Houston. It's the first time I will have seen her in 30 years, but I recognize her instantly and greet her with a hug. She is as beautiful as ever, and we spend a couple of hours enjoying each other's company. It's wonderful.

Paulette is able to connect me with other friends from my youth and it motivates me to spend a few hours searching online again through hundreds of people to find the friend who I stayed with the weekend my mother died. I eventually find her. Thirty years of distance, time, and missing these people evaporates in less than a week. I don't know if it's closure, or a new beginning, but it gives me peace.

By the time we get back to Billie's at the end of the day, the weather has started to turn, changing from dry cold air, to mist and dark clouds on the horizon. The forecast calls for an ice storm, and in Texas that's not a good thing. The evening news' weather map looks ominous, as the storm moves toward Dallas.

While I hate the idea of not having more time with Billie, I don't have any idea when the roads might clear up after this storm, so we have to keep moving. We decide to ride to Austin, since it still seems to be in the blue portion of the weather map instead of the pink, icy part. I say my goodbyes, and hug Billie extra tight before we go. I'm grateful for every moment of this healing time in Texas.

Austin is a good refuge for one night, but no more than that, while that silly storm stays on our trail. We ride to San Antonio and enjoy an evening stroll on the River Walk before heading west through the Hill Country toward a rendezvous with two of my cousins in west Texas.

Abbie picks me up at our hotel and drives me out to see her sister, Brie and her family near Seagraves for a wonderful evening at their home. I pack up early the next morning and cringe at the smell of natural gas that hovers in the air while I tie my luggage onto the bike. Fracking in the area makes for two days of smelly riding.

We ride to Fort Stockton on a road that gently turns toward the southwest and Big Bend National Park. I message a fellow rider who is wintering near Terlingua. He invites us to camp nearby. Ara, a gourmet chef, and his rescued Pitbull, Spirit, have travelled by motorcycle for several years now, and I'm beyond happy that I will finally get the chance to meet them both. Ara is one of the people who really inspires me.

Spirit rides in the motorcycle's sidecar while wearing dog goggles. They spent the past summer in the mountains of Colorado, Wyoming and Idaho. Ara frequently posts photos of fresh-caught trout frying in a pan or of cotton-candy sunsets.

The roads of Big Bend are freshly asphalted and the jet-black runway provides the perfect background for cinnamon-colored tarantulas to sun themselves on cool days. I see each giant spider nearly a quarter of a mile before I get to it. I park and walk over for a photo of one. Being an arachnophobe, this is a big deal for me. I've decided they look like a stuffed animal-version of spider, soft and cuddly, and for some reason that makes them less intimidating.

Brian leads us up a gravel road at the west end of Big Bend, the Mavericks Road, which makes my pulse quicken a bit. It's good practice for what lies ahead and it's a gorgeous road. At the far end, we stop in Terlingua long enough to load the GPS coordinates that will hopefully lead us to Ara and Spirit.

Eventually, we wind our way across the desert and off the main road to a trail. It dissolves into a series of gaps between scrubby bushes until finally the GPS says we have arrived. For a moment, I think it must be wrong, but then Spirit peeks out from behind a mesquite and I know we have arrived.

Ara welcomes us warmly. It's late on this December day, short on daylight, and we need to get settled and make dinner before dark. I produce two cans from my pannier (saddlebag), intending to heat up soup to go with the fresh rolls we bought in Terlingua. Ara, being a highly-regarded chef, cringes at the sight and directs me to put them away. He says it goes against his being to see someone eat anything from a can in his presence, much less in his home. He has a pork loin and vegetables, which he baked in a solar oven, and offers Brian and I some of the finest cuisine we've had in weeks.

Ara is working on a book of his life and the past seven years of traveling he has done with Spirit. His quiet oasis seems the perfect place to do it. He regales us with a few stories and offers some suggestions on where to ride as we continue to make our way toward Arizona.

Brian and Ara discuss Brian's rotting boots which seem to disintegrate more with every mile. Ara wanders over to a storage container and comes back a few minutes later and presents Brian with a new pair of boots to try. Almost unbelievably, they fit perfectly. Ara wants nothing, just for Brian to pay it forward to another rider down the road.

We carry on, west along the Rio Grande, coasting just feet from Mexico for miles and miles. We turn north and decide instead of crossing into New Mexico near El Paso that we will go to Carlsbad to see the famous caverns. On the way, we stop in a small town for our usual mid-morning bathroom and snack break. As we get back onto the highway, two fat dark javelinas trot across the road in front of us, the first I've seen on the trip.

Montana claims with its state motto to be Big Sky Country, but I think Texas gives her a run for her money. Each plateau offers endless views to the next. We wind our way west, then north, and finally reach Guadalupe National Park and adjust our direction to Carlsbad. We spend a day riding out to the caverns and exploring them, which are well worth the time. Then we head west over the mountains, by ski areas that already have snow starting to linger, and down to White Sands before crossing into Arizona.

My aunt and uncle have a guest room waiting for us when we ride into Phoenix. It's wonderful to spend some time with them before we leave the States. I feel lucky to spend the holidays with my family this year, another benefit of our new timeline.

We work to get ready for the next leg of our journey. We stock up on parts and pesos. Friends of a lovely Aussie couple we know have introduced us online to friends of their who live in Phoenix too. They generously offer us the use of their garage and tools so Brian can give the bikes one last service before we cross into Mexico.

Bevan and Clare are good people, as we say in South Dakota, and I like them immediately. We decide we need to come back for at least one more day of work on the bikes, and Clare's good cooking, before we head to Yuma.

7 MEXICO

Aún no tienes alas y ya quieres volar. (You don't have wings yet, and already you want to fly.)

-Mexican proverb

Allan, the rider we met at Cape Spear, Newfoundland, has a winter home in Tucson. He's offered to cross with us into Mexico to show us the ropes. Although Brian rode across Mexico when he came up from Argentina, he only spent four days doing it. We appreciate Allan's offer.

Christmas gives us a few wonderful days with family and friends, before we pack up and turn toward Yuma just three days into the new year. Hard to believe it's already been six months since I left home, and I haven't even made it to Mexico.

Thanks to the hospitality of friends and family, I haven't spent much of my budget yet. I haven't decided how long or far I will travel since I'm so far behind my original schedule. For now, I will just keep going, still aiming for Ushuaia.

Allan meets us at a hotel in Yuma. It's wonderful to see him. I'm nervous, and having someone else with us gives me comfort. I don't have much of an appetite at dinner or the next morning. Allan can sense my nerves, perhaps due in no small part to the fact that I pepper him with questions, openly discuss my near-panic level of fear, and outright say I might throw up as we cross into Mexico. He's so insightful.

He does a good job of calming me which I appreciate. His plan is to ride south to Rio Colorado. We'll cross the border one at a time, ride under a gate and over a set of topes (a.k.a. row of chrome domes mounted to the road intended to act as a speed bump) before parking just inside the border at the Aduana (customs) office to import our bikes. Allan says that the topes will be a little disconcerting for me if I've never ridden over them before. The metal domes are close together and there isn't room for a tire to fit between them and get traction on the road. Instead my tire will slide around on smooth metal looking for grip.

After fueling up, Allan leads us the dozen or so miles to the small border town, through a couple of backstreets to a gap between cars, saving us time in line. We stop and start our way to the border. Allan goes through first, riding ahead, over two topes, and turning to the right. I can't watch his route because the border guard asks for my papers. I produce my passport with a trembling hand and stuff it quickly back inside my jacket when she waves me through. Everything from here on out, is entirely unknown, unfamiliar to me, and out of my control. I'm scared witless.

Two rows of zig-zagged metal domes, each the size of half a soccer ball, lay in docile wait about 10 feet ahead. As I let my clutch out and ease over the topes I catch a glimpse of Allan waving to me from my right periphery. He's done a 180-degree turn just past the topes and turned into a parking area beneath the awning we just rode under. I turn to look at him and try to figure out how to get there, in the process awkwardly grab a handful of brake and turning my head to the right. My non-existent speed over the topes now comes to a complete standstill, causing me to drop my bike slowly onto its side.

I step off it, seemingly in slow motion, and stand there for an instant as Brian rides around me to the parking lot. Two kind Mexicanos rush to my aide from either side of the street and pick up my bike, righting her as quickly as I had dropped it. My first words in Spanish for the trip turn out to be "thank you" to these chivalrous strangers. So much for my fear that Mexico is only a dangerous place.

Brian digs for his camera to document my flashy entrance into Mexico, before noticing that my bike has already been righted. I ride the bike the last 20 feet to the small parking area and bring it to a stop, more gracefully this time. Allan strolls over and pats me on the back, knowing how jittery I must be. He breaks the ice by saying, "Isn't it nice to know you can dump your bike without breaking a leg?".

My laugh evaporates the last of my nervous mood. For the first time in a couple of days, I relax.

"Welcome to Mexico", teases Brian.

Even though I've spoken a little Spanish since middle school, and have been practicing for this trip, I feel completely lost when we venture into the Migracion to get ourselves processed into Mexico. Allan keeps us pointed in the right direction though, and before long we ride to a gas station just a couple of blocks away. Shortly after, we ride onto a fresh stretch of Mexican highway headed for Baja.

I've calmed down enough to ride, but am still a bag of raw nerves. The day flies by without me having noticed much of it. Just before dusk we arrive at San Felipe and wind our way up the malecon, past cafes and bars, looking for a motorcycle-friendly hostel that Allan has heard about. This town isn't big enough to hide anything, but we still wind around it a couple of times before finding a sign that leads us the right way. At what seems like a relatively cheap price to this gringa, I opt for a room instead of camping.

I unpack my bike and enjoy a hot shower before we walk into town for dinner and celebratory Margaritas. I've just survived my first day in Mexico.

But I can't say the same about the night. What started out as "a"

Margarita finished somewhere after four or five, along with tasters of tequilas, including one that had a name like "Quite a Penis". The combination results in a horrible hangover, sour stomach, and my first "day off" in Mexico. It's all I can do to choke down a few saltines by early afternoon the next day.

It was worth it.

Allan leads us south, trying to make a dent in the 1000-mile length of Baja before he turns back to Tucson. He's chosen to take us over a slightly more rugged road than Mexico's Highway 1, opting instead to ride to Coco's Corner. After I spend 24 hours properly rehydrating, we ride out of San Felipe to Puertocitos where we stop for a beer. I love Mexico.

We continue down Mexico 5, following the eastern coastline to Gonzaga Bay where the highway dissolves into a construction project followed by a sandy windswept airstrip, and stop at Alfonsina's for their famous fish tacos. I watch pelicans dive into the bay for fish, and enjoy a few minutes' reprieve from my heavy black riding jacket. Even with all the vents open and my zipper undone, I'm baking in the sun.

The road beyond is challenging. It sets off my nervous ticks about dumping my bike again and I have to consciously work to avoid going into death grip mode, although not always successfully. The first several miles out of Gonzaga are loose sand, and the three of us more or less wiggle our way up the road. While Allan and Brian have ridden in it before, sand riding is a new sensation to me, not one I'm even remotely comfortable with. I feel like I'm waterskiing up the road, about to tip over at the tiniest hint of imperfect balance. Thankfully, the long flat stretch of sand gives way to a rocky dirt road that begins to wind up and over rolling hills.

The sun is low by the time I catch a glimpse of quarter-mile stretches of silver garland strewn along the sides of the road. As I get closer, I make out the sun-bleached gleam of now brand-less beer cans strewn along the fence which create a grand entrance to Coco's world. Golden dirt roads give way to refreshing golden lager, and relief in knowing that I've made it halfway across this dirt section, my first dirt riding in a while.

Coco himself greets us and offers us access to a cooler in a storeroom in the back of a lean to. It's self-service on the honor system here, since Coco doesn't get around as easily as some. Well, that's not entirely fair. He gets around very well for someone who has had both of his legs amputated above the knees.

When we arrive, he's seated on a makeshift plywood patio at the back of his camper/home entertaining another motorcyclist. Lee, from Canada, is riding south to Mazatlan for the winter and will be camping here tonight too. Coco has a small collection of abandoned campers and toppers that serve as a campground of sorts. He offers shelter to his friends, even brand new ones like me, and in return we leave him a few dollars to help him with buying supplies, etc. He allows us the use of the gas stove inside his camper to cook our dinner. Coco's English is good and we enjoy an evening of talk about each other's travels and Coco's life here in his oasis.

Coco lets me explore his library of registration books. Over the years his guests have written Coco thank yous and drawn beautiful sketches in the books. Each is an amazing, colorful memento from one of the thousands of people who came through here.

Lee rides out with us the next day as we carry on to Bahia de Los Angeles (BOLA) and find a beach camp spot under shade trees, for $5 per night including toilets and cold showers. Allan opts for the comfort of a room instead, but joins us for dinner after we settle into our respective lodgings.

He's decided to turn toward home, having already been gone nearly a week. We thank him for being a great tour guide. I wish he could stay longer. We decide to spend another day at BOLA. Lee is due for an oil change and has found oil in the small village.

I'm blown away by the spectacular sunrise that awakens me the next morning. As I turn over in my sleeping bag to relieve the stiffness of the half of my body closest to the ground, a bright orange-magenta glow in the tent's small window catches my eye. I sit up and peek through the plastic and out across the bay. I've never seen such vibrant colors in the sky. It's beautiful enough to make me wiggle out of my cozy bag, grab my camera and crawl out of the tent into the early morning air. The sun climbs quickly and I worry I won't be able to get a photo fast enough to do it justice. I can actually see the sky changing before my eyes.

I trot down to a rickety wooden pier, with its Pelican post caps perched and dozing, and snap a couple of quick pics before it's too late. Sherbet orange and hot pink give way to daffodil yellow and cornflower blue, melting and writhing together in a beautifully soft-brushed heaven above. I'm so engrossed for a few moments that I don't notice Lee is already out too, and enjoying a cup of coffee with his morning view.

Lee continues south with us for a couple of days, but we split up before Mulege as he rides off to see a village he's heard about. Brian and I have plans to meet someone from ADVRider.com for a place to stay.

Tim and Lenae have generously offered us their home for a week in return for dog-sitting. They live walking distance from a gorgeous beach and have kayaks and snorkeling gear stashed for us to use. It's like a 5-star resort…for free. We take full advantage of the bay with its shallow beach and short kayak paddle over to a neighboring beach for Sunday Bloody Marys. As I comment to Brian on the hundreds of birds around us, a sea lion pops out of the water near our kayak. The Sea of Cortez and wildlife around Baja are second to none. It's whale season and I hope to visit one of the whale nurseries on the other side of the peninsula after we cross into the southern half of Baja.

Our genial hosts return after a few days and we enjoy them so much we ask to stay a couple more days to hang out with them. They introduce us to other people in the small community of expats and take us to see the local sights – fish tacos and homemade coconut ice cream in Mulege and movie night at Coyote Beach. We enjoy a wonderful evening with their friends while one prepares us a meal from her home in the Philippines.

Brian and I purchased insurance for the bikes the night before we crossed into Mexico. We both thought 30-day policies would provide us more than enough time to cross the whole of this enormous country. Now we find we've used half of that policy and are only halfway down Baja. We might have miscalculated this a bit.

We ride south to Loreto and take an early morning detour up to San Javier, thinking it's a dead-end road and that we will have to come back to the highway. The fairly short distance is slow-going thanks to road construction and heavy equipment. Once we make our way to a higher plateau, every mile or two presents a vado (water crossing).

While most are dry, a few have a lazy-moving layer of water running across them for as much as thirty feet. Brian pulls over to warn me to take them easy, so I do, and focus on keeping my balance. I don't feel even the slightest wobble but I see Brian's bike slipping sideways ahead of me as he hits an invisible, slimy, algae-covered patch of concrete. After seven crossings, we arrive in San Javier.

We wander through the small pueblo's church and have lunch before turning back to the highway. As we make our way back across the vados, I have no trouble until my 13th crossing of the day, which catches me completely off guard and slaps me onto my left side. A white car filled with people drives slowly past me while I crawl out from under my bike. They all stare.

Brian watched me go over in his mirror, pulls to a quick stop, and drops his kickstand while stepping off his bike to run back and help me. But he finds as he leans his bike over that he kicked his kickstand down so hard it bounced back up. Down goes his bike too. A few minutes later, we are righted and riding on.

Perhaps a mile further, we start the descent to the lower coastal plain and meet two riders coming up the hill. We wave and pull in our clutches to see if they will stop. Both sets of riders watch their mirrors for a sign. One of the four of us touches a brake and we all take the cue and pull over. They are Markus and Karin from Switzerland on a round-the-world (RTW) ride, and are bound for Ushuaia. We chat for a few minutes, enough time to form an instant connection and swap email addresses to stay in touch.

After Couchsurfing with a sweet man and his two dogs in La Paz, Brian and I make our way through Baja California Sur and loop around the bottom of the peninsula before boarding a ferry to the mainland, arriving at Topolobampo.

As we arrive in the dark I'm suddenly glad I thought to reserve a room near the port, instead of wandering along the highway in the dark. Mainland Mexico already feels much less like gringo-land than Baja. I want to get tucked into a hotel as soon as possible.

From there we head north and stop for a night in Los Alamos, we ride north through Sinaloa to Sonora and turn off the main highway, opting for more direct but rougher roads as we make our way to Chihuahua and eventually to the north end of Copper Canyon. Flat desert scrublands give way to rolling pine covered hills that remind me of the Black Hills. We misjudge the distance from Los Alamos to San Nicolas late in the afternoon and find ourselves riding twisty mountain roads in pitch black, a combination of everything we know not to do – ride after dark, ride after dark in Mexico, ride in the mountains after dark in Mexico.

We arrive at a police checkpoint only to be chided by an officer about being out at this time of night. He urges us to get to Yecora quickly, since it has the only motel for miles around. We have to carry on another 25 miles in the dark, finally riding up to a blockade at the entrance of the next small town. Note to self – no more riding at night.

There is indeed a small motel with an open room, but the place is dark and eerie. I'm uncomfortable but this is the only choice we have. We pay and ask about food. The woman at the inn points to a small house across the gravel parking lot with a light in its window.

There's no sign and I quickly figure out that we're just buying food from a local woman's kitchen. I'm happy to do so, I might add. Brian locks up the bikes and we settle into our room, happy to be off the road. While I like spicy food, my stomach, a veteran of many years of stressful work and subsequent ulcers, hasn't begun to toughen up for my new spicy diet. I swear that while I polish off the last of the flaming hot pork-something dinner that my stomach has already started holding a grudge.

After a stop to see the falls at Bassaseachic, we turn south toward Creel, a bit of a tourist trap, and continue to the road that leads down into Copper Canyon and the village of Batopilas. We've been warned the road is closed for construction and that heavy equipment will keep us from getting down the steeply switch-backed canyon, so we aren't overly surprised when we arrive and find this to be true. We ride to the edge of the canyon but can go no further, so turn back to the main road.

We ride to Guachicho and take our view of the canyons from a private ranch near Sinforosa. I read somewhere that the Copper Canyon network is made up of six enormous canyons, each larger than the Grand Canyon, which blows my mind. The view from the edge of this branch of the canyon is awe-inspiring.

On our way to Hidalgo del Parral we stop at the small town of Balleza for lunch. Colorful tents are set up where farmers have come to sell their livestock. Any fear that I ever had of roadside food, and I'm not sure I ever had any, was forgotten within the first day or two of crossing into this beautiful country. We keep up our brave, and naïve, exploration of the local food scene with a round of street tacos.

A young man who looks like he suffers from an advanced aging disease walks over and tries to chat with me as I suit up to go. I take my helmet off and remove my earplugs to hear him but still don't know what he's saying. He finally makes a hand gesture like he's revving a motorcycle throttle and says, "cool" in perfect English. He gives me a thumbs-up and smiles, and I smile back and thank him.

He's made my day before wandering back to his perch on a concrete wall in the shade, and relaxing with his two companions.

We ride south through mainland Mexico across the grasslands. As we ride through a small village and out the other end I twist my throttle and speed up, but then feel suddenly dizzy. Brian is ahead, shrinking into the distance. I feel like I'm going to pass out and pull over as quickly as I can. I put down the kickstand and hop off, worried I might black out any second. I've had this happen before, but not for a while, and it catches me off-guard.

When I was 30, a doctor ran some tests for a problem I was having with a ringing in my right ear. Through the battery of tests, he randomly discovered a hole in my heart, which was unrelated to the problem with my ear. Around the same time, I started having bouts of dizziness caused by supraventricular tachycardia and arrhythmia, which was likely caused by the stress of having found out I had a hole in my heart. Kind of a chicken-and-egg scenario.

My atrial septal defect was closed five years later with a titanium and Gore-tex umbrella device, which made my heart itch for weeks. It was like I could actually feel the patch in the center of my heart, irritating it. After a year or two, my heart rhythm seemed to level out, and I haven't had more than a handful of "episodes" in the past few years.

But when one occurs, a single wonky rhythm seems to slow my heart down, making me feel like I'm going to pass out, before kicking off my adrenal gland, causing my heart to race. Usually it's triggered by high stress, heat or dehydration, sometimes even by lack of sleep. But I don't think I'm dealing with any of those things at the moment.

Brian rides back and sits while I take 15 minutes to lie down and decide if I can carry on. The only cure out here is a moment of quietly calming myself and breathing deeply. After a while it passes and we decide to go on.

The land south of Hidalgo transitions from flat high plateau and grassland into something resembling a set from a John Wayne movie complete with red mesas and winding river valleys. It's gorgeous. Just as I finish this thought, we come to yet another of the dozens of bridges today. Each bridge is named, and the sign says this is the Puente John Wayne. Someone must have read my mind.

Small villages can be seen more easily from a greater distance because of the church bell tower inevitably parked on each main plaza. The highway serves as the main street of almost every town we pass through, and three topes usually warn us to slow down as we enter, while another three keep us from speeding up too quickly at the other end.

Durango, our next rest stop and turning point, provides a dilemma. We must choose one of the two Espinozas del Diablo (Devil's Backbone) to ride west to Mazatlan. The older road winds and climbs over hills and down canyon walls while choking with truck traffic. This "libre" (free) version of the road is legendary, but a dangerous route. The other option is the new "cuota" (toll) road, and is said to be an engineering marvel, but expensive to use. Perhaps I haven't learned the budget nuances of long-term travel well enough yet, but I opt for the latter. I'm more of a fan of enjoying the route than of having to fight truckloads of slow-moving cargo on a twisted hilly highway. As we come to a fork in the road and turn toward the first tollway, I notice that all the traffic is going the other way, opting to drive one of the most dangerous roads in the world instead of paying the expensive tolls.

Having opened only a few months ago, the new Espinoza del Diablo has roughly 115 bridges and 61 tunnels dotted along its 140 miles. It's as pristine as a race track with curves and turns more perfectly graded than most roads we've ridden lately. I see very little traffic moving in either direction. After the first two or three toll booths, I start to figure out why. The tolls add up quickly - 29 pesos, 38 pesos, 121 pesos, and so on. All said, it costs me roughly $70 USD to make the traverse. Since it feels a little like a grown-up version of an amusement park, I'm willing to pay something, but that's too much.

A handful of ultra-modern suspension bridges gracefully span the chasm at Baluarte before the highway disappears into a series of tunnels. Eventually there are no more tunnels or bridges, and we come out on a ridge which offers a view of the Pacific coast, and Mazatlan in the distance. We descend to a lower altitude than we've been at for a few weeks, and into more heat than we've experienced so far.

Lee, who we last saw on Baja, messaged Brian to let us know he's staying at a hotel near the old city center. He and Brian have managed to discover that they share the same birthday which is coming up in a couple of weeks, and they've hatched a plan to celebrate it together.

We ride straight to the hotel in hopes of finding a vacant room, which, luckily, we do. After negotiating a price for a two-week stay, we settle in. The room reminds me of Cuba in the 1940s, not that I would know. Bare stucco walls with high ceilings and a slow-moving ceiling fan form a canopy over flower-covered painted concrete walls and dark wooden furniture. Our room has a private bath, but no shower curtain, the norm in Mexico.

It's wonderful to see Lee, and we celebrate the reunion with a few beers from the local boteleria. Lee isn't the only rider who has found shelter at this lovely old, colonial style hotel with its formidable exterior walls and plain interior courtyard.

Billy and Trish, an Aussie couple with matching crew cuts, have a room on the other side of the courtyard. Dwight, another Canadian, is wintering here too. And Wolf, a German rider, is here for another day before carrying on. We meet lots of lovely people over the next couple of weeks, including Sandra, and Shoe, who regales us with his fiddle playing from the balcony most evenings. A lovely Malaysian couple, Alex and Allison, arrive days later.

Lee has the place dialed in – lunches at the corner cocina economica, cheap beers from the boteleria, a hike up to El Faro or the hill just west of Centro, dinner at the Mercado or whatever else he discovers. We follow in his footsteps the first few days and enjoy relaxed evenings on the veranda sipping cold beer. We all form a perfect combination of stories and personalities.

Billy and Trish are incredibly interesting, having ridden the better part of 7 or 8 years. Maybe longer. Their stories are inspiring – Trish's emergency appendectomy in southeast Asia, Billy's broken wrist in South America, meeting up with an arms dealer someplace in north Africa, and even their lives back in Australia.

Brian and I settle into a routine – breakfast of fresh mango and other fruit in our room, a walk along the beach or up the hill each day, lunch at the Mercado, dinner someplace cheap. We've stumbled upon a great little street food stand near the electrical meter on the outside of the city's central market, which we dub Electric Tacos and revisit nearly nightly for two weeks. We stock up on supplies, including new socks and underwear. It's amazing how good one new pair of socks can make you feel after six months of the same old ones.

With the good wifi, I spend time working on blogs, catching up on emails and communicating with people back home. My sister, Stephanie, is worried, so I email her to say how safe I feel, and try to put her mind at ease.

She replies by sending me a link to an article about an American motorcyclist who has disappeared in Mexico, somewhere further south, in an area that Brian and I plan to visit. Harry Devert's name pops up in more than one conversation with fellow riders this week. He rode a Kawasaki KLR, like mine, and was travelling solo from the U.S. to Brazil for the World Cup in June. His blog gives the impression he's a risk-taker and partier, so I hope he's only gone on a bender and will resurface soon.

This place has become such a comfortable oasis of friendship and relaxation, that it's hard to move on, but after a couple of weeks, and the guys' birthdays, we must go. It's been nearly eight months since I left home and we haven't gotten a fraction as far as I had imagined we would in that time. Besides, I've got this crazy idea involving butterflies.

When I was a little girl, my mother, knowing my love of nature, bought me a subscription to the kids' version of National Geographic Magazine, World. It was one of the best gifts I ever received.

One particular issue about Monarch butterflies showed photos of giant evergreen trees covered in swarming masses of Monarchs clumped together, in their newly-discovered wintering grounds high in the mountains of Mexico. I've been telling Brian for a while that I'd like to add a visit to a butterfly sanctuary to our route. Time is running out for this year's wintering, and I don't want to miss it.

We ride south along the coast to San Blas and then to Puerto Vallarta, before turning east to cross the backbone of the country again, on our way to Tequila. As the name suggests, this is the heart of agave country, and home to the beverage of the same name. There's several local distilleries open for tours.

We opt for a second-floor room off the busy main street. Early one morning as I lay in bed drifting into wakefulness, I hear three loud bangs and come full awake with a start. I slide off the bed and onto the floor, lying flat to avoid any stray bullets. Brian laughs so hard that he shakes the bed, and rolls over to peer down at me and ask why I'm so afraid of fireworks. Maybe this Harry Devert thing is scaring me more than I want to admit. Or maybe I'm just a paranoid American in scary old Mexico.

We visit Guadalajara, Leon and Guanajuato, a beautiful, colorful city with mazes of tunnels under its old city center. I plan to do some volunteer work while there but it falls through at the last minute. The day we ride out of Guanajuato I'm caught up in thoughts in my helmet.

On this day, 31 years ago, I lost my mom. I hope I'm a person she would be proud of. That's silly, of course. My mom would have been proud of me no matter what. That says something about her, not me. My mother left behind a beautiful jade butterfly necklace, which I keep in my jewelry box. I remember her embroidering a Monarch once. Perhaps I acquired my love of butterflies from her.

We camp next to a tennis court in San Miguel de Allende one night before riding south to Angangueo, a small village in the mountains west of Mexico City near the El Rosario Santuario de Mariposa. I'm going to see my butterflies.

Brian leads us down the highway and through a few road changes until finally we reach the state line, taking us from the state of Guanajuato to the state of Michoacan. As has often been the case at most of the dozen or two state lines we have crossed in Mexico so far, a police checkpoint awaits us. Brian parks and shuts off his bike while a heavily armed young officer walks over to him to ask for his papers. An older officer approaches me to do the same. I politely turn off my bike and work to remove my helmet while explaining that my Spanish isn't great, and that I cannot hear with my helmet on. Just as I remove my ear plugs, I hear Brian bark at his policeman, "What?!"

His officer isn't impressed and is a bit taken aback. He looks to the officer helping me, who clearly is his supervisor, for direction.

My officer, who has a small stash of English saved for just such an occasion, smiles at me and shrugs towards Brian, "Why is he angry?"

Thankful for my quick reflexes, and my willingness to play airhead when it serves me, I smile and respond, "No, he's fine. He isn't hungry. We ate this morning. But thank you."

"No, I said 'angry'. He sounds angry." He again indicates Brian by nodding toward him. I'm thankful that his version of "angry" sounds fairly similar to my version of "hungry".

I smile and keep pretending not to understand. I call up to Brian and tell him the guard has asked for his vehicle import permit and passport. I retrieve my own, smile and bat my eyelashes at the superior officer, and go into the details of our lovely breakfast.

"You have excellent English skills. It's much better than my Spanish. Thank you for making it much easier for me by speaking my language even though I need the practice."

He reviews my papers, which are all in order. I say how much I love his country, which I do. He wishes us well, or maybe just me, and waves us on.

Angangueo's small white homes and the large church and municipal buildings on the central plaza are all painted with Monarch butterflies. It's lovely. I arrange for Brian and I to catch a bus to the top of the mountain and drop us at El Rosario by 8:00am. We want to get there early and hike up to the highest protected groves to witness the waking of the swarm.

Each evening, millions of butterflies cluster together on the trunks and branches of the giant evergreen trees in order to stay warm. They stay there, gathered tightly, until the next day's sun warms them enough to wake them and release them in flight.

At over 10,000 feet, I huff and puff as we climb the trail and hurry to meet our guide, Jose Luis, in the mountaintop meadow above. He leads us further, and higher. On the way, he explains the life cycle of the Monarch, saying it takes four generations to make each one-way trip of the annual migration to the summering grounds in the U.S. and Canada, and that scientists still don't know how the next generation knows where to go. He talks about their diet, how to tell which are male or female, and so much more, but I only understand about half of what he tells me.

As we walk up the dirt path, the forest gives way to a small clearing. Jose Luis points out frost on the ground, indicating how cold it gets here at night. He whispers and moves very gently, careful not to tread on any of the butterflies which litter the walkway.

He stoops to ever-so-carefully pick one up and places it between his cupped hands to offer a gentle warm breath to awaken it. After three or four breaths, he opens his hand to reveal the butterfly, which I had thought might be dead. It has revived and is slowly opening and closing its wings. Jose Luis walks over to a small shrub speckled with the sunlight that pierces the canopy, and places the butterfly gently on a leaf in the sun so it can continue waking up.

He leads us along the main path and points out trees in the shadows to our left. At first glance they look like old-growth trees with deformed limbs. But when I look more closely, I see the limbs are bent from great clusters of butterflies gathered on them. I look closer still and see the trunk of the tree isn't covered in bark as I'd first thought, it's covered entirely with butterflies. Because their wings are closed their brilliant orange color isn't showing and instead we see the softer muted version of the undersides. I watch in awe for a few moments. This is the realization of a lifelong dream for me.

We linger half an hour more as the rising sun continues to warm and wake the butterflies who start to rise in great clouds from the forest floor and trees. Butterflies flitter to and fro, landing on each of us. One lingers in my hair for a moment while I enjoy the soft fluttering sound it makes.

Before I know it, a class of students arrives, breaking the spell.

As we pack up to leave Angangueo, it occurs to me that Harry Devert disappeared not far from here. We're in Michoacan, one of the statistically deadliest states in Mexico, and I will be happy to ride out of it.

We carry on around the Arco Norte, opting to bypass the capitol of Mexico City on this trip. Brian went through it on his ride north and has strong feelings about not wanting to go back. I don't mind much. I'm on a butterfly high.

We scoot across central Mexico fairly quickly, stopping in Veracruz, and Tuxtepec, before crossing more mountains on the way to Oaxaca. There, we meet up with the former president of the BMW owner's group, Ruben, and his lovely wife for drinks one evening. They're wonderful people. Ruben takes us for an incredible Oaxacan breakfast and then to the ruins at Monte Alban. We spend our nights in El Tule, home to the biggest tree in the world.

The Swiss couple we met on Baja, Markus and Karin, are camping here as well and Karin whips up dinner one night using a local Oaxaca delicacy, fried crickets. I don't mind the small ones, because the legs don't seem to get caught in your teeth as badly. But either the bugs themselves or the scrambled eggs she mixes them in, don't agree with me. Regardless, we enjoy spending time with them and the campground's snaggle-toothed dog.

After a week in Oaxaca, we ride south toward the Pacific along Highway 175 which tickles the spine of the country for more than a hundred miles. Cloudy mist covers the road for miles but breaks now and then to offer a glimpse of the dense forest around us and the deep lush valleys descending from both sides of the ridge.

We stop to warm up and have a bite in a small village just after noon. After enjoying a hot cup of tea, I ask to use the café's bathroom before we carry on. The hostess says they don't have one. I must look mildly panicked at the thought of riding another few hours after a cup of tea without the luxury of a bathroom break before we leave. She takes pity on me and leans in closely to ask, "Solo pee pee?"

"Si, solo pee pee," I reply. She says the toilet isn't working well right now but that as long as I'm only going to urinate, she will allow me to use it. I smile and nod to express my gratitude.

We spend a few days in Puerto Angel and the hippy town of Mazunte. One night, while I sleep under a mosquito net to avoid dengue and malaria-carrying mosquitoes, I hear something rustling in my belongings and wait nervously for it to stop. In the morning, I find a rat has eaten half of a banana that I'd bought for my breakfast.

We ride east to Tapanatepec and up into the hills to San Cristobal de las Casas. Markus and Karin come here too. So begins the narrowing of the land mass, the reduction of road choices and the development of the clearly defined Gringo Trail which allows us to interlace routes with several friends from here to the bottom of South America.

We carry on to Palenque and camp with Markus and Karin, and another Swiss couple. We all rise early to a chorus of howler monkeys which are silhouetted against the trees, backlit by the early dawn. I can't see what I'm taking photos of, but try to zoom in closely, only to find later I have twenty photos of sagging monkey testicles.

Before the heat of the day, we hike into the park to see the ruins which remind me of an Indiana Jones movie set - covered in tree roots, jungle vines, tropical flowers and armies of insects.

The two Swiss couples and Brian and I have a potluck dinner at camp. Delicious as it is, I come down with a stomach bug in the middle of the night. Half-awake, I crawl out of the tent, and race to the communal bathroom at the end of the field before my illness takes over. Thankfully, none of the other five diners come down with anything. The mysteries of bacteria.

Our route takes us across the Yucatan and passes through lovely colonial cities, including Campeche and Merida. We stop for a night in a village near Chichen Itza so we can spend a full day at the ruins, despite the ever-increasing heat and humidity. After Chichen Itza we ride to Puerto Aventuras where Aussie friends, Ken and Carol, have rented a condo for a month.

Brian and I set up camp in their living room, sleeping on the comfy sofas and sharing the only bathroom via their bedroom loft. The day we arrive, I'm not feeling altogether well, and by nightfall I'm starting to feel downright miserable. Something I've eaten in the past few days seems to be causing me problems.

At about midnight, hours after we've all gone to bed, I'm awakened by terrible lower abdominal cramps and know I need to get to the toilet immediately. But I'm mortified that to get to the bathroom, I have to climb the spiral staircase and tiptoe past Ken and Carol's bed as they sleep. Worse still is the knowledge of the horrible sounds and smells I will create just three feet from my slumbering friends when I get there. A happy thought occurs to me, perhaps if I just lay here, I will die instead and save myself the embarrassment.

After surviving the horrifying experience, I crawl back into my sleeping bag, only to have to do it all over again at 4:00am. I'm so embarrassed. I don't care that Ken and Carol, and Brian, are all experienced world travelers and have each, no doubt, had travelers' diarrhea more than once. I want to crawl in a hole, or at least get a room with a private bathroom so I don't inflict my agony on other people.

I start a round of Cipro with my breakfast and opt for a nap in the condo while the others go out to explore the area. Thankfully, a day or two of meds stops the crisis.

The morning after we arrive, we find a note stashed on our bikes, inviting us to stop at a nearby restaurant. Dan, one of the owners, is a fellow rider and wants to meet us. He and his wife, Pamela, spoil us with great cooking (they are both chefs) and good company. We spend a few days here and get to see fellow travelers, Simon and Lisa Thomas, and meet new ones. A dozen motorcyclists gather around a table at Dan's restaurant one day and it occurs to me that this is something special, this brotherhood of bikers.

At some point in our cocktail-fueled conversation, we talk about the missing rider, Harry Devert, who still hasn't turned up after disappearing more than two months ago. His mother established a Facebook page and campaign to try and uncover any clues that might help get him home. Nearly every rider has a theory: Harry had an accident on a two-lane road; Harry is intentionally building drama for a book he plans to write; Harry has found a paradise of his own with no wifi and will show up eventually. I'm hoping for the latter.

Brian and I have a date with friends in Belize in a few days, so we decide to keep moving south. We say "hasta luego" and ride out, passing the Lake of Seven Colors before arriving in Chetumal, our last stop before crossing another border.

My three months in Mexico, have been amazingly beautiful. I've enjoyed nearly every moment inside its borders and I'm thankful to be delivered safely to the next step in my journey.

8 BELIZE

Adventure is worthwhile in itself.
-Amelia Earhart

The border crossing goes smoothly, both the Mexico and Belize sides. Our bikes get fumigated and we buy mandatory motorcycle insurance at an office near the border. I find it funny that the English spoken here now sounds foreign to me. Three months of Spanish immersion has taken a deeper hold than I thought.

We ride south, bound for San Ignacio, but don't make it far before stopping to get a cold beverage to fend off the oppressive heat and humidity. I notice the difference in the gas stations and restrooms immediately, and later comment about it in a blog which offends some guy who takes the time to post a comment about my shallow observation. I wonder if he's ever been deprived of some of the small luxuries of life long enough to appreciate them differently.

This is definitely not Latin America any more. It's more than just a language thing. Everything from the products in the stores, the styles of architecture and the faces of the people reflect the impact of the imaginary line drawn between countries.

Belize feels, sounds and tastes Caribbean. Accents have a Jamaican lilt to them, and while Spanish influences can be found, the remnants of centuries of English and West Indies cultures still linger in every part of daily life. Reggae music can be heard in the shade under plantation trees and bursting out of boomboxes strapped to mopeds. Everyone wears flip flops.

After setting up camp, we walk into San Ignacio to find some dinner. It's stiflingly hot and I pick up two one-liter bottles of cold water to take back to camp to get me through the night, tucking one under each arm as I lay uncovered on my sleeping mat. I wake sometime after midnight in a puddle of sweat and am more uncomfortable than I've been since the hospital in Newfoundland. The thermometer says it's 95 degrees in our tent.

My best friend, Heather, and her boyfriend arrive and splurge on a hotel room with air conditioning. They invite us to stay. Without hesitation, or manners, I say yes. Not just for the AC, although that's a luxury. I've missed Heather and am excited to see her. We follow them to Placencia and spend a week as beach bums.

Bruce and Heather take dive trips during the day and we gather each evening for a stroll up the boardwalk to a beach café for umbrella drinks and Caribbean food. We sample homemade bitters in a bar one night, from a jar of murky liquid filled with hunks of firewood and tree bark. We sample seafood, including infamously venomous lionfish, but avoid the local delicacy of cow-foot soup. We soak our feet in the turquoise Caribbean. Brian and I take a snorkel trip to an outer reef in hopes of swimming with whale sharks, but have to settle for the massive emptiness of the deep blue water beneath us instead.

I spend an evening researching the pros and cons of taking malarial prophylactics, and am more confused after my reading than I was when I started. We are deep enough in the tropics now that I need to decide what to do. Somewhere in the bowels of my luggage is a $750 bottle of pills that will protect me for several weeks, but by now I know that with our slow travel pace that won't be long enough. The crazy side effects described on some websites don't make it appealing enough to start taking them yet, so I leave the pills buried.

Heather and Bruce bring us much-needed supplies from the U.S. Brian, at my horrible suggestion, installed new inner tubes on our bikes in Guadalajara, only to find out before the Yucatan that they were an inferior Chinese make which were disintegrating inside our tires, more with every mile. I had a flat tire in San Cristobal, which led to the discovery. I messaged Heather and asked her to make room in her luggage for new inner tubes for both our bikes. Brian sets to work installing them. The week flies by, much more quickly than I feared, and before I know it, Bruce and Heather are headed home.

Brian and I ride back to San Ignacio. This time Brian has arranged for us to meet friends of the campground maintenance man from Happy Valley-Goose Bay. Alain, and his wife, Mary Lee, include us in a weekend gathering with their friends and make us feel very welcome.

Alain owns the Black Pearl Harley-Davidson dealership, and his friends are, of course, Harley riders, but they overlook the make of our bikes and treat us like old friends. I've developed a fondness for Canadians, and by now I'm developing one for Belizians too. A few days of homemade traditional food, drinks and good company is enough to make me forget the heat.

Belize is a surprise to me, a mix of so many things. Local markets owned by Asian families and Mennonite colonies dot the countryside. Beachfronts are lined with tourist resorts and bars, while inland mountains hide Mayan ruins and rugged landscapes. After a few days in San Ignacio, we decide to move on again. Half an hour up the road is our next border crossing.

9 GUATEMALA

Everyone is the age of their heart.
-Guatemalan proverb

We're back to using Spanish, although not very successfully. For some reason, I find it difficult to understand the money changers outside the Migracion office as I haggle with them to convert our remaining pesos into Guatemalan Quetzales. If I listen very closely, I can pick up a few words here and there, but I feel like I've completely lost all the ground I'd gained in Mexico with regard to language. It's like I'm starting all over again, and it's frustrating.

Eventually, we get our paperwork sorted, get the bikes fumigated and ride off toward Tikal National Park. This part of the world is littered with the ruins of past civilizations, and I'm hoping to see as many as possible. Tikal is quietly famous for a small part it played in the Star Wars movies, a fact I didn't know before visiting.

We set up camp behind a café and book ourselves for the evening's guided tour, as well as the sunrise tour the next morning. It makes for very little sleep, but in this heat, it wouldn't have been quality sleep anyway. It's a real splurge to do both, but we can't decide between them. We enjoy a quick lunch and surf online a bit before meeting our guide for the evening tour. We come prepared with headlamps and bug spray.

Caesar leads us, and half a dozen other guests, away from the café and up the trail to the entrance to the park. Once through, we follow him to three different groupings of buildings, each larger than the last. Caesar tells us about their construction, the civilization and its history, and the land. We watch coatimundis, long-nosed cousins of raccoons, wandering through the jungle, as we hike.

Just a few minutes before sunset Caesar leads us to the Gran Plaza, to a terrace on the north side. We climb the steps as high as possible and look west toward Temple 4. The sun is setting right behind it, providing a stunning vista for the end of this day. Twilight doesn't last long, and we make our way back toward the drop-off point in the dark. Caesar stops to point out an all-spice tree and shows us how rubbing a leaf between your fingers releases the beautiful aroma. We carefully step over a leaf-cutter ant super-highway which bisects our trail.

Early the next morning, we rise before the sun to meet our guide and hike to the Temple 4 complex which we'd seen illuminated so beautifully the night before. The jungle is silent. Everything is still asleep in the darkness.

As hints of light start to show in the sky, a cloudy mist is revealed. We climb the stairs of the temple and find a seat on the terraced steps, facing out over the jungle. Everyone is half asleep and silent, which allows us to experience something special. The higher the sun climbs, the more the animals of the jungle awaken. At first, we hear distant bird calls, and then squeaks and chirps of other animals. Dozens of species join in with new sounds nearly every minute for more than half an hour.

Howler monkeys start their deep, roaring calls off in the distance, and are later answered by others from somewhere else. It's an orchestra of sounds, all of nature making up the show. It occurs to me that this is Earth Day, and somehow seems like the perfect way to start the day.

Later, we pack up our camp and ride out the way we came, re-joining the highway and carrying on to the town of Flores for a night. A brief stop for lunch at El Remate gives me a chance to practice my new version of Spanish, Guatemala-style. I've started to figure out that I hadn't forgotten my Spanish while we were in Belize, it's just that the Spanish is different here than it is in Mexico. Guatemalans use different nouns and verbs than Mexicans do, and I need to expand my vocabulary.

I order a whole fried fish with rice and tomatoes for lunch and watch a stray puppy nose through the trash in the ditch while I wait. At first glance the puppy appears to be thin, but as he moves to another place to scavenge, I can see him more clearly. He is positively skeletal.

I touch Brian's arm to make him look over, and regret it instantly. There's nothing to gain from seeing this poor animal's suffering, and I shouldn't have shared the sad sight with him. The pup wanders to our side of the street, looks up and sees that I'm watching him. His ears soften and lower in submission to me as he wags the bony string of vertebrae that comprise his tail.

When I coo softly to him, he comes closer, responding to the kindness he must see so infrequently, and tucks his body lower as a sign of both his fear and respect. He is utterly pathetic, nearly bald from mange and covered in scabs. Taking my bottle of water from the table, I walk out and find a piece of plastic wrapping in the ditch and form a small bowl for him. He quickly laps up the cool water I pour for him, so I pour more. And then more.

Stepping back into the open-air café, I grab some bread and take it out front just to have something to fill his poor empty stomach until I can get him some meat from the kitchen. But when I return, he has gone. I step out onto the street in hopes of drawing him back for a good meal, but can't see where he wandered. I return to the table, and Brian teases me for crying for what must be the hundredth time for parasite-ridden dogs in this part of the world.

For a long time, I begrudged the locals not taking better care of their animals and for what I judge to be a lack of humanity. But later I begin to see this as a part of local life. People in this part of the world literally struggle to have enough food for their families and often have children suffering from parasites and diseases for which they won't be able to afford treatment. When you recognize the struggle they face simply to keep themselves and their families alive, you soon understand why animals don't rank among their concerns.

We ride to Flores and find a hotel, only to find out later that it also serves as a brothel which explains the large numbers of construction workers staying here too. Ken and Carol mentioned the town to us, and suggested we visit the small island connected to Flores by a bridge. We waste no time and ride over the same afternoon.

Boatmen offer rides on Lago Peten Itza for a small charge, and I decide to treat us to one as a way to see more of the island from a different perspective. Manuel, our gondolier for the day, is accompanied by his grown son, Manuel, who appears to have Down Syndrome.

Manuel, the father, shyly explains that his son is special and doesn't "have many words", and that he only uses small ones. The father says that his son is an excellent swimmer, and even won a few awards. He is obviously very proud of him. I smile and clap for him and the son beams proudly, as does his father. There are few things as inspiring in this life as that of the limitless love shared between parent and child.

Manuel guides the boat across the lake toward a sandy point, and shows us the Gallo Cerveza plant on the far side. Instead of rounding the point to rougher open water we make our way back to Flores, trolling along the shoreline.

At one place along the shore, two tall wooden posts rise about 6 feet out of the water, while a third spans the gap between them. A knotted rope dangles from the center of the structure and 3 young boys take turns climbing the rope to stand on the wooden goal post and launch themselves into flips before splashing into the lake. Looks just like something we do at home. The boys wave to us while bobbing in the water, and Manuel says these are his grandsons. He calls out to a woman who is painting a small wooden boat that has been dragged onto the sandy shore. She smiles and waves in reply.

Not having much insight into the best places to visit in Guatemala, we opt to take a wide route around the country and see what there is to see. From Flores, we ride south to Rio Dulce, a hot and not-so-scenic town. There's a fair going on with a small rusted Ferris wheel that's so rickety it's braced against, and wired to, a bridge so it won't collapse as it rotates.

I can't remember ever being as miserably hot in my life as I am in Rio Dulce. I take three showers in the one day we stay in town only to be miserably sweaty again within minutes of drying off.

My electronics apparently aren't tolerating the combination of sauna-like humidity and heat either. My phone, camera and laptops all seize up, the first time for each of them on the trip. I seal my phone and camera in a large plastic bag with a handful of dried rice, a trick I've found online, and try the same with my laptop in a grocery store bag. After two days, they all seem to come out of it.

Alain, from Belize, had suggested a visit to a hot spring and hot waterfall, somewhere on the road from Rio Dulce to El Estor along Lago De Izabal. We watch for signs as we ride west but can't find the place, so we carry on.

The paved road stops somewhere before El Estor and is replaced with a freshly packed dirt road awaiting its new concrete cover. Rounding a corner, I'm greeted with a face-to-face view of a bulldozer and gingerly move to find a way around it without slipping off the 2-foot-high ledge of the new concrete road.

We cross Guatemala from east to west by bisecting the country on a gravel road for more than 100 miles, enjoying the steeply rolling hills and views from their tops. I see skinny cattle, skinny horses, or skinny dogs nearly every mile. There's certainly no shortage of food here, so maybe parasites or the heat (or both) keep the animals from putting on weight.

Guatemalan women dress differently than their neighbors wearing traditional dress of a beautiful dark woven wrap-around skirt and a colorful peasant blouse. Little girls dress like miniature versions of their mothers, and they all often carry baskets balanced on top of their heads. I admire the colorful fashion show put on by women walking along the roadside from one farm to another as I pass by on my motorcycle.

Village names sound more Mayan than Spanish to me – Uspantan, Sacapulas, Chichicastenango. The latter is a village we ride through late in the afternoon on our way south to Lago Atitlan, one of the more popular places with visitors.

As Brian and I discuss whether I can have a few minutes to go shop the famous market of Chichicastenango, I unknowingly drop my keys. Instead of having a few minutes to browse the local handicrafts, Brian and I spend a panicked fifteen minutes digging through a metal grate in the gutter to fish them out.

We arrive in Panajachel late in the day and settle into a backstreet hostel with a tiny courtyard just big enough for our bikes to squeeze in between flower pots and the courtyard's iron gate. After lugging our bags upstairs, we very nearly fight over who gets the first shower. That is, until we see it. I've been hearing about the infamous "suicide showers" of Central America, but had yet to see one, until now.

I wasn't sure I would recognize one, but this one is pretty obvious, even for a layperson. A standard-issue metal pipe protrudes from a hole in the stucco wall of the bathroom and is capped with an enormous shower head. Also protruding from the hole in the wall is a single, heavy-gauge electrical wire which connects to the shower head with a couple of loose wire caps.

The shower head serves as a sort of flash heater to instantly super-heat the water as it comes out of the pipe. Very clever when you consider you only have to have cold water to supply buildings.

But even with my very limited electrical and plumbing knowledge, I recognize this as the obvious hazard it appears to be.

Drawing the short straw, I have first dibs. I spend an extra amount of time sorting my things and preparing for my shower, but in the end, I can't stall any longer. I turn on the tap, which automatically turns on the shower head and close my eyes as I stretch out my hand and put it into the stream of water. Nothing happens. At least nothing unusual. The water is warm, and my hand gets wet. In I go; my first suicide shower.

Tammy, the woman who generously took Brian and I in after my accident, wrote me a few weeks ago to say she's taken a job and relocated. Funnily enough, she's living in Guatemala. She's renting a cabin on the north side of Lago Atitlan, in a small village only accessible by boat, and invites us to stay.

I've arranged to do some volunteer work for Mayan Families and we plan to be in the area a couple of weeks, which will be a wonderful chance to catch up with her. We find a place to stash our bikes, load our luggage and gear into one of the small lanchas (boats), and pay the fare for the trip to Jaibalito.

Our lancha pulls up to the rickety wooden pier as a helper steps off and ties a rope around a post. Brian and I throw our bags onto the dock and step up off the bobbing boat as it retreats into the lake bound for its next stop. Three hens run by as a rooster half-heartedly follows in warm pursuit.

We climb the concrete path toward the center of the village which is more or less a crossing of two sidewalks and turn left. This is Tammy's street, since there are no streets in Jaibalito. After dropping our luggage off just after sunset, we walk back 200 feet, nearly to the sidewalk crossing, in search of dinner.

Tammy looks at home here. Her skin is golden and her smile more relaxed. It's wonderful to see her and our threesome falls back to its comfortable routine within minutes. It feels like it's only been days since we last saw her.

Jaibalito is a quirky little village filled mostly with locals, and a handful of ex-pats. A German named Hans runs a small hostel and café, which is where Tammy dines most evenings. The word "café" might be a tad generous, but you can buy food and drinks at his place.

A stone house made up of only a few rooms, one of which is a small kitchen with high ceilings, opens onto a concrete patio covered with a tin roof. The "café" is the patio, and the house kitchen is the source of all its offerings. Chickens, ducks and geese peck away at the black soil under the tropical trees and weave amongst the legs of the tables and diners in hopes of finding fallen treasures. It looks to me like the aviary genepool isn't wide enough here, forcing these birds to create a few wart-covered new species – dickens, chucks, and geeks.

Tammy takes a seat at one of two wooden tables, surrounded by a dozen chairs, and we follow. We each order a beer to celebrate our reunion. I ask which of the handful of men is Hans, but Tammy doesn't see him. She leads me off the patio fifteen feet to a rickety wooden shed belching smoke into this tropical paradise. Inside is a tall bearded man stirring a cauldron with a wooden paddle. Hans is roasting coffee.

One of my favorite things about life in Latin America is the availability of local produce in nearly every part of its countries. Most homes, even the small ones, have fruit trees, vines and small gardens, all within arms' reach. Tammy's cabin is surrounded by a papaya plant, passion fruit vines, orange trees, mango trees and tropical flowers. Hans' café is shaded by a giant avocado tree, which drops rich green bombs onto the tin roof of the café's patio every few hours, each with an enormous bang. Hans also has coffee plants, whose produce he is roasting in the shed.

Along with the rich flora, come an assortment of fauna. Dozens of species of insects I've never seen before make their homes in every cubic inch of this place. There are stick insects, iridescent green beetles and butterflies in every shade imaginable, all residing on the porch. Giant spiders, well at least by my standards, live in the concrete bathroom of the cabin and I keep an eye on them every time I shower. I count a dozen different types of hummingbirds fluttering around the liquid feeder, and hear strange animal calls from the trees on the hillside above us. Guatemala is teaming with life.

It never ceases to amaze me how each place I visit at length seems a like theater to me, complete with its own unique cast. Posada Jaibalito is no exception.

Colin stops in from time to time between online consulting jobs, having abandoned an office for this particular jungle. Carlton pops by between magic mushroom trips to chat or go for a walk. A man named Dennis is having a party this weekend, which must be de rigueur in this Gilligan's Island-like gathering of huts. Norm, the baker, lives just up the sidewalk and says he will try to honor my request for a coconut cream pie while I'm here. Scott is here with his German Shepard, his straw derby and his Columbo-like trenchcoat, which I find endearing and eccentric in the tropical heat.

Scott has lived quite the life, which he shares between "medicinal" trips to the bushes one evening. After asking where I'm from, he confirms that he has been to South Dakota. He once visited his brother in Nebraska and asked him, "What's the best way to see Nebraska?"

To which his brother replied, "In the rearview mirror with your foot on the gas."

Scott started his vagabond life as a young man living in New York City. He didn't like the structure and confinement of a typical job so he decided to do something about it. He says many people have commented over the years how much they envy his freedom and wish they could do the same. He doesn't have patience for the blathering of wannabes and insists that if you hate the place where you live, you have no excuse to not do something about it. He sums it up by saying, "Just pack a sandwich and start fucking walking."

He used to travel a lot across the United States and remembers Deadwood, South Dakota as the most dismal place he's ever been. During the early days of legalized gambling Deadwood had $5 limits which he saw as puny and pointless. He talks a bit about Kevin Costner having big plans for business ventures in Deadwood but then letting his idea die after he traveled there to see Deadwood for himself. While he isn't exactly right, he is highly entertaining.

I catch the early morning lancha back to Panajachel each day and walk through town to the Mayan Families office. Apparently, my social media and scrapbooking skills have finally found a use, because I've been offered a project for the week helping to build more online presence for this charity. My host and supervisor, Hannah, gets me sorted within a matter of minutes.

As I work at her desk each day, I watch local families come and go from the compound, here to collect much needed food or to seek medical care. The charity helps with a variety of projects, mostly to support the children and the elderly in the local communities.

Later in the week I have the good fortune to tag along on one of the delivery runs to outlying villages around Panajachel. We take supplies to a food bank in one village and books, food and water to two small rural schools where smiling brown faces greet me and my camera. It's an incredible experience. I wish I could stay longer.

One of the more popular reasons to have an extended stay in Guatemala is the great availability of language schools within its borders. Guatemala is a relatively inexpensive place to travel, or to live, so spending weeks or months here is easily affordable by Western standards.

After completing my week at Mayan Families, I enroll at a Spanish school in Santa Cruz, a twenty-minute walk by trail and wooden boardwalk from Jaibalito. I really enjoy this temporary life – rising early to the chatter of jungle birds, walking along the lakeside cliffs to school, chatting about local life while practicing my Spanish, before wandering back to this peaceful village and stumbling over to Hans' for a beer and the plato del dia(special of the day).

Locals have small businesses and a system of bartering

established. Someone produces almost everything you could need, if you know who to ask. There's a baker and a butcher, a man who sells homemade goat's milk yogurt and fresh triple-washed salad greens. An old woman and her grandson stop by to sell wooden carvings, beaded necklaces and bracelets. We have the chance to buy homemade cheese from a woman, who also offers magic mushrooms that she flashes from under an embroidered cotton towel that lines her cheese basket, as she smiles and winks.

Tammy, her sister who is visiting from Canada, and a friend accompany me to my first day of school. We climb the steep hill out of Jaibalito and follow the narrow rocky trail along the cliff overlooking the deep dark blue waters of the lake. Three enormous and stereotypically cone-shaped volcanos stand as guardians on the other side. We pass a few homes perched precariously above the waters' edge and wind around a handful of points before seeing Santa Cruz in the next inside corner. The trail descends the equivalent of a few stories before depositing us on the shores of the lake at a wooden boardwalk.

It's ridiculous how beautiful it is here. Tall reeds cozy up to the edges of the boardwalk while the water laps at the posts holding it up. Flowering trees arch overhead, showering the walkway with lovely jasmine-scented blossoms, while fishermen mend their nets in their hand-carved wooden dugouts in knee-deep water. The boardwalk meanders through the reeds and tall grasses, across open stretches of shallow water and over small streams descending from springs higher up the mountain. Our foursome walks single-file at a slow pace to more fully enjoy the beauty of this path.

Finally, we arrive at the boat dock, which I have stopped at many times while travelling back and forth to Panajachel in lanchas, and just a bit further ahead is the small hotel where I am to meet my tutor, Lydia. She's already waiting, dressed in a traditional wrap-around woven skirt and bright pink, short-sleeved peasant blouse. A woven fabric belt tied around her waist makes her look faintly reminiscent of a Geisha. She's beautiful.

We sit at a table under the shade of a meandering tropical tree and sip fresh passion fruit juice while she assesses my current level of Spanish. Growing the remnants of my 7th-grade knowledge by three months in Mexico, has given me a fairly good rudimentary vocabulary. She asks me lots of questions to which I reply as clearly as I can. We work up a lesson plan for one week. Sadly, this will be my only week with her. My shortage of time is the only thing that keeps me from staying longer. I could rent a lovely lakeside cottage and take private lessons, all for less than $180 U.S. dollars per week.

I retrace my steps to Jaibalito late in the day carrying my homework assignment. The lovely lakeside trail is lit differently in the afternoon sun and entrances me completely.

Such is my week. I'm amazed how much more comfortable I feel after only a few lessons. Lydia and I spend the first of each 4-hour lesson in conversation. She asks about my family and travels, and in turn, I ask her questions about life in Guatemala. At some point, I tell her that I love working with crafts and she tells me her mother-in-law is a talented local weaver.

On Friday, Lydia makes plans for a special treat for me. She offers to welcome me into her family's home so that I can experience some of their culture and life. I take a lancha early in the morning to the far west side of the lake where she meets me at the dock. We walk up the hillside and make our way through the narrow streets to a long low building with a gated yard. Inside we find Lydia's mother and sisters-in-law.

Many generations of families usually live together. When Lydia married her husband, she moved into her mother-in-law's home. Each of the family's couples has their own bedroom just off a small concrete courtyard which serves as the outdoor living space for everyone to share. An open-air kitchen is tucked under a lean-to on the back of the courtyard. Chickens wander through as they please.

Lydia's mother-in-law has her loom set up in the courtyard and has started a piece which will become a table runner. While she quietly listens to my lessons, her leathery and gnarled arthritic fingers continually work the fine threads into a textile. When I finish my last lesson of future-tense verbs, I'm offered the chance to try the weaving myself. At first, I politely refuse, worried that I will in some way harm the beautifully smooth pattern she has already worked so hard on, but they insist.

I straddle the wooden stool as Lydia ties the bottom end of the loom around my waist. The matriarch speaks more native language than Spanish, but we both work hard to find our common ground. She uses her hands to instruct me how to weave the shuttle back and forth and then tighten each row with a long wooden blade before reversing the process and tightening it again. She's an excellent teacher, like her daughter-in-law, and in the end, keeps me focused enough to not show much difference in the pattern between our work. It's an incredible experience.

Back at Tammy's, Brian has been taking advantage of the rare luxury of internet signal at the cabin and has reserved space for us and our bikes on the Stahlratte, our way around the Darien Gap, the missing section of Pan-American Highway that every traveler must navigate around when crossing between North and South America. The ship sails in just over a month and we have five countries left on this continent. We'd better get moving.

Our English friend, Pete, whom we met in the Yucatan, stops to see us at Tammy's a few days before we leave. He forgets his full-size umbrella at her house. This becomes a constant source of teasing for Pete, as he seems to forget something of his at every place he goes. I find his forgotten umbrella very odd though, considering it's nearly 3-feet long and cumbersome for a motorcyclist to carry on a bike.

We stop in Antigua long enough to return it to him and meet his friends, Mateo and Pam, a French man and American woman, who are traveling south on his bike. It turns out they and Pete are booked on the Stahlratte with us, along with the Swiss couple from Baja. We enjoy a couple evenings of dinner and drinks with our small moto group.

Antigua is a lovely colonial city nestled into the base of a conical volcano. Its cobbled streets are lined with beautiful old buildings and dozens of chapels. I buy a small watercolor painting from a man who captures an archway covered in bougainvillea perfectly. Holy Week festivities here are world-famous for their beauty, but sadly I've missed them by just over a month.

Just to show what a small world it is, I email a woman I used to work with at Holiday Inn who now lives less than an hour from Antigua. She drives up to see me and we enjoy dinner together. It's surreal and wonderful that I never seem to be alone.

10 EL SALVADOR

I believe the world is beautiful...
-Roque Dalton

The border crossing goes smoothly, and before we know it Brian and I are headed southeast along the coast road to La Libertad, a ride suggested by Billy and Trish at the hotel in Mazatlan. It's a gorgeous road and includes nearly half a dozen long tunnels that arch gently enough to be taken at speed.

About halfway down the coastal stretch, I get passed quickly by two men on BMWs who disappear before I catch sight of their license plates. They pass Brian too, then pull over and flag him down. Hugo and Javier are enjoying the beautiful day by riding their bikes from San Salvador on a 150-mile loop to the coast. They're on their way to a fairly famous restaurant which overlooks the sea and invite us to join them. It's all I can do to keep up with them the few miles it takes us to reach it. I appreciate their perfect English and hospitality. It's a wonderful welcome to this small, beautiful country.

In the early afternoon, we make our way to a beachfront hostel which also serves as a surf school. My idea for a stroll up the beach is forgotten when I wander out and find it's made of giant gray baby-head rocks and is impossible for me to walk on. Three small green parrots pester us in the dining room, hopping across the table top to beg for food within inches of our plates. One sits on my hand, having become very comfortable with gringos, in hopes of a treat.

Brian wants to head south along the coast and then duck inland and parallel our way back north so we can see as much of El Salvador as possible. He leads us southeast to Usulutan before turning north over a ridge of lush hills. We double back on the central highway and pass San Salvador before opting for a loop around Cerro Verde National Park. At a small stand in the park, we share a single piece of chicken and some rice and salad for lunch, which makes me sick within an hour but strangely doesn't affect Brian.

Somewhere along the way today my odometer quits, foiling my attempt to keep a daily log of miles ridden. I pester Brian for his mileage instead.

In Santa Ana, we have no luck finding a hotel, hostel or campground, but do stumble across a "love motel", one of the unique treasures of Latin America. My first experience with one wasn't far into Mexico, somewhere on Baja. People say they are typically rented by the hour for extra-marital affairs, but I've also heard that young married couples frequent them to enjoy some privacy that they can't get at home with three generations of loved ones under the same roof.

Most have a private garage for each room, allowing guests to hide a vehicle, something motorcycle travelers appreciate. Despite their common use, these are some of the cleanest lodgings I've found in this part of the world. I've come to appreciate them, and this one is nicer, if a little stranger, than most. The satin covered bed is dominated by a large mirror on the ceiling, and comes with wall-mounted toilet paper dispensers on each side of the bed. For the purposes of privacy, money is paid through a wooden door and you only speak with the staff via intercom, never actually seeing anyone face-to-face.

We ride to a UNESCO world heritage site, perhaps the only one in El Salvador, at Joya de Cerren to see the ruins of an ancient civilization. Late in the day we plan to ride closer to the border with Honduras and prepare to cross over, but Brian isn't feeling well. Maybe that chicken finally caught up with him. We settle into a hotel and he gets sick during the night. I spend most of the next day walking to stores to get him juice, medicine, yogurt, and anything that sounds good to him.

The next day we ride northeast to La Palma and spend an evening in the cute village known for its painted murals. Two busloads of students unload at our hotel, changing the atmosphere of the relaxing lodge. We decide to hole up in our room and pack and prepare for the border.

11 HONDURAS

Every time one laughs, a nail is removed from one's coffin.
-Honduran proverb

Google and travel blogs are my main resources for travel tips, and information on how to cross each border. But even these don't have much to offer for the backwater crossing from La Palma, El Salvador to Ocotepeque, Honduras.

This border crossing is a slow one, at roughly three hours, during which I wander around (to a copy shop, to the bank to pay fees, to an office to obtain permit stamps, etc.) while Brian stays with the bikes. Eventually we get through, and ride northeast toward La Entrada before turning to Copan Ruinas. Friends say the ruins there are some of their favorite in this part of the world, and we find it's worth a two-day trek in the wrong direction.

Brian leads us to Canoa and then turns southwest. We get stopped at a military checkpoint, present our papers and explain where we came from and where we are headed. We are quickly waved through and opt for an off-the-highway route so we can enjoy the scenery before rushing off to the border on the other end of Honduras.

After a day spent admiring the craftsmanship of a lost civilization, we start plotting our route south. I debate about trying to get to Utila or Roatan to do some diving, but we don't have time. We have a ticking clock in front of us with the Stahlratte sailing and have to keep moving south.

Place names in Latin America can be mildly confusing, for a number of reasons. Sometimes they're spelled differently on road signs than they are on maps, or from other road signs. I noted 4 different spelling for a small village near Mexico City after I finally figured out the various spelling all phonetically referred to the same town. Sometimes names are abbreviated, and often not in a way that I'm used to. Sometimes there are several towns with the same name in one country, each differentiated by adding the name of the state or area, like a surname, to the city name. In the same way that there seems to be a Buffalo in every state of the United States, there seems to be a San Miguel around every corner in Latin America.

Microscopic distinguishing characteristics which Brian and I overlook, can make all the difference when trying to navigate. Of course, you only learn these nuances through trial and error. In Honduras, we find ourselves with no shortage of towns name "Comayagua". As we haven't yet learned the way that this country manages its place names, we hit a minor stumbling block.

Brian wants to lead us toward "Comayagua", which he scouted on the internet and looks like a decent-sized place to stop for the night(likely to have hotels or campsites). The internet doesn't seem to agree with either our printed map or our GPS in pinpointing exactly where Comayagua is located, partly because Comayagua is actually the name of the state and not a specific city. Unknowingly, with the aid of our non-Spanish-speaking GPS and maps, Brian leads us up a gravel road to San Jose de Comayagua instead of the central city of Comayagua. And here begins a small adventure within our bigger adventure.

I have a moment of pause as he turns off the highway, and leads us through a village and out a bumpy dirt road at the other end. The deep ruts in one shady section of the road and subsequent stream crossing only make me question the road choice slightly. In this part of the world, you never know what you're going to get for roads, so I don't really doubt that this one will lead us to our desired destination.

After six or seven miles of bouncing along we come to an even smaller village, one with only a single street through the middle of it. We traverse the town and at the far end find the road dissolves into a trail. Doubt finally takes over. This doesn't look right.

Brian consults the map, and tries to get it and the GPS to agree. After zooming the GPS in as far as possible, he finds he has taken a wrong turn. We need to double back to the highway. He turns around and leads us back through the village. We pass two small children playing in the ditch to our right, while up ahead on the left a police officer stands on the steps in front of a small police station.

As we approach, I watch the officer pull his pistol from his holster, shoot his gun at the police station doorway, re-holster it and turn quickly around to face us as we near him. He holds up a hand and yells for us to stop. My heart skips a beat, and then sets off racing. My Spidey senses kick into overdrive.

Brian does as directed, and instinctively shuts off his bike. He must think this is going to be a routine stop to check our papers and that we will need to hear and speak. I hesitate for a moment, not wanting to shut off my bike because I'm afraid of not being able to get away if something happens.

The officer looks strange to me, drunk or high, and not quite all there. His eyes are glazed over, but he somehow also looks arrogant, like he's looking for a fight. He calls out an order to Brian which Brian doesn't understand. I don't hear because I have my earplugs in. I roll to a stop and leave my bike idling in neutral.

The officer looks back and forth between us and is clearly trying to process something. He looks angry and agitated, like he's about to pounce. I raise my visor and can see and smell the freshly-discharged acrid gunpowder lingering in the air. I'm not sure that the officer knows I'm a woman, and decide to reveal it in case it keeps him from doing anything aggressive. In my girliest, high-pitched voice, I call out, "Hola, buenas tardes! Como estas?", which stops the officer in his tracks.

He turns sharply to look at me and pauses for a moment, blinking, processing. He looks completely caught off-guard that I'm a woman. I ask if he needs to see our papers. He continues to stare at me, lost in thought.

His bloodshot yellow eyes aren't entirely focused, but I recognize that he is struggling with what to do. He looks back and forth between Brian and I for a moment, which seems like an eternity as I run scenarios in my head. Should I shut my bike off? Should I ride up beside Brian and tell him in English that we need to get out of here ASAP and risk the officer understanding me? Is this it? Is this where I die?

He doesn't say another word, but slowly raises his hand and waves us on. Brian takes a moment to restart his bike and then pulls away. I follow suit, hot on his back wheel, shaking as I ride. I keep watch in my mirror until the street curves and the officer, who is still watching us, disappears from my view as I round the bend. I worry the entire time that he will shoot me in the back.

Brian rides slowly and steadily along the dirt road, with me crowding him more with every inch. After half a mile, a white pickup truck starts to follow us, and when I see it I get another hit of adrenaline. I know Brian can ride faster and only assume he's trying to keep a reasonable, steady pace to keep me from getting too anxious and overriding my current state of mind.

After what seems like hours, we round a final bend and I see the small village at the edge of the highway. The white truck has fallen back somewhere behind us. I think Brian will sprint to the highway and put some miles between us and that last village, but instead he pulls over to consult his map yet again. I ride up next to him and ask why we wouldn't put more miles between us and that nut job, but he has no idea what I'm talking about.

It turns out that Brian had been looking to the right as we

approached the police station, watching the children playing in the ditch. He thought the loud bang and smell were from fireworks that he thought the kids must have been playing with. He hadn't seen or known what happened until I told him.

"Well, no wonder you were riding my ass. I haven't seen you ride that fast in ages," says Brian.

All I can think of is poor Harry Devert.

12 NICARAGUA

Eyes that see do not grow old.

-Nicaraguan proverb

Crossing out of Honduras takes only minutes. Crossing into Nicaragua goes smoothly, aided in small part by two young boys, who I dub Fat Jesus and Johnny Fever. Fixers will, for a small fee you should negotiate up front, help direct you to the correct offices, in the correct order, and (supposedly) expedite border crossings for you. I'd been able to manage on my own to this point and had no intention of using fixers this time either.

Fat Jesus is a chunk of a kid, and already a good businessman. He approaches us as we park in front of the Migracion and Aduana offices on the Honduran side, offering to act as our fixer, a common employ for grown men in border towns. Johnny Fever, by contrast, is a slender young man whose rapid-fire speech keeps me uninformed about anything he tries to tell me.

Again, it feels like I'm being hit with an entirely different version of Spanish in this new country. Johnny offers to watch our bikes while Jesus escorts us through the offices. I admire their confidence and have a hard time refusing them. I insist we don't need anyone to watch our bikes, but also hate to invite any spiteful behavior by not at least offering some token of goodwill.

Jesus is actually pretty handy, once he and I figure out which verbs and nouns I can understand in his native tongue. He runs off to get us cold waters and change. While we wait in line, Johnny tells me he is sick and has a fever, and asks me to touch his forehead as proof. I thank him, but decline. I'm probably packing enough bacteria of my own, thank you.

Jesus returns a short while later and gently nudges us between windows, lines and offices until we are finally finished. I'm impressed with his patience and professionalism. He must be all of ten years old.

Back at the bikes, Brian is not bothered by a language barrier, and introduces the boys to his detachable finger trick by folding back the end of his pointing finger at the first knuckle on one hand, and using the same knuckle on his other hand to make them think it's detachable as he slides it back and forth. They launch into hysterics and pester Brian to show them the trick. I think this would be payment enough for their help, but we give them a few dollars for their time anyway. They trot off happily afterward.

An overlanding couple living in Leon offers rooms for travelers, which is where we stop for our first few nights. Jurgen rents out motorbikes and his wife, Eli, teaches Spanish. I think they've made the perfect life for off-the-road overlanders.

My friend, Jen, flies down from the U.S., bringing us parts, and me some much-needed conversation and companionship from home. Brian services the bikes and installs my new speedo cable, which will allow me to track my own mileage again. We hang out at a nearby beach and then hike Cerro Negro, a small active volcano not far from town. While the tourist guides encourage people to surf down the side of the volcano on boards, Jergen teaches us how to run-slide our way down the crumbling slopes instead. It's fantastic fun, if more than a little dusty.

Another guest arrives, Shannon from Victoria, British Columbia, and gets to work building her Spanish vocabulary before setting off on a solo motorcycle adventure. I'm impressed by her spirit. The three of us leave Leon together riding south through Managua to Granada, up to the rim of a sulfur-belching volcano, and on to Ometepe Island.

Ometepe, in Lake Nicaragua, is formed by two adjoining volcanoes creating a slanted figure-eight. We take a ferry from San Jorge and wind halfway around the eight before stopping at a hostel for a couple nights. We lather up with bug spray, having moved even deeper into dengue and malaria country.

We enjoy our last day with Shannon, in San Juan del Sur, playing in the surf of the wide beach and having beers, before taking opposite roads. She rides back north and we turn south to cross into Costa Rica, passing a wind farm on the way.

13 COSTA RICA

Some die. Some bloom.

-Costa Rican proverb

Sandra, a lovely woman we met at the Hotel Lerma in Mazatlan, is from Costa Rica. During our time with her I sat down with a map and asked her for good places to visit in her country. But unfortunately, we have neither the time or the energy to take the scenic tour. We had hoped to cross into Costa Rica along the Caribbean coast via an old wooden bridge that I've seen in various blogs, but it's a long way out of our current path so we decide we will have to miss it.

The crossing into Costa Rica is by far the worst so far. The combination of heat, humidity, heavy bike gear and the five-hour wait in lines, probably skews my opinion slightly. There's nothing like the frustration of yet another version of Spanish combined with a complete lack of organized office locations and procedures, and epic border staff lunchbreaks, to frustrate you. But eventually persistence pays off.

We continue to avoid as much of the Pan-Am Highway as possible, but the narrowing of the continent this far south makes that increasingly difficult. Brian chooses a road that parallels the Pan-Am to its east and we quickly turn off the highway.

This land is a combination of hilly grass pastures and lush river valleys. Gravel and asphalt carry us south to Guaybo. After which, we wind our way along and ride a small stretch of the Pan-Am before turning east toward Lago Arenal.

Somewhere on a two-lane road Brian chooses a beautiful freshly-asphalted black raceway of a lane, and for a few minutes I'm in absolute heaven...until it ends at a rugged dirt road. According to the GPS, the road will lead us the right way and come out on the only road to Arenal, so we keep riding.

At some point the scales tip from rough dirt road, to descending a mountain, nearly rappelling, and I wish we had turned back before. But now we literally have no choice. There is no way to pull over or to park, or even to stop. We have to ride out the three-quarter mile steep, rocky mountainside until it comes out at the road below. I can't tell if it's actually a road or the remnants of a landslide. It's so steep that I can't get my bike to stop for a momentary rest, because gravity keeps pulling me down the hill. Instead I have to power through and bump over the baby heads and ruts and try to keep Betty upright en route to the bottom. It always looks worse from the top, and as much as I get scared of something, I feel a sense of accomplishment when I'm through it.

There's a German Baker in Nuevo Arenal who is also a motorcyclist. We stop to say hello, but he's busy feeding a busload of tourists, so instead we sit and enjoy pan au chocolat with a warm drink and wait to see if he will be free to talk in a little while. But his business seems to be booming, so we ride somewhere else for a beer.

Costa Rica is everything I've imagined - green, lush, and littered with volcanoes. We ride past Volcano Arenal toward San Jose before turning west to ride along the coast for a couple of days.

One evening we arrive at a small hotel in Golfito just minutes ahead of a thunderstorm. As I watch the torrential downpour from the comfort of our small room, I'm grateful to have learned the habit of getting off the road before the daily afternoon tropical deluge.

14 PANAMA

Half of a beautiful orange, tastes as good as the whole.
-Panamanian proverb

If crossing into Costa Rica was bad, crossing into Panama is exponentially worse. I must have jinxed myself by complaining about the last border crossing.

Border guards and customs officials are kept busy with cargo trucks driven by lazy truckers who are notoriously bad with paperwork. As a result, the staff are in very bad moods. The woman at the customs office yells at me for being ignorant about the vehicle import process when I ask her to repeat her instructions, which were, of course, delivered in yet another new version of Spanish. As I walk away to sulk, Brian announces he will just copy whatever I do because he's too afraid to approach "that bitch".

Four hours, nine hundred swear words, and one illegally-obtained stamp later, we ride into our last new country of this continent, Panama. It introduces us to its altogether worse version of jungle heat, complete with adult diaper rash. It seems strange to me to think that the Atlantic Ocean is north of me and the Pacific is south or even east at times, going against years of elementary school geography lessons.

We meet up with yet another motorcyclist couple in Panama City, and enjoy the chance to spend time with them. Carlos and Alison invite us to their apartment to watch a World Cup game and meet another rider who is staying with them. I love the easy mixing of cultures that you see in most of the world. Everyone is so open and comfortable. As we watch the game, I enjoy the mix of a German, a Colombian, an Englishman and two Americans sharing this experience together as if we had known each other for years. I love this world of overlanders and motorcyclists.

I spend my birthday enjoying a movie and a hot shower, luxuries these days. Brian and I ride out to the Miraflores Locks to experience the impressive Panama Canal during its 100th anniversary year. We watch construction on the far banks and see the plans for the canal expansion in the visitor center. We buy a few last-minute supplies and enjoy a night in a good hotel before riding to meet the Stahlratte at Carti, just a couple of hours from the city.

After fueling up, we ride east on the Pan-Am. We get just under halfway to Carti when we run into a road block, a routine occurrence in Latin America. As we pull to a stop in the now halted line of traffic, I see another bike ahead of us, a Triumph, ridden by a cute, shaggy Californian. Ryan is already talking with the protestors, asking if we can be allowed to pass.

Mat and Pam, who we met in Guatemala, and Pete, the Englishman, arrive shortly after. Now we are numerous enough to be a biker gang. We sit and relax on the guardrail while Ryan continues his bonding and pleas, to no avail. I worry for a moment about missing our scheduled departure time, but then remember that there are six of us stuck in the road block which is hopefully enough to make the Stahlratte's captain wait.

After an hour, and the involvement of local police and media, we are finally allowed to go. Mat and Pam take the lead, helping us to cover some fast miles. A left turn takes us off the highway onto Kuna land, a local tribe's property, before delivering us to the coast. We are the first to arrive. All the other riders were stuck further back in the protest blockade. Shortly after we park, a string of bikes rides up the beach onto the concrete pier, and lines up behind us. Markus and Karin are here, our Swiss friends, as well as a South African and French couple, another California man, and a Coloradan with a Carolinian drawl. We take a moment to introduce ourselves to each other before being called to work.

We begin to strip each bike of luggage which we hand over to the crew to be loaded by hand. Our ship's captain, Ludwig, maneuvers the Stahlratte into position and anchors her at the end of the pier. He climbs down and begins to secure lift ropes onto each bike frame which will be connected to a boom, lifting each in turn onto the deck of the ship. Each rider waits nervously for his or her turn.

Even though I know they've completed this maneuver dozens of times, I feel a sick pang as my beloved Betty lifts free of the concrete pier, flying high into the air and swinging out over the water. A moment of holding my breath lands her safely on the deck, and I finally exhale and relax.

One by one, the bikes are arranged on the ship's deck and lashed to her railings before being covered with tarps to protect them from sea spray. The crew carries our panniers and gear bags below decks to the common room which is surrounded by double-bed sized bunks, one for each couple. I abandon my shoes for the journey, and go settle in and change into something more appropriate to the heat and the sea.

Our first night is spent on a Kuna Island, in the San Blas Islands, where we are entertained by young dancers before retiring to small grass huts. We are each offered space in a local home, along with the family who lives in it, to experience the culture and way of life. There is no electricity or running water on the small island, and the only toilet is what my grandmother refers to as a "longdrop", an outhouse, perched over the rough surf at the end of their concrete pier.

The island is hot and humid, languoring in its tropical lagoon. Small black flies emerge at sunset. I'm reminded that I haven't started my malaria meds yet. While that makes me a little nervous, Simon Thomas put it in perspective when he said that malaria is treatable anyway, and that the real problem is dengue fever. I'd better put on pants and long sleeves.

The following day Ludwig, who has abandoned his pants along with dry land, thus earning the nickname Captain Underpants from me, turns our ship toward three small islets perched just inside a reef in turquoise shallows. We anchor for two days of swimming, drinking, barbecuing and shenanigans. The Stahlratte crew are great people and incredible cooks, which nearly helps me forget how awful the desalinated water is on board.

I spend my time snorkeling and exploring our small island, reading, sunning and chatting with fellow passengers. There's a rider from Mexico who has been on board for days. But not all of us are riders. There are two overlanding couples on board who shipped their vehicles by container and will retrieve them in Cartagena, Colombia, on the other side of this 5-day crossing.

All in all, it's a fantastic time, mostly due to the people we share the experience with. The crossing is smooth except for the last 36-hours which isn't unbearable, especially with the help of some anti-nausea meds.

On a Friday afternoon, I catch my first glimpse of the Colombian coast. It looks so modern and Miami-ish with its high-rise towers spanning long beaches in the distance. When I think of the Colombia of television news reports from my youth, I still recall Pablo Escobar, guerilla kidnappings and cocaine being the common themes. I spoke with my grandmother recently and decided against telling her I was coming to Colombia for just that reason.

15 COLOMBIA

Wings that traversed unexplored valleys…
- From "Butterflies" by José Asunción Silva

The grand dame, Stahlratte, drifts lazily into port and anchors in the small harbor not far from a boat ramp. Captain Ludwig expertly transfers each bike onto a floating barge, and shuttles them to the landing, where we take turns riding our bikes onto the new continent via a narrow plank. It's all a very hurried process as we try to get to the Customs office before the close of business for the week. All but four bikes get processed, but those four owners have to come back the next day, Saturday, to finish their paperwork.

Nearly all the riders trail along together to a narrow street near old Cartagena where we pile into a handful of hostels, within walking distance of each other. It takes us nearly two weeks to slowly drift apart and continue our individual journeys, as if the newly formed brethren don't yet want to break the happy spell of comradery. Nearly every day we meet for drinks or dinner, or to watch a World Cup game together. We sit on verandas sharing stories and discussing routes.

One afternoon during a visit to see fellow Stahlratte-ers at a hostel a block from ours, Brian and I are introduced to a bicyclist from Minnesota. Jim has cycled from Alaska, is bound for Ushuaia like us, and is raising funds for cancer research. I like him immediately. He's a mellow and easy-going guy, bearded, shaggy and smelly, just as he should be on his type of journey. While he sits quietly enjoying a smoke on the balcony, we chat about our travels, and about Midwestern life in America.

There's a sort of hierarchy to overlanding – top dogs being the Unimog, MAN Truck and Land Rover types, followed by 4X4ers, VWs and other "cool" rigs. Then there are the people who travel in converted soccer mom minivans, shelled-out trucks or other hodgepodge vehicles. Then there are motorcyclists (which have their own smaller internal hierarchy of sorts moving down from BMW snobs, to likeable BMW people, to dual sport riders, and on down to riders of anything on two wheels, etc.). And lastly, there are the cyclists.

I love traveling by motorcycle and wouldn't trade it for anything. But I will admit to having envious thoughts as I watch friends park up in a VW van with a small cooler and a mattress to sleep on. No tent to set up. No rain to deal with. Room for spare fuel and water. Time spent with your partner in conversation and mutual experience rather than alone in your helmet for months. Someone always has it better.

Traveling by motorcycle naturally doesn't allow for many comforts, certainly not as many as a vehicle allows. The experience is entirely different on a motorcycle – solitary, exposed and involving more work. But as many times as I have sat in a wet tent surrounded by lightning, envious of people tucked inside a dry truck, I have as often passed a cyclist on an uphill road and watched them standing and straining to make the grade, while counting my blessings for having an engine to carry me up. Someone always has it worse.

If all goes well, Jim plans to be in Ushuaia by February, just over seven months away. That's the timeline I'm working toward too, and I'm instantly struck by the thought that Jim can cover as many miles as me powered solely by his own body. Factoring in the type of terrain we will be covering in the Andes Mountains, and I'm suitably humbled.

The old city of Cartagena is beautiful. Inside the cannon-topped fortress walls of the original colonial city, houses stand shoulder to shoulder, draped in bougainvillea, with wooden balconies overlooking the narrow cobblestoned streets. I spend an afternoon lazily wandering them while shopping for tiny, lightweight souvenirs.

We have to buy insurance for our bikes and luckily get a company name from some shipmates who obtained theirs first. We should take a taxi to the office since our bikes aren't legal until after we get coverage, but we choose to ride instead, thinking the odds of having a problem in the mile between our hostel and the office are low. Apparently, we are wrong.

I see the road block from a quarter-mile off and look for a way out, but the median prevents my escape. I get flagged down by one of the officers. He asks for my papers, so I hand over my import permit for the bike. He requests my passport too, so I hand it over as well.

Then he requests my insurance papers, for the policy I haven't yet purchased. I happen to have a 23-page printed copy of a blanket policy I purchased for all of Central and South America and decide to present it to him. Never mind the fact that it excludes six countries, one of which is this country, and that the policy is in English, and that he can't read it. Another officer asks Brian for his documents as I translate for him. Cars start to line up behind us. Thankfully, the 23-page policy does exactly what I had hoped. The officer doesn't feel like spending time with us and waves us through.

After riding the last half-mile to the insurance office, we are disappointed to find that this office doesn't sell vehicle insurance. We have to go back through the city to another office. As we prepare to get back on our bikes, the skies let loose with a torrential downpour. We lurk in the lobby of the insurance agency for nearly

30 minutes while the deluge continues. Water starts to build in the street and overflow the gutters. It's not getting any better. In fact, I'm worried about how bad the flooding will get. We decide to chance it and get out of this low-elevation part of the city. We ride off in 12-inches of muddy running water, bumping over unseen objects in search of the correct insurance office.

A few days later, we ride into the small marijuana-infused beach town of Taganga to settle into a room overlooking the pool of a noisy party hostel. Rarely have I ever felt so old and uncool, but I really couldn't care less. My days of all-nighters are behind me, mostly, not that I ever partook of orgies and experimental drugs like these people do anyway. I'm just happy for a room and a place to park my bike off the street. We meet up with Mat and Pam from the Stahlratte, so that Pam and I can take advantage of the cheap scuba diving here. She and I spend a day interviewing dive guides and inspecting shops, and book a dive with the cleanest and most modern of the two dozen or more dive shops in town. I haven't been in the water for a couple of years so it's wonderful to have a friend along for my refresher dive.

Days later, we ride an hour up into the mountains to Minca, a sleepy village, where we meet half a dozen other overlanders, including Markus and Karin, Tom, Pete and Juan, all from the Stahlratte. Mat and Pam arrive later in the day. We settle into a nice campground complete with a Macaw, who both seems to like me and get annoyed with me. The open-air kitchen and views of the coastline below are perfect. There's yet another overlanding Swiss couple here (those Swiss really get around) traveling by Land Rover, Michael and Simone. Michael seems to be the Macaw's first choice for companions.

Brian and I plot a route to Venezuela, much to the surprise of most of our friends who are all turning to other parts of Colombia before crossing into Ecuador. I think Brian has big plans for trying to cross Venezuela and take the eastern route to Ushuaia, but we aren't hearing good reports about the road conditions in the Guyana region, so will have to decide later when we have more news on the rainy season roads. It takes us two days' easy riding along the northern coast of Colombia to get to the Venezuela border. While riding, I catch occasional glimpses of the muddy brown Caribbean to my left through the trees.

Somewhere east of the industrial port city of Barranquilla, the land gives itself away to the sea except for a narrow ribbon of land that supports the road. As we approach Cienaga and more shacks and lean-tos sprout up, I'm struck by the incredible amount of trash that lines both sides of the road on the salt flats surrounding the highway. It's as if we are riding through a garbage dump. And it makes me sad. Literally, semi-load upon semi-load of plastic bottles, plastic bags, and other debris fill the ditches and low spots…for miles.

We debate about trying to ride up to the end of the Guajira Peninsula, the northernmost point of the continent, but hear it's rough going. Instead we spend a night in Maicao and walk the beachfront enjoying the breeze coming in from the sea. I stock up on groceries and fill my bike with fuel.

Helmet thoughts:

- Buddhists kick ass. Well, not literally…that would be weird. But I like the philosophy (which happens to be the word that knocked me out of my fourth grade spelling be in the semi-final round…why couldn't it be philosiphy?)
- Some guy passes me on the two-lane road and dives back into my lane just missing my front wheel. My reaction is to think, "No offense, but you're offensive."
- The road less traveled…should be traveled more.
- Why is it that every time I notice a mile marker sign or some other sign, it almost always seems to be the number 78?
- I'm still not digging the Latin music. I wish I could get into it more, but it's just not my thing. Today's song of choice in my helmet is Banana Pancakes by Jack Johnson.

There isn't much information available about riding into Venezuela. Despite a week of surfing online and searching, I don't feel as prepared as I would like. It's obvious that not many people ride there. One blogpost I find walks me through the nerve-wracking process of black market money exchanges, skills I intend to use first thing tomorrow. I feel less than minimally prepared for the crossing.

Brian found a blog somewhere. He decides that after we cross into Venezuela, we will aim for the coastal town of San Rafael to try to find the posada mentioned by a fellow rider.

After I spend a few minutes sorting through my American money making some quick calculations and notes about currency exchanges, we ride out early in the day, bound for Venezuela. Both sides of the highway are lined with impromptu gas stations.

Post and palm leaf palapas shade large drums of fuel that has been freshly smuggled into Colombia. Thanks to government subsidies, Venezuela has notoriously cheap fuel, so much so, that its residents fill their cars with their weekly allotment and promptly drive to Colombia to syphon it out and resell it for 20 times what they paid for it, or more. Business-minded Colombians syphon the fuel into drums and sit in the shade waiting to resell it. There is a booming black market for fuel.

We ride to the border and park our bikes in front of the Colombian Aduana where we will cancel our bike import permits. But first, we want to be sure we can get into Venezuela. We walk over to the Venezuelan side, a hundred feet further up the road, and inquire about entering the country. We are asked for our passports.

Fairly quickly, one officer seems to take us under his corrupted wing to guide us through the crossing. He explains the process to enter Venezuela takes time, paving the way for a personal "expedite fee", and that we will need his assistance to have even a small chance of entering Venezuela. He escorts us away from the guard booth on the road, into the main building and to a bench where we are directed to sit down. I'm not sure where the Aduana or Migracion offices are, or if this man can even help us.

The officer asks if we have a letter of invitation to Venezuela, which we do not. He asks if we have any business to transact in Venezuela, which we do not. He asks if we have a hotel reservation in Venezuela, which we do not. Friends had warned us that we would need a reason to enter the country, so this isn't surprising. I hadn't reserved a room in a hotel, which could qualify as a business transaction and allow us to enter, because I wasn't sure we could get in. It presents a dilemma – I can't get in without a hotel reservation, but I don't want to book and pay for a room I may never get to use if I can't get into the country.

I ask if we can get into Venezuela if we have a hotel reservation, and the officer says he thinks it will be likely but could still take a few days to process, as far as the paperwork goes. Despite feeling like I'm starting over with yet another version of Spanish, I get his message loud and clear. He wants an "expedite fee" (bribe) in order to get us across the border today.

In a moment of haughty judgmental-ism, I try to gather my limited Spanish vocabulary to impart the proper words to reflect my frustration and distaste of his thinly-veiled request. I tell him that I'm very sad that Venezuela is hurting its people by keeping tourists out, tourists who want to celebrate this beautiful country. I explain that bribes will keep people from coming here, which will hurt the economy.

He listens quietly and is wholly unaffected. I can pay him the "expedite fee" for the paperwork to enter Venezuela or I can turn around and go away. He doesn't care either way, and thus has the upper hand in this poker game.

Brian and I talk for a few moments, and decide we will pay the bribe because we want to cross the border. I'm incensed, but am still curious, still a traveler. We tell the officer that we would like to apply for entry. He sets to work, while we return to the Colombian side to get processed out, and stop off at an internet café to book a room at a hotel in Maracaibo which will serve as our reason for visiting Venezuela.

16 VENEZUELA (AND COLOMBIA)

There is nothing hidden between heaven and earth
-Venezuelan proverb

We haggle in the parking lot of the Colombian Aduana to buy Venezuelan Bolivianos before riding over to park at the Venezuelan offices. Current blog posts have given me a fair idea of what price I should pay, but I don't feel like bargaining. So instead of pushing for the top price, I settle for roughly 90-95% of the going rate. We swap U.S. Dollars for 15 million Bolivianos and wander back to the immigration office.

The officer doesn't want to talk to me, not so much from my obvious desire to lecture him, as out of deference to the Latino culture's belief that business should be conducted between men. Brian slides one of my $20 bills across to the officer in a cliché handshake maneuver. We wait for less than ten minutes to get the proper stamps and permits to resolve it all to a successful conclusion. Welcome to Venezuela.

We ride out of the frontier and down the highway toward San

Rafael, passing dozens of 1970s American muscle cars waiting their turns at long fuel pump lines before crossing into Colombia to unload their oversized fuel tanks. Riding east for an hour and a bit leads us to a turn to the village where we hope to stay tonight. But a quick lap of town reveals not a single hotel or hostel. We stop and ask a few people, at least the ones who don't scatter quickly away and ignore us, but no one can point us in the direction of lodging for the night. Mind you, this isn't a small town. There must be more than 10,000 residents.

Brian leads us all the way around town to check out the smaller side streets, and river and beachfront areas where we're most likely to find something. But there isn't anything here. The more we ride, the more uncomfortable I feel. People are staring at us. There aren't many restaurants, gas stations, or shops, much less hotels, which I would normally expect to see in a town of this size. After a quick roadside huddle, we decide to ride on to Maracaibo. I hope we can make it before dark.

Another hour brings us to the outer edges of the city and still we don't see any tourist services. I've not seen anything like this before. We decide to head for the Holiday Inn where I had booked our "business transaction" reservation for two days from now in hopes of getting a room there. It's all the way through town. The streets are quiet, and the sun is getting low. I'd planned to cancel the reservation, but now it may be our only hope.

We arrive at the hotel, but have a hard time getting into the property itself because it is surrounded with a high concrete security wall topped with razor wire. It's more than a little unsettling. After a full lap of the block, we finally find the gated entrance and go in. Thankfully, the hotel can check us in early, and we unload our bikes onto a luggage cart.

A bellman who helps us to our room is overtaken with curiosity and wonders aloud why we would come to Venezuela. He warns us more than once to not wander around at night, and not leave the hotel at any time at all during our stay unless we leave Maracaibo. In an instant, I feel trapped and nervous. He says the entire city is very dangerous and we shouldn't linger.

My years of hoarding hotel points finally bear fruit in the form of a comp night in good hotel, and we get upgraded to boot. I'm not sure what I was happier about, the Jacuzzi tub or the beautiful pool. My riding jacket and pants are long overdue for a bath, not having had one since Belize. The Jacuzzi tub serves double duty as a lovely soaking oasis for me, and later as a spinning and bubbling washing machine for my gear. The laundry water is black with dirt and grime even after a half dozen rinses. I scoop up a handful of dirt from the corners of the tub when I'm done.

We walk over to a Subway restaurant in the hotel complex to get a sandwich to share. Trying to get my bearings with the local currency, and especially with our black-market rate, I run a quick calculation on what the sandwich has cost, just shy of $5 USD. Then I check the number again using the rates I would've paid if I hadn't used black market money. If I had paid with a credit card or gotten money from an ATM, that same sandwich and drink would have cost nearly $50 USD. I'm blown away. No wonder tourists don't come here. How could they possibly afford to?

I've been told the Venezuelan government, even with Chavez gone, isn't supportive of foreigners visiting the country, so it intentionally sets the monetary exchange rates at impossibly bad rates to discourage tourism. That's not the only thing that's strange about this place or its government. Fuel prices are subsidized to the point that gas is virtually free, but the effect is that the country is nearly bankrupt. There are very few shops to be seen and everything seems to be in short supply. The Subway only had three sandwiches on the menu.

We hear on the evening news that the airport in Caracas, the country's capitol, has shut down, for who knows how long. The handful of tourists and business people visiting Venezuela have to take boats to nearby islands, like Aruba and Bonaire, to get out of the country.

There's an oppressive air to the place. Everyone seems suspicious and wary, of each other and of us. We draw a lot of attention. While I'm accustomed to some, being a 5-foot-8-inch tall white girl traveling on a big motorcycle (at least by local standards) in Latin America, this attention is different. I can't tell if the locals think I'm predator or prey.

Brian and I aren't getting along, and I wonder how much of it is road weariness or the glumness of this place. One day he notices a hair of mine stuck to his shirt, scowls and says in a disgusted way, "What's the deal with your hair?"

To which I reply, "Sorry,", my usual response to whatever sets him off.

If one stray hair stuck to his shirt is grossing him out, I can only imagine how he must have felt about the handfuls of hair I lost in Newfoundland after my surgery. We've been on the road for just over a year now, which has helped to rub some of the rough edges off the two of us. But long hot days and the stress of this not-quite-comfortable place finds new ones.

Recent photos of the roads through Guyana, Suriname and French Guiana look horrible. Knee-deep, bike-swallowing mud ruts don't appeal to me with my heavily loaded bike. After a short discussion, we agree instead to head into the mountains south of Maracaibo and make our way back to Colombia to take the western route through the continent to Ushuaia.

After a soak in the pool, a soak in the tub, and a good two-night rest, we pack up to ride out of Maracaibo to the mountains, the top end of the Andes, and begin our travels south. We ride out of the hotel parking lot in search of fuel, for first time since entering the country.

Brian quickly spots a gas station with dozens of cars lined up at each pump, and turns to find our place at the back. Attendants pump the fuel, which is customary in Venezuela, and finally when it's our turn, we ride up and park, shutting off the bikes.

Our attendant asks Brian something, clearly avoiding talking to me, but Brian can't understand him or respond. I ask him to fill our tanks but the attendant just stares for a moment. Cars are impatiently waiting behind us while he seems to want something from us. Finally, he lets out a deep frustrated sigh and begins to fill our bikes. I hold out a bill to him to pay and he shakes his head, and instead reaches for a much smaller one. I thought he had asked for 30,000 bolivianos, but he wants much less. He takes the bill out of my hand and returns some coins to me and waves us on, happy to be rid of us. Everyone within a block has been staring at us the whole time.

On our way out of the city, we ride over the 5-mile-long General Rafael Urdaneta bridge, crossing over the estuary of Lago Maracaibo where the sea pours in and out of this enormous brackish bay. If this really were a lake, rather than a bay, it would be the largest in South America. At its southern end, there's an incredible natural phenomenon I want to see, the world's longest running lightning storm, at Catatumbo. More lightning occurs there than anywhere else in the world, and the several-hundred-year long storm has been the world's largest producer of ozone.

But our recent dose of good internet and free time may have put a stop to that idea. One evening, I stumbled across a list of the highest murder rates of various countries around the world. Venezuela is number 2. Unknowingly, I've ridden through all of the top five and now have entered my sixth of the top ten. Quite an eerie collection. Within the report, I also see the murder rates for each province within these countries, and find that the province around Maracaibo is the worst part of Venezuela. The areas around Lago Maracaibo, and especially near the Catatumbo River, are supposed to be notoriously dangerous. Well then, no lightning show for me.

As we cover 50 miles, I'm surprised by how few places I can see to buy fuel or food. There only seem to be small villages, occasional farms, and clusters of run down cinder block and corrugated tin buildings which I think must be homes. We finally find a small truck stop and pull in for a snack and a cool drink, before carrying on. I have a chance to use my calculator app and figure out that we paid just under three cents (U.S. dollars) to fill the two motorcycles back in Maracaibo. I double and triple check my math, because I can't believe it.

In Valera, we stop in traffic for fifteen minutes to watch a funeral procession, which in this part of the world takes place on foot. A wagon serves as a hearse while friends and family walk behind it from the church to the cemetery.

Every mile from Maracaibo seems to get greener and more lush. The road starts to climb up into mountain valleys, through the village of La Puerta, and eventually climbs up the side of the mountain, tracing back and forth in long angles on the mountainsides forming long, loose switchbacks. Tin-roofed shacks line the roadways on both sides, one perched on the edge of the downward slope while the other backs up to the mountain. Children and skinny puppies play in the road until they see us coming then step out of the way.

We continue to climb higher. After the road snakes back to the inside corner of a valley, it turns onto the next mountain ridge and continues to another outside corner and then around the back of the next mountain. Instead of tight switchbacks, the mountain spines are deep and long enough to allow us to climb in long stretches, make a single turn and then carry on to another long straight stretch. I'm in awe of the incredible views I see as we continue to climb. Somewhere down below is the village of La Puerta which I thought was relatively high when I rode through it just half an hour before.

Troncal 7, which takes us through several small towns including Timotes and Chachopo, is absorbed by each village as the main street when it traverses them. I'm treated to views of the town squares and main cathedrals as we pass. The slices of life I see seem much calmer here than in the coastal areas of the country far below. What's true in my home, is probably true in most parts of the world – life and people are better in the rural areas of a country.

It's getting late in the day and we still haven't seen any form of place to stay. High above us at the top of the mountains, clouds gather and fog starts to cascade down from above.

Not far out of Chachopo, Brian passes a small collection of buildings and rounds a tight corner, but then pulls off the narrow road. I pull in behind him and he waves me to turn around. He leads us back down the road and turns into a gravel lot in front of what appears to be a small café. I'm not sure that it's open, but I walk over and try the door.

As we rode higher the air cooled noticeably, which makes the inside of this small German café especially pleasant and warm. I smell rich meaty stew and fresh baked bread, and am reminded that we haven't had a meal since breakfast. We decide to sit and warm up with a hot drink and meal.

When the woman working in the kitchen comes to take our orders, I inquire about the sign that caught Brian's eye and caused him to turn back to this place. They have cabins to rent. But the woman looks at me a little suspiciously and says the cabins are very expensive. She thinks we can't afford one, or else she just doesn't want foreigners here.

"How much?" I inquire.

"Un million," she replies. $1 million Bolivianos is roughly $20 U.S. dollars with the black-market exchange rate. We accept. Knowing we have a place to settle in for the night puts my mind at ease in an instant. Rain is coming, and now I know we will be tucked in before it gets here.

We enjoy our Latin version of a German meal of pastel carne with salty boiled vegetables and a tangy vinegar slaw, before riding our bikes up the grassy lane between the café and the farmhouse where the woman lives with her elderly father. Their handful of cabins are lovely and cozy.

Once unpacked and relaxed, I admire the beautiful valley below, the steep mountainsides on which we are perched, and the lush green slopes covered with grazing dairy cows. This place reminds me a little of Switzerland. We have a small woodstove which warms the timber and stucco cabin nicely. I work on my journal and make a cup of tea, while the rain starts. It's a subtle and soothing sound, which continues all through the night, but at times becomes more of a roar with heavy downpour.

In the morning as I load my bike, I watch the old farmer lead cows, one by one, from a pasture above our cabin, to a small milking shed just below it. His yellow rain poncho reminds me of the yellow rain slickers that ranchers wear on rainy days at home. He stops, bows, and wishes me a good morning and safe travels ahead. I smile and thank him.

With the night's rain the mountains have been so thoroughly saturated that water can no longer soak into the land. Waterfalls have formed all over the ridgelines above, making it seem as though we are riding our way up the tiers of a freshly iced cake. Culverts are so overwhelmed by the volume of water that water has had to invent new crossings which appear all over the roadway.

Off we go, up over the next ridge to a high bare plateau and then onto the next higher ridge. Fog settles in around us and the rain continues off and on. Finally, we reach Pico Aguila and stop for a photo and a bathroom break before carrying on to Merida for the night. A sign along the roadway says there is a Condor sanctuary here, but it's closed.

Merida is a lovely city, and seems much more tourist-oriented with its hotels, cafes and shops. We settle on a hotel with a parking garage below. The World Cup games are still on, which we watch in our room.

Graffiti around the city extolls the locals love (or mandated support) of former President Chavez. I see anti-American graffiti too, but am reminded how much propaganda this part of the world has been fed about my country, not that we haven't earned our reputation as materialistic and arrogant.

While the people don't seem as wary of us here, most aren't overly friendly. But at least people don't stare, so I relax. The atmosphere, while still a little depressed, is completely different than in Maracaibo.

We stop for ice cream at a local shop which holds the Guinness Record for the widest variety of flavors, with over 1000 of them, including meat and Viagra. As we walk out with our cones, a local man smiles and tips his hat at me and says, "Welcome to Venezuela," confirming the thoughts I have just been having about this lovely part of the country, and making me smile.

My crazy GPS, which Brian rarely uses but is as we leave Merida, guides us up a narrow mountainside road above town in the complete opposite direction of where we want to go. Eventually Brian ignores it and finds what appears to be an abandoned road to bounce down to return to the main highway.

Troncal 7 follows the Rio Chama west toward Lagunillas and Tovar before climbing high up the mountains again to cross to La Grita. While our ride in the valley was graced by a warm sun, clouds and fog return as we climb. The tradeoff is a spectacular view of a rainbow just below us, not the usual perspective of them, which is stunning.

A few miles above La Grita we see signs for a finca (farm), and stop to see if there are any rooms open. Luckily, we find one and settle in just before a dark cloud opens up over the mountain.

The young woman at the office is the only person here, selling and cleaning the place by herself each day. When I inquire about a market nearby she says there is nothing here and that the closest place to buy food is La Grita, down the mountain. With my stores on the bike having been depleted due to fewer grocery stores, I don't have much, but I do have enough for dinner. She asks if we have food. I say we won't for breakfast, but, I tell her, we can ride down to La Grita in the morning and eat there. She smiles and nods. After I cook dinner, do the dishes and have a shower, I wander back to the office to ask about directions and services along the route ahead. The young woman and I spark up a conversation about life in our respective countries, and about my trip.

Jocelenda has never met an American before, much less a woman traveling by motorcycle. She says she has always dreamed of travel, but that it isn't possible in Venezuela. Her grandmother lives in Colombia, which to my mind is relatively close, but to her might as well be on the other side of the world. What has been a benefit to me, is a curse to her, in the form of that crazy black market exchange rate. While it helps me afford to travel here, it means that it's nearly impossible for her to get any value out of her Venezuelan money if she wants to visit any other country.

Jocelenda works 7 days a week, 12-14 hours each day, and is grateful she has a job. Her sister had a hard time finding work in the area after finishing her university studies, so she moved to Caracas. Jocelenda and her family worry about her all the time because Caracas a very dangerous place. I'm reminded how good we have it in America. Her conversation is a gift for me, hard-won through six months of struggling through learning Spanish. This is exactly what I'd hoped to experience on this trip, a sharing of cultures and experiences with another person, and my studying feel worth it.

In the morning, as I stop by the office to let Jocelenda know we are leaving, she invites Brian and I to come in for breakfast. Before coming to work this morning from her home in La Grita, she stopped at a panaderia and bought us two breakfast arepas. The moist ground white corn bread is topped with chicken and cheese. She kept them warm for us and even brought us small bottles of orange juice, recalling a comment I'd made the night before.

I'm overwhelmed by her kind gesture and what must have been a huge expense for her. As a thank you, I leave her a $20 USD tip in our room with a note suggesting she try to find a way to exchange it on the black market for $1 million Bolivianos, the going rate. We are running low, so I can't spare any Bolivianos yet, even though they're worthless.

La Grita is three miles down the road. Apparently, that's 1.5 miles ahead and 1.5 miles down, if judged by the grade of the road. It's the steepest road I've ever seen, much less ridden on. It's enough to expose one of the weaknesses of my model of bike. KLRs are notorious for weak brakes. As I descend the wet, paved road, I consciously try to minimize the use of my brakes. But with the sharp turns and steep grade, I will careen out of control if I don't use them enough.

Brian rides ahead and makes it down to a level place to stop and wait for me. Despite using first gear, I notice that my rear brake is gone completely, and is being followed quickly by my front. I get the bike to a complete stop using what's left of my front brake and my thick-soled boots, but the bike continues to nudge forward an inch at a time. I'm afraid I won't be able to hold it much longer. I shut the bike off and release the clutch assuming my gear will help hold the bike in place, but it's not doing much good against the steep grade and my bike continues to roll a few inches ahead every several seconds.

Holding the brake allows the heat to transfer from the pads of my red-hot disk into the brake lines. The heat is so great it boils the fluid which causes bubbles to form, causing my brakes to fail. It's a recipe for disaster. I've heard of it before, and have had nightmares about a ride without brakes. I've worked hard to never be in this situation, but this road has beaten me entirely.

I stand still on the steeply-pitched single-lane road and brace my legs against gravity, trying hard to keep the bike from rolling forward while I figure out my exit strategy. Brian rides back up to chew me out for the delay, and discovers my quandary. He parks his bike and walks over to pour water on my front and rear disks, which instantly bursts into a cloud of steam, and stands to admire my literal hot mess.

Although Brian agrees that this is the steepest road he's ever seen too, he shakes his head, and is clearly frustrated with me. I sit tight, not that I have any other choice, for 10-15 minutes, until my legs are exhausted and finally Brian thinks I can give it another try. The stop was just enough to get me down the rest of the mountain into town.

We stop for fuel in La Grita and are asked if we have permits for the bikes, which we do not. Perhaps this is what the gas station attendant back in Maracaibo was asking about. The pumps only activate when they sense a permit disk, and won't operate without it. Since we don't have one, we will have to wait for a local person to fuel up and then quickly remove the free-flowing nozzle from their car to cram it into our bike's fuel tanks while fuel sprays all over. It's the only way to fuel up and sounds horrible.

A small rusted white car pulls up to the pump in front of me and I push my quiet bike as close as I can to their rear bumper and ready myself for the exchange. The attendant gives me a nod and quickly jerks the nozzle from the car and aims it for my tank, as fuel showers all over my bike and hot engine. Thankfully, he does it as quickly as he can, and I don't burst into flames.

I ask how much I owe for the fuel, and prepare to pay so that the driver of the white car isn't stuck paying my bill. He's already been more than generous by allowing me to fuel up on his permit. But he waves his hand and smiles, and drives off. All in all, my 1000 kilometers (600-ish miles) in the country has cost me just under five cents for fuel. Incredible.

Leave it to me to notice silly little things to find something entertain myself while in my helmet. As we make our way down the Andean spine of the continent, we have crossed back into Colombia on a different road. It occurs to me while I ride, that I woke this morning in the village of Pamplona and am headed for Berlin, while riding on Route 66.

Despite my boiled-brake incident a couple of days ago, I find that I'm already addicted to the mountain riding of South America. From what I hear, it only gets better from here on. We cross from Cucuta to Bucaramanga and then to Barranca Bermeja. I love practicing the names and grade school Spanish lesson conversations in my helmet, all the while exaggerating my accent. I hope I sound like Salma Hayek.

After a couple days' riding we finally push through to the highway to Medellin where we will meet up with a couple of Stahlratte friends for dinner, and shop for bike parts. The last couple of hours of riding toward the city, we follow a muddy brown river which bubbles and foams with chemicals and soap that have been dumped into the river by small villages for hundreds of miles above. The valley is filled with the strange stench of sewage and soap bubbles, making me feel sick.

Medellin is beautiful, if a little run down, which spills up the mountainsides on either side of a wide valley. We take a cable car to the top of the ridgeline on the eastern side of the city. While the view of the valley is spectacular, the closer view from our car, of the endless terraces of slums just below, is infinitely more interesting.

I watch a mother wash her little boy in a small blue plastic bucket on the rooftop of a cinder block home. Dogs meander through the narrow spaces between shanties and nose through endless piles trash for something to eat. Barefoot and dirty children run and play while their grandmothers watch wistfully out of windows.

After a few days, we ride to the village of Guatape, to see the famous monolithic rock that towers strangely over the green lake-strewn district. We go for a hike with people we meet at a hostel there, and finally get the chance to connect with an Australian couple we've been hoping to cross paths with in our opposing routes. As we sit around the common room one night, the four of us discuss the big news of the day. Harry Devert has finally been found.

It's heartbreaking to hear that his bike and two plastic bags of dismembered human remains have been found. While that happened several days ago, DNA tests confirmed in the last couple of days that the remains are those of Harry Devert. Harry's mother has been an inspiring force, pushing hard to keep the search going for her son. There's a Facebook page, with thousands of followers, dedicated to keeping him in the media spotlight in hopes that officials in Mexico would be pressured to help solve his disappearance.

I'm numb. I never met him and I don't think we shared many traits. But we did have a motorcycle journey through the Americas in common. While I'm sitting here enjoying time with new friends, I now know that his parallel journey has ended tragically. Life is like that. Random. Unexpected.

This news, to me at least, reinforces my belief in my need to be here. Cliché as it is to say, life is short. While taking a trip like this may put me in harm's way at times, who's to say I would be safe and healthy in South Dakota. I'm glad I've taken this chance to live a life I had only ever imagined. It won't be forever, but this is how I'm living for now, and I'm going to make the most of it.

Brian reaches out to a coffee farmer on Help Exchange and lands us a gig working on a coffee plantation a few hundred miles down the road. It sounds exotic and mildly romantic, to pick red coffee berries in the mountains of Colombia. But I'm quickly put off by the heat and the bugs, and the not-so-teddy-bear-like spiders, and even more by the lazy farmwife who mildly abuses our help. I'm glad it is only for a week. The Zona Cafetera itself is a beautiful region, covered in lush vegetation and steeply rolling hills that are packed together tightly.

We carry on through the coffee highlands and make our way south through the center of the country, bound for Ecuador. I hope to stop at a UNESCO site, the ruins at Tierradentro, but the FARC are active again in that area. One night Brian plots a route to the archaeological park, only to find the next day that the road no longer "exists" according to the Colombian government. Somehow, it has even been removed from some online maps. Such is life in this part of the world.

A blog I stumble across while reading up on salsa dance lessons in Cali, mentions the risk of borrachero being higher at the moment, which gives me pause. The horrifying possibility of having this drug slipped into your drink and you being completely at the mercy of anyone giving suggestions is crazy to me. It describes those who are on it as being "zombie-like", and reminds me why I'm paranoid at times.

We stop in Salento and camp on the grounds of a hostel, taking a day to hike up to see the famous and spectacular 200-foot-tall wax palm trees that only grow in this part of the world in the Cocora Valley. The following day we opt for a rest day, to recover from the hike. It's time for laundry anyway. And as it dries in the sun, I sit quietly inside the farmhouse to surf online.

Two other people sit silently in the cool breeze of the room with Brian and I, a platinum-blonde American motorcyclist, and a girl from who knows where. As we all journal or surf, or read Facebook posts, it doesn't occur to me that the woman might speak English. In hostels, many times visitors may not share a common language, so a smile may be all the exchange you get from your roommates.

The girl tinkers with her iPad and then suddenly starts to speak through her headphones, obviously on a digital call. It quickly becomes clear that she is American. But more than that, she starts talking about South Dakota. Brian looks up at her and then turns to me to see if I'm eavesdropping enough to have caught the name of a town, Spearfish, located just twenty miles from my hometown of Sturgis. I heard her, but I can't believe my ears.

First of all, there aren't that many of us from South Dakota. There are even fewer of us traveling out of the state at the moment. Exponentially fewer must be the number of us in Colombia, much less the small mountain village of Salento. I can't imagine the odds of finding someone from Spearfish, South Dakota sitting in a chair in a tiny hostel not ten feet from me. It's crazy.

I wait politely for her to finish her call, but am on pins and needles in anticipation of telling her. Before I can say a word, Brian springs the "small world" revelation on her. We laugh out loud and can't believe our luck. Jackie and I burst into a conversation of local friends and connections, trying to find our common ground, while Brian laughs at how similar our accents and vocabularies are. Finding her is one of those serendipitous moments you have, more often than you think, while traveling. We spend an afternoon together, sharing lunch and a stroll through Salento's central plaza to shop the jewelry makers' wares. A few hours with this sweet and bubbly stranger renews me enough to keep my homesickness at bay for at least a few more weeks.

Markus and Karin arrive in Salento, along with other friends, and we walk into town one evening to try a game of Tejo, which is sort of like shuffleboard but with explosives. I don't know how I could ever feel homesick with friends like these crossing our path every few days.

Brian and I make our way south along the Pan-Am highway, stopping for a night in Popoyan, where we meet a Russian rider on his RTW ride. As I prepare breakfast in the hostel one morning, I overhear two French women wondering about the market in town. Hoping to offer some insight to them, I try to explain what I know in my remnants of French. But I find my practice of that language is so neglected that what comes out is a version of Franish that makes us all giggle. Instead I draw a map on a sheet of paper and smile, achieving the desired result anyway.

Brian hasn't developed a fondness for the local cuisine yet. We usually cook our own meals except lunch on riding days, which we buy at any café we can find along our route. In Popoyan, I order fish soup while Brian opts for the cuy soup, a real leap of faith for him. I question my choice when my soup turns out to be milky, fishy broth loaded with four-inch bones and nickel-sized scales.

The next day we try again at a roadside stop. I can't keep up with the woman's quickly-mumbled description of what our choices are, but did catch "chicken soup" as an option, so we order two bowls. This soup arrives in large deep bowls, and looks pretty good, until I dip my large spoon into the milky broth and pull up a spoon loaded with a small potato and a large clammy chicken foot. I must have missed the word "foot" in the description she offered. We eat everything but the feet and leave the six or so feet we each have lying on the tray our bowls arrived on, much to the chagrin of the other diners. I'm sure they thought we were very wasteful and rude.

On the following day, we ride through another stretch of two-lane mountain roads, stopped at yet another café and are offered soup. As cool and damp as it has been the past few days, it still sounds nice, even after the past two episodes. Hopefully, the third time is the charm.

Our two bowls arrive, each filled with broth and the large meatless ribcage of a chicken. Nothing appeared to remain of the meat, until I went to remove the rib cage from my bowl so I could eat the broth. Just then a burgundy wobble revealed itself to be the chicken's heart, still attached to the rib cage by a narrow tendon.

Brian's dish matched mine perfectly. Maybe that's enough soup.

We carry on through Pasto and camp at a state park at the base of a volcano, before riding to Las Lajas to see the famous and stunningly beautiful cathedral which spans a narrow canyon, just a few miles from the border of Ecuador.

I'm only a day's ride from the Equator.

17 ECUADOR

A man who dares to waste one hour of time has not discovered the value of life.

-Charles Darwin

Green Colombian patchwork hills, deep river valleys and canyons dissolve into gold and peach-colored arid mountains as we cross into Ecuador. This next country holds a feather for my cap, the chance to ride over the equator into the southern hemisphere.

Not more than an hour into the country, we ride past three cyclists on the highway, and Brian promptly pulls over and turns around. He leads us back to a small roadside café and pulls off his helmet, announcing that he thinks we just passed Jim, our new cyclist friend who is pedaling his way to Ushuaia. A few minutes later they roll into the parking lot, having descended the hill into our path. I can't believe Brian recognized him. It's wonderful to see Jim, even though it's only been a few weeks. We catch up over cold drinks and then go our separate ways, hoping to cross paths again somewhere further south.

We carry on along the Pan-Am highway, to a town near the equator where Brian stayed in a hacienda on his way north from Ushuaia to Alaska. The great estate and buildings of the Hacienda Guachala are incredible, but it's sad to see them empty. I think visitors should be admiring the nearly 500-year-old ranch, thought to be the oldest Hacienda in Ecuador which at one time had more than 120,000 acres. We wander through the cobblestoned courtyards, old stable and rooms of a chapel.

We stay the night and make the obligatory photo stop at the stone tower that marks the midpoint of our planet before carrying on to Quito. The road carries across an enormous valley before starting the steep climb to the great city itself. The main highway bores through a mile-long tunnel before depositing us into the bowl-shaped city center. But just on the other end is a confusing roundabout which skirts us right back into the long tunnel only to have to take a third run through it all in the course of fifteen minutes.

Brian and I head straight for a hostel where Stahlratte friends have been staying, in hopes of catching up with them, but we miss them by a few hours. We find a cheap backpacker hostel with a small parking area off the street and settle in for a week or two. I have an idea that I presented to Brian a few weeks ago, and need a few days to work on. I'd like to go to the Galapagos Islands.

The day after we arrive I start making the rounds of local travel agencies to find out about cheap last minute tours. Our Aussie friends came back from the Galapagos a few weeks before and gave me all the details. Although it's a stretch, I think we can make it work. It's a once-in-a-lifetime experience, and we are so close that I think we should at least try.

Within a couple of days, we book a trip to fly from Quito to the islands, spending two nights on land before boarding a backpacker-class boat for a 4-night island-hopping cruise. All told, it's just $1500 per person.

Even after only a few days, Ecuador is quickly becoming one of my favorite countries so far, for a number of reasons. Fuel is cheap, at around $1.25 per gallon. Food is cheap too. I walk to local produce markets from our hostel and carry home two plastic bags stuffed with fresh fruits and vegetables – potatoes, carrots, zucchini, apples, avocados, pineapple, mango, strawberries, onions, bananas, tomatoes, lemons, garlic, peppers, and more – all for about $4 USD.

Each day I prepare fresh meals for us in the hostel kitchen and make the most of the fantastic produce. Although that's been our habit since leaving the United States, it's taken me until Ecuador to notice how much better I feel. Even though I indulge in sugar and alcohol, the greatest part of my diet is natural food. In Latin America, food products aren't filled with chemicals or preservatives like they are in the United States and my body feels immensely better.

The hostel agrees to keep our bikes stored and safe for the week that we will be gone, and we pack only what we need for the islands. The flight from Quito takes a few hours and provides a stunning view of a volcano erupting in the distance, a black cloud rising from a peak that pierces the fluffy white blanket of clouds.

The Galapagos are more incredible than I would ever have guessed they would be, and I'm so glad we added this detour to our travels. We spend our mornings snorkeling in deep blue waters off several different islands, followed by a hike with a naturalist guide across a red sand beach or over a jagged black lava flow. At lunchtime, the boat moves to another anchor-point or island, and we repeat the routine somewhere else in the afternoon. In between each exploration, the crew fills us with spectacular food, and we share great conversations with our companions.

A dozen of us fill the few small cabins of the King of the Sea as we explore this incredible treasure of flora and fauna. Each person on the boat is thoroughly enjoyable and hilarious, including the crewmen. We swim with sharks and seals, spy chocolate-chip starfish on the sea floor, dive with penguins, and watch dolphins playing in the open water. We explore lava tubes and watch black iguanas and red crabs try to camouflage themselves on the rocky shore. And we climb the rock pinnacle on Bartolome for a view of the half dozen islands we've explored.

When we return to Quito, we are rested and excited for the next leg of our journey. We stop for the second time to see the owners of Ecuador Freedom Bike Rental, not far from our hostel. When we stopped the first time to say hello, they were warm and welcoming, giving us free t-shirts and bandanas, and tips on where to ride while in the country.

We want to get more details about a route they suggested just south of the city. They call it the Lago Quilotoa loop, and it sounds incredible. Court points out the route on a map and offers suggestions for places to stay, and hikes to take in the area if we can spare a day or two. He points out that we will pass Cotopaxi on the way in case that's another stop we want to make. Cotopaxi is the second highest point in Ecuador at nearly 20,000 feet, and is an active volcano.

We pack up and ride out of the city, dropping down from the city itself to reach the Pan-American Highway near Tambillo. Even after the descent, we are still at a high altitude. I watch for Cotopaxi on our way, but it's shrouded in clouds as we pass. Less than an hour ahead, Brian turns off the highway onto a dirt ramp, which, it turns out, is what an exit looks like in Ecuador. We ride toward Sigchos, and up a twisty road, through a lush valley.

Sigchos itself appears in our path just in time for a late lunch. We ride through town trying to find an open place. Nothing is marked as a restaurant, even on the town square, but I spot someone through a big window spooning soup into her mouth and pull over. I climb off my bike and lock my helmet to my bars, as usual, and walk over to see if we can have a table. Resting quietly on the sidewalk in front of the café is a large slouched canvas bag with the perky head of a rooster peeking out, the zipper open just enough for him to look around and breathe while securing him from escape.

We find one of the few empty tables and inquire about lunch. The waiter (or owner?) nods and disappears. Instead of returning with menus, we are each served a bowl of soup. I ask about choices for food and am told there aren't choices, only the plate of the day. A few minutes later the man returns with two plates filled with rice and sections of fried plantain. The rice is covered with a golden gravy and what looks like large chunks of swollen, soggy tortillas. But I'm skeptical. The rice, gravy and plantain are delicious, but as I feared, the tortilla pieces turn out to be big chunks of pig fat. Not having acquired a taste for boiled chicharrones, I leave most of mine on my plate. When the waiter isn't looking, I stuff a few pieces into a napkin to feed a stray dog somewhere down the road.

With less than 20 miles to Chugchilan, our stopping place for the night, we carry on along the gravel road out of Sigchos. Just a mile or two ahead, the sky opens up and drenches us. Rockier sections of the road get a little slick, but thankfully the sand on the road holds up better than the clay and rich dirt that we have ridden on in other places. We stop at a place suggested by Court, and quickly settle into a room in the giant chalet-like lodge. Somewhere below our room must be a woodstove. The stovepipe pierces our floor and travels up through our room, through the ceiling to the room above us, providing heat for the guests on all the floors.

After grabbing a beer from the office, I settle into a warm upholstered chair in the great room, making time to journal, A couple from Evergreen, Colorado spark up a conversation with me. They saw my license plate and ask if I'm really from South Dakota. That's a common question, and my confirmation usually raises a few eyebrows. We go sit for a while at a picnic table outside, enjoying the afternoon sun, and exchanging our top five travel places. They focus theirs on the southern half of South America so that I have new places to add to my "must see" list.

I sign into my email and find I have a message from my attorney back in South Dakota. My old bosses, the brothers, have made a settlement offer conditional upon my release of my claim on their father's estate. I'm surprised by how far removed I feel from all of that now. And I'm more surprised by how quickly it comes flooding back, dragging me down into a bad mood.

Brian and I catch a bus early the next morning to a small village a few miles up the road. Conejito is perched high on the rim of a dormant volcano, Quilotoa, which is now filled with a sapphire lake. Hiking trails lace around the crater rim and down the hillsides into steep ravines on the slopes of Quilotoa.

I'm shocked by how cold it is, and stop to buy an alpaca scarf and hat at a hotel coffee shop where we warm up. Across the road, a sign points the way to a windy overlook, where we snap a few pics before setting out on the trail toward Chugchilan.

The wide sandy path leading out of Conejito quickly narrows to a slender track lined on both sides with scrubby brush and golden grass. Quilotoa's shoulder falls away quickly to my left and rises high above me to the right. We wind our way around a quarter of the rim before the mountain falls into itself, sinking into the crater of the dormant volcano. Suddenly, our trail is left straddling a thin knife-edge between a deep ravine and the deep blue lake inside the crater which reflects the dark clouds looming overhead. Ecuador is stunning.

When Brian rode to Prudhoe Bay a few years ago, he stopped at a sign marking his crossing north of the Arctic Circle. At the same time, another rider stopped for a similar photo and introduced himself. Julio and Brian have kept in touch for the past few years, and Julio has invited us to stay with his family in Ambato.

We arrive sometime after lunch. The GPS, surprisingly, gets us to our target after only a handful of wrong turns. Brian rides onto the sidewalk to get out of the way of traffic, but is barred from pulling into Julio's parents driveway by a big iron gate. We barely have our back tires out of the street. Brian climbs off his bike, presses the buzzer and waits. After a few minutes, he tries again, but nothing happens.

A slender older man trots toward us from across the street with a big grin and a hurried Spanish greeting. He speaks so quickly that I have a hard time catching it all, and have to ask him to repeat himself. He knows we are looking for Julio. He lives across the street and is a friend of Julio's family and has been watching for us. We are to wait at his house until Julio returns from work.

We push our bikes out into the street between bursts of traffic and dart across, following this enthusiastic ambassador of ours. He turns into a gated driveway just three houses up, waves his arms to herd us inside and briskly closes and locks the gate behind us. Taking for granted that our new friend doesn't speak any English, I joke to Brian that it would be ironic if this turned out to be one of those kidney-harvesting places you hear about in urban legends, and us so eager to cooperate. He laughs.

We are ushered quickly into the house, leaving all our gear outside, and are told that the locked gate will keep our things safe from passersby. Our new friend is fidgety and energetic, a bundle of nervous excitement. I like him immediately. I introduce Brian and myself as we cross the threshold into his lovely home. Our guide says his name is Pancho, but everyone calls him Pancho Loco. Crazy Pancho, indeed.

He pulls us through the living room and into the kitchen, up to a counter where two of his sons are slurping soup as we sit down. A small, dark-haired woman smiles to us as she ladles two bowls of warm broth with vegetables and chicken and sets them down in front of Brian and me. Martita, is Pancho's wife. Without a moment's hesitation, we are invited to dine with their family.

The highway from Quito had been covered in sun, but I'm still a little chilled. The hot soup cures me immediately. Their sons finish their soup and are served entrees while we dine on our first course, which is also quickly followed by the main meal. Martita has made rice with vegetables and tuna and places a freshly fried egg on top of it all. The dinner is delicious and filling, and greatly appreciated. The boys, both grown men with families of their own, bow their farewells and head out to finish their workdays. I love the family luncheon that is a tradition in Latin America, and wish that it was tradition in my country too.

Just as we finish lunch, Julio arrives. He and Brian embrace. He's incredibly friendly and smiles broadly as they catch up for a moment. But he cannot stay long and leaves soon after.

Late in the afternoon he comes to usher us back across the road to his parents' home. We ride through the gate, down a grassy hill behind their large home and park in the garden, out of view from the street. We carry our gear through a side door into the basement, which serves as both Julio's dance studio business and guest quarters for traveling friends.

Brian and I take a few minutes to settle in and freshen up before walking around to the front of the house, to be formally received by Julio's parents. While we wait, Julio invites us to sit in the living room. I hear a woman working in the kitchen, and later find out it is Martha, Julio's mother, who was starting tea.

When she is ready, Julio introduces us to his mother and she escorts us into the dining room. Martha serves tea and sweets as we settle into a polite conversation and wait for Julio's father to arrive. She has the kindest eyes, that sparkle a little as she quietly adds a few words of English to the conversation. Many people in Latin America, and indeed all around the world, are shy about practicing their English with visitors. I appreciate her welcoming us with the English words she knows. Julio's father, Fernando, arrives and welcomes us too. He's a sharply-dressed, sophisticated man. At first, I feel like we should be more formal, but soon find us all relaxing into a comfortable conversation.

A planned "few night" stay turns into more than a week. In Latin fashion, the family welcomes us into their home for meals as well as a place to stay. We enjoy tea and most breakfasts and lunches with them. Julio suggests a couple of day rides to take from his home. We make time to ride around the perimeter of the volcano Chimborazo, which rises to over 18,000 feet. Vicuñas, relatives of camels, line the roadways as we climb in altitude near the entrance to Chimborazo National Park. At 12,000 feet, there are no trees here, only a windswept plateau.

During our stay, Julio and his parents spoil us with local cuisine and good conversation. His father introduces us to a local "medicine", aguardiente, a kind of licorice-flavored alcohol. They say that each village is known for its own individual concoction. It's not bad, but I don't think I need to try them all.

Martha makes homemade meals. One of her soups is made with fish and yucca, and is delicious. At most meals, we are served wafer-thin slices of onion and fresh lime wedges which are used to flavor dishes instead of salt and pepper. One meal is accented with a small bowl of freshly popped corn and a bowl of unpopped corn kernels which turn out to be something like Corn Nuts. We try humitas which are like cornbread steamed in corn husks, similar to tamales. They serve us choclo, an ear of corn with kernels each as big as almonds. No more than 8 to 10 rows fit around the cob. Everything is wonderfully delicious and I appreciate them sharing their food and culture with us.

Brian catches a stomach bug and spends a day in bed. Within a couple of days, it's my turn. Julio's mother makes soup to help with our recovery. Martha is the epitome of a loving, caring mother. Perhaps it's the loss of my own, which makes me more sensitive to and grateful for the kindness that other mothers have given me.

Brian and I are both tentative at best, at least stomach-wise, but we know we have to keep moving south. We set a date to leave, and decide to tackle two remaining "to do" items for our visit to Ambato in one outing. We invite Julio and his parents to a traditional cuy, roasted guinea pig, dinner which we wanted to try, and which we think might be a small way to show our gratitude to Julio and his parents for their generous hospitality. Unfortunately, my stomach only has one day to recover from my illness before the day of the dinner arrives.

We walk by several large open rotisserie grills on our way into the restaurant as cuys and rabbits, impaled on metal rods, sizzle over the open fire. Good as it probably looks and smells to locals, it makes my stomach churn a little.

Julio's father, who we have lovingly nicknamed El Presidente, sits at the head of the table and orders for us. We will share a single guinea pig, which will be cut into five pieces and served with potatoes and peanut sauce. Martha asks if she can have the head, since it has what she believes to be the best meat of the animal, the delicate facial muscles.

Our dinner arrives on a silver tray and I see immediately that the four chops of the machete haven't done anything to disguise the fact that this is guinea pig. For some reason, seeing the face and tiny paws of something I am about to eat really puts me off. We each take our section. The skin of the guinea pig has burned into a thick crunchy rind, sort of like the texture of peanut brittle, which cracks into shards when I bite it. I break a piece off and try it. It tastes like pork rinds. I try some of the meat, which is dark and lean sort of like dark meat of a chicken, but darker, leaner and slightly more gamey. I bathe it in peanut sauce, which I normally like, but which doesn't sit well with me today. It's not bad, but I'm just not feeling well yet. To be polite, I power through a few more bites and then give up. Everyone else really enjoys it.

We enjoy one more breakfast with the family before riding to Baños, which isn't far down the road. Fernando gives us each a hug, a kiss on each cheek, and a sweet smile, before leaving for the day. Martha goes into a bedroom and comes back with something in her hand that she slips into mine. She tells me in Spanish that she wants us to be careful and that they prayed for us in church this morning. I look at what she has placed gently in mind, and find a small blue glass-bead rosary. She says either to keep it with me always or that she will pray for us always, my Spanish skills aren't good enough to tell the difference. I'm on the verge of tears and it's all I can do to say thank you. They have been so kind to us and have made us feel like family. I'm grateful and am going to miss them immensely.

The ride to our next stop takes only a couple of hours. This next small town is nestled in a narrow valley below an active volcano, Tungurahua, which we watched steadily spewing ash and steam into the atmosphere from Ambato. Baños is famous for its thermal baths which are fed by springs that bubble up from the lava flow not far below ground. This town is popular with tourists, which means lots of t-shirt shops, taffy stands and cafes.

After spending a morning at the public baths, and stewing in the stinking, clouded, sulfur-infused water, we make our way up the hill to the famous tree swing perched on the side of the volcano. We catch a ride in an old pickup truck and get dropped off on the side of a dirt road at the beginning of a well-worn trail that leads to the Casa de Arbol.

A short hike in, we come out at a clearing with an open-air hut built on the edge of a precipice. A large tree growing right at the edge of the ridge has been burdened with both a small tree house and a large swing that dangles from its outermost branch. Said branch happens to be dead, which does nothing to excite me about taking it for a spin. We sit and watch while two or three people wait for a turn to climb into the swing and fly out over the ledge. It's all an effort to get the gut-wrenching adrenaline rush that the drop below the swing provides as you reach the outer edge of the arch. I hesitate for a moment, but then get in line and wait my turn. A sheet of plywood laid beneath the swing on the hillside provides a brake of sorts and is where you prepare yourself for the ride. A second later, I'm off.

Within a fraction of a second I go from having my feet on the ground, to swinging out over a lush green gorge below, one of the eroded runoffs from the high mountain above. My stomach lurches and goes back to the hillside to wait for me. I swing back and forth for a couple of minutes, reminding myself how much I loved this as a child. But after a moment of relived youth, I reach back at the properly timed moment and plant my feet on the ground and dismount. Brian takes a turn while I snap some photos. I walk to the edge of the hill to get the scariest camera angle to accentuate the thrill. Before we know it, we are done.

A trail leads down to the village by traversing the ridgeline and then dropping into the valley. It's not that late in the afternoon, but the sun is quickly making its way west and won't be high enough to penetrate the valley for much longer. The trail leads us past farms and a small group of plastic greenhouses. Every now and then a hand-painted wooden sign keeps us on the path. The trail is worn so deeply in some places that it becomes a trench, muddy in its shadiest corners. Fences line one or both sides of our narrow path keeping us out of pastures. Some of the fenceposts have taken root and sprouted leaves and branches.

Flowers line both sides of our path, bursting from nearly every plant. As I stop to take my umpteenth photo of a wild orchid, Brian snaps "What are you, Lewis and Clark or something?" showing his frustration at how slow I am today. His attitude encourages me to slow down even more.

I look back and see plumes of gray ash and smoke billowing from Tungurahua, which gives me an eerie feeling. But I'm told you should be more nervous about the volcanoes that aren't releasing pressure regularly like this one.

Lush grass gives way to groupings of cactus and 3-foot deep piles of vines lining the edges of the trail, which has begun to descend the mountain in switchbacks. My knees complain about the steep angle of descent. We reach an overlook and take a photo of the village below. I'm amazed how it sits virtually straight below us, and how far we have yet to descend with little forward movement left to make before we get to the edge of town. It takes more than two hours to climb down, and by the time we reach the western edge of Baños, it's nearly dark. One last look at Tungurahua reveals a deep red glow lurking behind the tower of steam and ash.

The Ruta de las Cascadas (the waterfall route) leads east of Baños along a river, and provides incredible views of waterfalls along the way. Strange that we are on the western edge of this continent but have already crossed east of the continental divide. From here, all waters lead to the Atlantic side of South America. Although we had already descended quite a bit from the higher altitudes of Ambato, we continue to drop as we make our way east to the headwaters of the Amazon River.

We arrive in Puyo around lunchtime and carry on to Macas for the night. Storm clouds on the horizon encourage me to walk across the road from our hotel and buy some yellow rubber pants to wear over my riding pants which started leaking recently.

Rain pours as we ride out of town the next morning and head to Bella Union before turning onto a freshly constructed Highway 40. I'm happy to have my bright construction worker pants to keep me dry. Between Macas and Mendez a couple passes me in a small silver SUV as the passenger rolls down her window, despite the rain. She waves, and gives me a big thumbs-up making my morning.

The road rises up from Bella Union, making its way along a river into the mountains. We cross the continental divide again today, which means twisty mountain roads and steep grades. I notice we've ridden two hundred miles since our last gas stop, which makes me worry, especially since we're in the mountains. I reach down and turn my petcock valve onto reserve so I don't have to worry about, running out at an inopportune time.

Each village has lots of moppy, poodle-like dogs, much different than most South American dogs. These are dirty and their hair has grown into long dreadlocks. Today's batch of dogs seems more aggressive than normal, which usually occurs in pockets along the highway. We can go days without seeing aggressive dogs, and then run into a two-hundred-mile stretch of nasty biters before running out of them again. Most of the dogs just run at you, and are easy enough to avoid if you watch their angle of attack and trajectory. Occasionally, I pull in my clutch which changes the engine noise and makes them think I'm stopping, and sometimes turns them back. Many dogs could care less and come at me anyway.

The road climbs higher and higher as we round dozens of bends. There are a lot of trucks on the road, including dump trucks which take corners wide, so I'm on high alert. I see an enormous dam across the valley which is where all the trucks seem to be headed.

Dozens of chickens and a few geese cross the road today. Just before Sevilla de Oro, I see a dead dog, and it occurs to me that I haven't seen one in ages. It's lying in the road just across from a group of school kids who wait for their bus. They don't seem to even notice as blood drains from its nose, running across the road.

The rain morphs into a light fog and the road dries a little. It's warm riding even on this drizzly day. As we ride through more villages, we hit the end of the school day. Small groups of uniformed children walk home along the highway.

Highway 40 leads us south to the inside corner of a mountain and bends sharply north. After an hour of riding we arrive at El Pan and find we have doubled-back to the outer edge of this narrow valley and are just across the deep chasm from where we stopped for lunch. We carry on to Paute, where Brian finds fuel that meets his approval, and fill up. I take my bike off reserve and have a stretch while he checks the GPS. This highway is in great condition, but it's still slow going.

Another hour delivers us to Cuenca. We find a horrible, cheap hostel on a side street and decide to take a room just to get settled for the night. It's filthy and old with a rickety wooden staircase that sways and buckles when we climb it, like one in a carnival spookhouse. I spend the evening searching for someplace else.

Julio put us in touch with a friend of his in Cuenca, Roberto, but neither Brian nor I want to stay in Cuenca long. We decide it would be rude to put a stranger to the trouble of hosting us for a night or two. And Brian is concerned that because he speaks little Spanish it will be difficult for him to converse with Roberto and his family. Instead we find another hostel and move the next day, after stashing the bikes at a garage.

In the meantime, Roberto has been on the lookout for us and sends me a message on Facebook asking when we plan to arrive in Cuenca. Brian and I confer and decide we will invite Roberto and his wife for dinner because we would love to meet them, but we will stay at a hostel. I send him a message to that effect. His reply directs us to pack our things because we WILL be coming to stay with him. Apparently, Roberto won't take "no" for an answer. As I give Brian the news, we laugh.

Roberto arrives the next the morning, and loads our bags into the back of his truck. He instructs us to follow him to his house and we ride quickly to keep up. Our meandering through Cuenca ends at a three-story stone building on the corner of two small streets. The ground floor holds a business that sells lumber, while the second floor holds a private residence and the third has a small apartment. All of this belongs to Roberto and his family. We park our bikes inside a small garage under the main residence and climb the stairs to the family's home where we are immediately seated for lunch. There's nothing quite like being scooped up by an Ecuadorian family, as we have now experienced three times.

Roberto quickly settles us into the third-story apartment and tells us to make ourselves at home. We are given a standing invitation to have all meals with his family. He and his lovely wife, Janeth, who is a firefighter, have three children. Their son Carlos and his wife have recently made Roberto and Janeth very proud new grandparents. Their daughter, Daniela, is a newlywed, and helps in the family business. Their youngest, Julian, practices his English with us and is funny and friendly. Roberto and all three of his kids are avid riders, and have raced motocross for years.

Daniela escorts Brian around Cuenca in search of parts and supplies for our next leg of the journey. Both bikes are due for full services, and Brian hopes to make use of the garage. He sets to work replacing my brake pads, tires and spark plug, as well as changing the oil and cleaning the air filter. There's a Kawasaki dealer in Cuenca, which thankfully has two oil filters on hand, one for now and one to carry with me.

I've been debating for some time about what tires to put on my bike. I've got a lot of gravel ahead of me, and I want something that will handle well, but that oftentimes comes with reduced life expectancy for the tires. My last pair of tires were Shinkos, which last for ages, but they don't offer the stability on gravel that I want for the rugged roads ahead. Online research leads me to a model of Pirelli tires. Since they are made in Brazil, I'm hopeful that if they do wear out before I get to Ushuaia, that at least I have a chance of finding more somewhere else on the continent.

I leave Brian at our new friends' home and fly to Quito for a couple of days to meet my friend, Jen. She brings me a few supplies, including a new camera and mounts. On our first morning, she searches online for the best cup of coffee in the city and we set out to find it. Not being a coffee drinker myself, I hadn't thought of what an exotic experience it could be.

We explore the historic city center and climb to the top of the Basilica of the National Vow. The view from above is spectacular. She and I chatter until the wee hours of the morning and finally force ourselves to go to sleep. Before I know it, we grab a taxi for the airport to go our separate ways.

On the trip back to Cuenca, it occurs to me that I'm missing yet another year of my sister's and step-mother's early September birthdays. I've made an informal tradition of taking them and my niece (whose birthday is in November) for birthday pedicures. I'm a little homesick at the thought of not being there to celebrate them, and miss them very much.

When I return to Cuenca, I find that Brian and Daniela have hit it off, and all his fears of not being able to converse with Roberto's family while I was in Quito are a distant memory. He's been practicing his Spanish because Roberto insists that Brian try to speak it in his house. We stay a few more nights and then plan to ride south to Peru, taking a dirt road to the border. But as the day of our departure arrives, Brian is under the weather again. This is getting to be a routine for us. He comes down with a stomach bug every three weeks, not that I'm doing much better.

In Ambato, Julio asked if we had tried anti-parasite medicines. Julio suspects that we may be carrying some bugs and need to do a cleanse. Something I read online suggests that while it's certainly possible, we can't know for sure without going to a doctor. To be safe, I pick up some de-worming pills at the farmacia (pharmacy) down the street from Roberto's to keep on hand. Julio suggested a certain medication, but warned that we can have absolutely no alcohol when taking the medicine, as it can be fatal. The pharmacist is adamant about this as well, and seems worried that I'm not clear enough on the warning because I'm an English-speaker. I assure her that I understand.

More online research shows there are some pretty nasty possible side effects from this medicine, so we opt to carry it along in case we need it later, but not take it now. Strange to me that in much of the world, even in developed countries, people cleanse their bodies of parasites/worms regularly. I remember visiting a friend in New Zealand once and running to the pharmacy to pick up her and her husband's de-worming pills.

Speaking a bit too frankly even to an old friend, I commented, "I think it's gross that you de-worm."

To which she replied, "I think it's disgusting that you don't." On further thought, I think she was right.

Brian recovers well enough for us to continue but we find now that it's hard to leave. We've become very attached to this beautiful family. We linger a few more days. Roberto and Janeth take us to Cajas National Park, a spectacular, mountainous region west of the city. It's rugged and rocky landscape, dotted with small lakes, is covered in clouds at its highest elevations.

In the evening, they take us to a thermal bath, changing my opinion of the thermal pools of South America entirely from the dirty public pool scene of Baños. This spa is elegant and relaxing.

A stone walkway leads past a courtyard and formal gardens to a locker room with teak benches. Ecuadorian music whispers from speakers hidden in the pristine landscaping while soft lights accent tall palm trees and flowering bougainvillea around the perimeter of the pools. There's a formal dining room with waiters on standby to mix cocktails. Roberto suggests alternating between the hot pool and the cold pool as a means of improving health and circulation, so we each give it a try. Brian's painful grimace as he enters the cold water doesn't do anything to encourage me when it's my turn, but I pluck up some courage anyway. It's generous of Roberto and Janeth to treat us to this experience.

Roberto asks about our travels. Brian told him about my accident and Roberto asks how I'm doing. I say that physically I'm well, but that I'm afraid of the road ahead. Ruta 40 in Argentina, the road we must take to get to Ushuaia, is famously bad. Even with hundreds of miles yet to go, I'm already dreading it.

The night before we plan to depart, we share a quiet dinner with Roberto and Janeth. Roberto says he has something he wants to say to us, and asks if I will translate for Brian. He starts by saying that he has always loved motorcycles and has taught his children to love motorcycles too. His lifelong dream has been to travel by motorcycle, as we are doing now, but he married young and started a family right away, and they is everything to him. He has, of course, no regrets, but still holds a small version of that dream alive. Roberto explains that this led him to share his home with motorcyclists who travel through Ecuador, which is why he invited us to stay.

Roberto goes on, slowly now, and Janeth and he hold hands while he speaks. His voice falters slightly, and I can see he is momentarily overwhelmed by emotion, which causes me to get a lump in my throat. He says that they've enjoyed having us, and that we are now dear friends of theirs. Then he pauses, changing the word, and says we are family.

I swallow hard and blink back tears, trying to gather myself and translate his words for Brian. But Brian's people skills and Spanish are good enough to have clearly understood the meaning of Roberto saying "familia". We explain how grateful we are for all they have done for us, and for their friendship. They have opened their hearts, their family, and their home to us, and it has meant the world to me. We ride out of Cuenca with full hearts.

The Pan-American Highway carries us south to Loja before we leave it near Vilcabamba. We've heard people talk about this village, famous for its ex-pat community and tourist-friendly cafes and hotels.

Since we have some dirt riding ahead of us, I vote for us to stay in a nice room at a hotel on the south edge of town. We only plan to stay one night. But then we get a message from our Swiss friend, Markus, that says he and three others have recently ridden the route we intend to take to the Peruvian border. He says the road is really hard work. It sounds like it's under construction for much of the 80 miles between Yangana, where the pavement ends, and La Balsa, where it begins again. It's only a dirt road, and with no gravel, rain turns the surface into a slippery mess. Brian suggests we wait a couple of days to let it dry out.

I've been following several blogs en route to Ushuaia, one of which is Song of the Road, named for a line from a Walt Whitman poem. Erica, of the couple who authors it, and I have been messaging on Facebook, finding we are taking a nearly identical route south. The extra day or two in Vilcabamba provides us a chance to meet Erica and her husband, Sam. They are from California and are traveling south in a truck with a camper mounted on the truck's flatbed. It's positively Hyatt-like compared to how we are traveling. The thought of having a dorm-sized fridge and a toilet seem overwhelmingly dreamy to me.

We enjoy a nice dinner together in our hotel's open-air restaurant, overlooking the tropical valley below while local dogs wander in and lay down on the cool tile floor by our feet. I like Sam and Erica immediately, and the feeling must at least be partially mutual, because we make plans to cross paths again and maybe even travel together a little in Peru.

With two or three dry days behind us and a forecast for rain coming, we push on to get through the dirt road. As I load my bike in the morning, I notice something unusual on the front faring. There's a grouping of the tiniest pale yellow-green specks laid out in the shape of a spiral. I'm instantly reminded of the Maori symbol, the Koru, which is meant to resemble an unfurling silver fern frond. It symbolizes growth, strength and new beginnings. I decide it's a good omen for the dirt road ahead of me, and my nerves settle a bit.

I lean down to get a closer look. Each of these crumb-sized dots is suspended about a quarter-inch above the surface of the plastic by a silk thread. I count twenty-one of them. "Perfect," I think sarcastically to myself. Some poisonous tropical spider has probably laid its eggs on my bike. But I decide to leave them alone and let the wind take them as it will.

The two-lane road is paved for a few dozen miles south of Vilcabamba, and enters distinctly jungle-ish country. I notice a yellow highway sign, not far down the road, warning of bears and wonder to myself if there is such a thing as a jungle bear.

Our fairly direct southbound road begins to climb and curve, leading us out to a point above the valley below. Rolling high hills are cleft in two by a deeply cut river valley in the bottom. Our road will turn up ahead and drop down to the valley floor to follow the river. A jagged red scar slashed into the lush green hillside, as far as I can see, shows where construction equipment has torn open the mountainside for the new road.

Pavement gives way to gravel, and eventually to dirt. Smooth packed dirt deteriorates into roads with deep dried ruts, remnants of the previous week's rain. We cross a few streams and keep moving, now starting to climb up the mountainside again.

Around one corner, we stumble upon the work crew. Spread out over a two-mile section of the road, they force us to weave our bikes between the enormous heavy equipment, while trying to be mindful of the steep drop into the valley below. Guardrails are non-existent in this part of the world, and no one looks out for each other. We hit a few slippery spots, where the wet clay creates a hazard, and I wonder how bad it was for our friends the week before. Perched on a ledge on the side of the mountain, I can imagine how easily a rider could slide right off.

We reach a long dry section of road, and see a few houses perched on the cliff. Corrugated tin roofs and thin plywood siding provides all the shelter you need this close to the equator. I watch small children in only t-shirts, no pants, playing in the vegetation at the side of the road. As I pass one hut, a lean dog trots up beside my bike, and without much effort, because of our slow pace, nips my left leg. I give my horn a little toot as he comes back for a second nip. I giggle and keep riding forward, grateful as always for my heavy boots, even on hot days like today.

The riding gets trickier from Zumba, the road having dissolved into a single lane with increasing frequency and sharpness of curves. After miles of bumping through the hot dry wild land we reach a security gate stretched across the road seemingly in the middle of nowhere. We present our passports and the guard raises the iron barrier for us to pass.

After two hours of riding, we start to descend a long, rocky hill to a river below. I look ahead and see Sam and Erica's camper parked below us at the bridge that will carry us into Peru.

I'm roasting, and have been the entire run from Zumba. A quick peek in my mirror reveals my beet red face is covered with big white splotches. I feel dehydrated, on the verge of heat exhaustion. My arms and legs are covered in giant goosebumps. I know better, but sometimes forget to hydrate while concentrating on the road. I need to work harder at it.

As we ride up to the small adobe buildings, two men come out to greet us. The older of the two men requests my bike import permit and passport. I climb off the bike, remove my helmet and hang it on my mirror, before walking into the small, open air office. There is only a single desk and a tall filing cabinet inside.

After reviewing my documents, the Customs Officer points out that my vehicle import permit doesn't have a required stamp, one I should have received when I entered the country. Brian and I were stopped by an officer on the way to Loja a few days ago, and he pointed this out to me too. But I play dumb, and smile. He reviews Brian's paperwork and finds it all in order. He says again that I need the stamp, but I just smile and nod. He thinks my Spanish isn't that good, and finally takes pity on me. He stamps my papers out of Ecuador and tells me that I need to walk over the bridge to the Peru side to have copies made to complete the process. This border post isn't integrated with the Ecuador National Customs Service electronically, so if I want to prove that my bike exited the country, I will need a copy of this exit form.

A small palm-leaf roofed pile of concrete blocks up ahead serves as both the last store and bank in Ecuador. I exchange some dollars (the currency of Ecuador) for Peruvian Soles, so that I can purchase my photocopies. I buy four cold bottles of water too, so I can get my overheating under control. There's a crowd of kids and adults hanging out around the shop, and my heavy black riding gear and taller-than-average height are drawing attention. I cross over the bridge while Brian stays with the bikes. It's not very far, but in this sweltering heat, I'm starting to melt.

Within a few minutes, I'm back at the Aduana. As I approach the office, I can see the younger officer sitting on my bike, and wearing my helmet. My instant reaction is to be unhappy. It's one thing to sit on my bike, but it's another thing entirely to put on my helmet. That's just gross, for him and for me.

Brian catches me and whispers that this turned out to be the son of the officer who was helping us, and he thinks the boy has Down Syndrome. I hadn't ever looked at him, but now that I do, it's obvious, and my grumpiness dissolves instantly. The boy is enjoying himself and asking for someone to take his picture, so we happily oblige him. His father smiles at us. The son pretends to rev the bike, even though it's not running, and stands on the pegs. It's sweet to see him enjoying himself, and ends my visit to Ecuador on a nice note.

We walk to the next office where a man stands on a chair and paints the world "Policia" above the door. Inside, an officer sits at a desk in front of a fan. He takes only a moment to process us out.

Ecuador has been one of my favorite countries of the trip. As we mount our bikes to ride over the bridge into Peru, I count 21 eggs still clinging to my bike.

18 PERU

Little by little one goes far.

-Peruvian proverb

I'm happy to see Peru. I've been to this country before, so it's not another notch on my travel belt that makes me so giddy to be here. It's the pavement.

We still have a couple of hours before we get to the first town that we hope has lodging. We'll likely be riding in the dark, but that's fine when the road is paved. The paperwork doesn't take long, once we actually get it started. The Peruvian Aduana is a one-man show, and this man happens to be nearly blind, so he lets me type my own data into the computer to speed up the process. Federal police require we register our entry into Peru at the office next door, and then we can be on our way. All the while, old leather-skinned men with bare feet sit in the shade of a tienda across the road and watch what must be a busy day at the border - two motorcycles and a camper lining up to get into the country.

As the sun sets over the western mountains, we finally ride free of

La Balsa, bound for San Ignacio, and hopefully, for a hotel. The road ahead is twisty. A couple of hours later we pull into San Ignacio and meander through its handful of streets before pulling over at the only hotel we see. My GPS app shows two others, but we've driven around the whole town and they simply aren't here.

A pleasant young man greets me as I catch my breath after the steep flight of stairs from the street. He has a room but no parking for our bikes, and we aren't comfortable leaving them on the street, especially in a new country and so close to the border. He asks me to follow him outside, around the side of the cinder block building and through an empty lot to the street behind the hotel. He knocks on the door of a corrugated tin shed. It slides open.

After a short conversation, in yet another version of expedited Spanish that I struggle to understand, I'm offered parking in this building for a nominal fee. While I think the young desk clerk seems nice, I'm too tired to think anything other than suspicious and defensive thoughts about anyone in an unfamiliar place. It must be mutual, because the woman who opened the door to the shed starts to backtrack and now says there isn't room for us after all. I take a deep breath and speak as politely as possible in Spanish, explaining that we want our bikes to be safely parked off the street. She ponders for a moment before saying that she will take us in.

I walk back to fill Brian in and let him make the call, not that we have any other options. We ride around to the garage so he can take a better look, and now a few locals have appeared in the garage. Someone introduces himself as the owner of a local radio station. The group seems like decent, middle-aged people. By now, as tired as I'm getting, if someone steals my bike, I won't lose any sleep over it until tomorrow. We decide to stay.

There weren't any services at the border, and this town is practically closed for the night, so we don't have Peruvian money with which to pay for tonight's room, but that doesn't occur to me until after we lug our baggage across the empty lot and up the long staircase to the hotel, and I go to pay. Thankfully, the young man's boss approves my paying with U.S. dollars, at a slightly degraded exchange rate. Even more thankfully, a shop down the street accepts dollars for bottled water and grilled carne and rice for our dinner.

In the morning, we plan to ride to Jaen in hopes of getting local currency and fuel, in that order. The desk clerk warns me that while San Ignacio and most of the other northeastern towns of Peru are safe, Jaen is not and we should be careful. His comments mirror things I've read online.

As we top the hill on the far side of town and wind into the jungle a mile or two, traffic comes to a stop. People have shut off their junky cars and small rusted pickup trucks, and are milling about in conversation on the road. I park and walk over to a small group of men to ask if we can ride through. Sometimes motorcycles are allowed to do that, and if we don't have to wait, we'd prefer not to.

One man speaks up and says that the road is closed for construction for the next few miles and that we have to wait for a pilot car. He points at a couple of motorbikes parked further ahead in line as proof that even bikes aren't allowed through. I thank him and walk back to tell Brian, taking off my helmet so I can breathe better in the heat.

A while later the men in the group call out to me and ask where we are from, and where we are headed. These are some of the questions we hear most often. I reply that I'm from America and Brian is from England. Then comes the next most common question, "Did you ride that bike all the way here?"

Brian is being anti-social and is draped like a rag doll over the gear bag on his bike. The chattiest of the group comments about it and says it looks like "muchacho"(boy) needs "descansar" (to rest). We laugh.

Conversation ensues. The guys are funny and entertaining. Without any hesitation or concern about impoliteness, they ask how much my bike is worth. I hate to lie too much and have them be suspicious, but I also don't want to declare a value that makes Betty a target, so I tell them she's worth $3000 USD, about half what I paid for her. They can't believe it and tell me that my KLR, even with thousands of miles, is worth three or four times that here. I'm shocked. For a second, I think maybe I should sell her at the end of the trip, but dismiss the idea as quickly as I think of it.

Our roadside neighbors peruse and compliment Brian's bike and then come to see mine. The most outgoing of the quartet notices the 21 eggs attached to my faring and smiles. He points them out, and tells me that they're butterfly eggs and are a sign of good luck. I smile. Knowing they are butterfly eggs, makes me want to transplant them to safer home.

A few days ago, I was thinking of the jade butterfly necklace my mother used to wear. I hope it's still safe in my storage unit. It's only now that I realize how much she loved butterflies. After my blog post about my visit to the butterfly sanctuary in Mexico posted, a friend sent me a link to a website about butterfly lore, and one particular post about butterflies being believed, in some cultures, to be the spirits of our lost loved ones coming to visit us. Aristotle gave the butterfly the name "psyche" which is the Greek word for soul.

Mayela and I have both lost our mothers, a commonality that bonds us closely, even though I have never met her. She tells me she has been seeing butterflies too and thinking of me when she does. She shares with me a personal story about her mother and a memory involving an American coin, a dime. Later in the evening after our online chat, I organize my tank bag and randomly find a U.S. dime in a corner of it. I sign back online to tell her.

Our pilot car arrives and the long line of cars starts to loosen and move forward, until finally it's our turn. We ride over the hill and through several miles of disrupted earth, dodging heavy equipment and oncoming cars. Finally, we are free of it, and can ride at a normal pace. My mind wanders until I remind myself to return to my helmet and pay attention.

Jaen turns out to be a busy place with all the things we need to be better prepared for our travels in Peru, like banks and insurance offices. I purchased a multi-country insurance policy which covered all but a couple of countries in South America, before we got here. But Brian chose to buy his in each country, which means searching for offices, translating documents and purchasing individual policies. His way takes more time, but is less expensive.

As I wait for him outside an office, I notice a young boy and girl playing behind the jail-like barred front of a small tienda across the street. They wave at me through the bars and climb up them like a ladder. The little curly-headed girl sings a song and dances for me while I clap for her. I walk over to buy snacks for our lunch, and a couple of bottles of water, now that I am flush with Peruvian soles.

Normally, store owners will hand you merchandise through the bars, rather than opening them, as a way of maintaining their safety. But their mother has been watching me, and opens the bars to invite me in to browse. I pick out a few things and pay for them, and find I have two American quarters in my change purse, which I offer to her son and daughter. They smile broadly. As any good mother would, she encourages them to mind their manners which results in a stereo-version of "gracias" as I wave goodbye and leave. I tuck my goodies into my bags and glance up briefly to see the youngsters blowing me kisses through the iron bars and waving to me.

We gas up in town, making use of our fresh money, and check the map. As Brian gives the bikes a once over, a small truck pulls up and a cute little boy in the back smiles at me, obviously enamored with the fact that I'm on a bike, or that I'm blonde. I smile back, finish packing up and put on my helmet to go. The boy calls out "Amiga!" to me and I turn to see him blowing me a kiss and winking, a little Latin lover in the making.

South of Jaen we turn east toward Bagua Grande and the land opens into broad valleys with lush fields of rice in various stages of growth, bananas and sugarcane crops creating a patchwork quilt of every shade of green imaginable. Pairs of mules drag heavy plows through the mud and graze in ditches between the fields. Rows of hills on each side of the valley rise in long successions of gray humps resembling a line of giant elephants walking in a trunk-to-tail chain along the horizon.

Dogs here are mange-ravaged and skinny, much different than just a half-day ride back, in Ecuador. It's amazing what a difference a border can make.

The further east we ride, the narrower the valley becomes, and the more pronounced and rugged are the canyon walls and mountains. Finally, we find ourselves in a narrow winding canyon, on a road that at times rides under the overhanging wall above. It's an eerie sight as my path leads me under an awning of stone that is capped by a mountain. But the road is gorgeous.

Helmet thoughts of the day:

- I spend much of the day singing my favorite songs in my helmet, which is a common past time. Sometimes I do so with a British accent, a Russian accent, or a French accent. Today I try on my best Kermit the Frog and Miss Piggy voices and laugh myself to bits. I can't imagine how I sound to the farmers we pass along the roadside.
- Ninety-nine bottles of beer on the wall, ninety-nine bottles of beer. You take one down, you pass it around. Ninety-eight bottles of beer on the wall. Ninety-eight bottles of beer on the wall, ninety-eight bottles of beer. You take one down, you pass it around. Ninety-seven bottles of beer on the wall…and so on. For the first time in my life, I actually sing the whole song down to "no bottles of beer on the wall". I must be bored. But really I'm not at all.
- Why on Earth would Brian have made the trip from Argentina to Alaska in 55 days? He stayed in Cusco on the last trip and was a half-day ride from Machu Picchu but didn't have time to go. I think it's a shame really, but am happy for him that he gets to come back and actually see something on this one.
- How lucky am I to be able to be here in this moment, on this incredible once-in-a-lifetime adventure? I'm blessed, and so very grateful.

At Pedro Ruiz, we turn toward Chachapoyas, passing the Gocta

Falls along the way. Little do we know at the time, but near there a rider who was somewhat famous with motorcyclists, the owner of Norton Rat's bar in Cusco, started building a hostel in the past couple of years. Sadly, Jeff died not long ago in a motorcycle accident. We'd hoped to stop at his bar and say hello, but instead will stop and have a drink in his honor.

Chachapoyas is perched on the ridge above the river valley, and we have to climb switchbacks to reach it. The low evening sun creates sharply contrasting shadows of my bike and I on the road. I watch myself in silhouette as I ride up the hill into town. It's a fairly touristy place, more than I'd expected, and there are plenty of hotels. Several offer off-street parking, and we easily find a room.

The altitude makes a big difference after the sun sets, and the warm day gives way to a chilly night. My scarf and hat come out from the bottom of my clothes bag for a night out on the town.

Brian and I walk to the main square, and walk around the perimeter to peruse our dinner choices. This town's Plaza des Armas (every town has one) is especially lovely with its large white colonial buildings standing shoulder to shoulder around the cobblestoned hollow square that encircles a lovely green garden and bronze fountain in its center.

We find a place that sounds good to us both, and each order lomo steak, fries and salad for 15 soles or $5 U.S. dollars. It's expensive, but worth it. While we wait for our food, I watch a small family (grandmother, mother and two small children) eating.

After we get our meals, a tiny hunchbacked man comes in through the front door. He's dirty, obviously poor, and has come to beg. Wondering to myself if the restaurant will ask him to leave, I reach into my pocket to see if I have a small bill to give him. The tiny man walks quietly over to us and shows me his empty hand and then rubs his fingers together asking for anything we can spare. I slip a 10 Soles note into his hand and smile warmly at him. He nods silently and moves along.

He walks over to the family who was getting up to go, leaving four plates, each with leftover food on them. The younger woman, mother of the young children, hugs him warmly in a gentle and close embrace and then guides him into her chair. Even though she's nearly whispering, I hear her tell him to eat all he likes and that no one will bother him. She walks over to the host and asks him to let the beggar finish their meals. The host nods politely.

It's sweet how gentle she is with this poor man, almost as I would imagine she would treat her own father. Even though she was obviously rushing off, she took a moment to offer him kindness and dignity.

The family bundles up and goes, leaving him to sit quietly. As soon as they are gone, he reaches out to each plate and begins to fill up on everything they left behind. After a while he gets up and pushes in his chair very politely. His deformed spine affects his walking and he struggles to get up, yet he has the manners to push his chair under the table before he goes.

Chachapoyas becomes our home for a couple of days while we go see the ruins of the fortress city of Kuelap. The road leading there is stunning in itself, and Kuelap is incredible. Archaeologists think it was a city long before Machu Picchu, all the more impressive that there is so much left to see. We walk out to a watch tower of sorts at the furthest point of the mountain ridge which resembles the bow of a ship. The vantage offered in nearly every direction must have made it easier to defend.

A guide shows us the ruins of a round stone house and the small arrangement of stones on the floor of what they believe was the kitchen or cooking area. These stones formed a cage for cuy, for the residents' consumption. I've seen small cages like these in Peruvian restaurants this week.

Back in town, Brian and I walk to the main plaza to get a snack. There's a political rally going on in the square with a stage and banners. Much like back home, it's common for political parties to have a symbol for their party. I've noticed signs with a hat, or a plow, or animals. As we walk through the square, I overhear two men attempting to converse in strongly-accented English. One sounds like a guide attempting to explain the happenings to another. He explains that his favorite candidate is the man whose face is shown with his party's symbol – a rooster. He says he intends to vote for the "man with the big cock".

When I get online, I see an email from my attorney. He wants to know what I've decided on the settlement offer. I'd nearly forgotten. It would give me a small sense of vindication if they have to eat their words, but I can't seem to focus on it at the moment. I promise myself to think about it later. For now, it's not important.

Our English friend, Pete, sent an email detailing his route south from Chachapoyas through the Andes. The pictures he posted are incredible and I'm hoping we can weave a route through Peru that includes the highlights he suggested.

Brian doesn't communicate with me much tonight and I finally ask him what's wrong. He says he isn't happy about my pace, not just that I ride too slowly, but that I want to stop too much. I want to stay a night in Lleymebamba which is only 50-60 miles south of here, and that, apparently, isn't far enough. He's grumpy. I'd wanted to go back to Gocta Falls, but don't mention that idea again after his comment.

We ride south the next day along the banks of the Utcubamba River on our way south to Lleymebamba. We will see what the day brings before deciding if we'll stay or not.

Along the way, I see cables draped across the river with iron gondolas dangling from them. These are used by locals to cross over to their homes. The river is high and moving fast. I'm intimidated as it is with no guardrail, and can't imagine crossing the river routinely to go home via a rickety rusted hand-drawn gondola.

The road varies from single-lane width to not quite two-lane, widening and narrowing at a whim for the entire trip to Lleymebamba. As I think to myself that I'm thankful there isn't much traffic on the road, a small cargo truck passes me. As so many cars in Latin America are, this one is decorated with a religious painting across the back, a guardian angel, who smiles beautifully.

At Yerbabuena, a big domesticated turkey stands in the middle of the road, with his tail and wings completely fanned out in a brilliant display. A small group of dogs, who would normally chase our bikes, is mesmerized by him. They simply stand and watch the show.

With ten miles to go, we hit rain. The road was wet for the last five miles, heavily so in some places, but I'd hoped the storm was passing us by. Brian pulls over to dig out his rain gear and suit up while I cover my tank bag. We chat for a moment, and he has decided we should stay in Lleymebamba for the night. We find a hostel on a hilly side street and settle into an upstairs room with a covered veranda overlooking the terraced village around us. It's cool in the mountains, despite our being in the Amazon region.

Since we have a few hours free this afternoon, we take a tuk tuk to the local museum where a collection of mummified human remains is on display. I'd read about them recently, which was why I wanted to stop in this village. The museum is impressive and modern. The mummies are respectfully displayed, and the entire collection is diverse and interesting.

The road leading out of Lleymebamba toward Celendin, which I fondly refer to as Celine Dion, disappears into the cloud forest high above the village. Terraced green fields fill the open spaces between trees. This road would be considered a single-lane road back home.

A few miles out of town it begins to drizzle softly. The higher we climb, the cooler the air feels. Layers of switchbacks lift us until we reach a rolling stretch of meadow that spans to the far side of a ridgeline. We cross to the other side, only to find another series of switchbacks, descending this time.

As we ride, I'm awestruck by the road. The mountain rises steeply above me on one side, while on the other, it falls away in a sheer drop. There is no guardrail, and the narrow road is open to all traffic, including buses and trucks. We have to be careful and ride defensively, but it's easy to be distracted, because the view is simply breathtaking. We drop below the clouds and into the deep canyon ahead with its walls shaded russet, salmon and gold.

At the bottom, we stop in a small village, where the temperature is at least 25 degrees Fahrenheit warmer than it was on top. We each have a frozen yogurt that a local woman sells from a cart, hand-mixed fruit and yogurt in slender plastic bags. They're delicious.

A bridge carries us over the Marañón River, a tributary of the Amazon, and our path meanders through the lower valley scrub before starting a long climb up and out of the canyon. As we crest the rim, we enter a high midland and face an enormous set of switchbacks lacing its way to the next higher mountainside in the west. It's spectacular, unlike any road I've ever ridden. The sheer scale of everything – depth of the canyons, steepness of the mountains, grandness of the wide valleys, and the miles and miles of panoramic vistas – is indescribable.

We hope to ride as far as Celendin for the night, but are comfortable enough in Peru now to wild camp if we find a place. Looking out at this landscape from a tent tomorrow morning would beat any hotel.

As we climb the midland to higher tiers of road, I look back at the river below and across the enormous slope we just crossed. I'm happy the single-lane road is empty so I can gawk. At the first turn of the switchbacks, I come upon an angry-looking cow tucked into the inside corner, facing toward me as I prepare to pass her. She gives her a tail a swish and seems to be sizing me up, so I hold my breath and steady myself to ride past. If she pushes me off the hundred-foot ledge now, at least I've had a spectacular day of riding to enjoy beforehand.

Celine Dion turns out to be a nice town with a busy central plaza, and makes a good landing place for the night. We ride to Cajamarca the next day, a much larger city, where we spend a day exploring the Incan ruins at Cumbemayo and the window-like graves carved into the rock face at Ventanillas de Otuzco. As we stroll through the central plaza one afternoon, I'm struck by the variety of hats worn by the women. It's as is each different kind identifies them as being part of a particular village or tribe and makes for an interesting segregated fashion show. There are tall pale straw hats with wide brims, dark-colored derbies, and small felt fedoras with pleated fans or feathers tucked inside the band.

After filling up at a fuel station, we have to wait to re-enter the flow of traffic between tuk tuks. Much to my selfish amusement, Brian has no patience whatsoever. After not much more than a minute of craning our necks to the left to watch for a gap in the vehicles, I hear a loud shouting stream of obscenity to my right and turn to see what all the fuss is about. Brian has apparently reached his limit and is yelling at the passing cars to vent his frustration. It's amazing how long it goes on, and moreso, how much joy I get from listening to it. I feel only mildly guilty, and hope he doesn't hear me laughing, if only so he doesn't start directing it at me. But part of me hopes the traffic stays thick for a minute or two longer. My sides hurt before I'm reduced to a snickering, heaving, teary-eyed giggle, like Muttley. I'm nearly out of air.

We ride west to Chilete and then turn south to Cascas. The road from Chilete is a quiet gravel road that offers some beautiful views. As is our usual habit, we stop to air down the tires for the gravel for better handling, and will air them up when we reach pavement again.

After a brief stop for lunch in the small village of Contumaza, we have to ask for directions to get out of the village, despite its only having two roads. We ride over a ridge and drop into the next valley on one of the most rugged rock roads I've ever seen. It's certainly the worst road I've ever ridden. This isn't gravel, it's more like a rock quarry. Chunks of rock the size of grapefruits and baseballs are common. Unfortunately, the rock is spread thickly enough on the road that I can't avoid them and my tire bumps and slides its way down the road however it can while I try to hang on.

As much as I want to take photos to prove how bad it is, I can't find a place to get decent footing and safely do it. So instead I carry on, hoping to stay upright, clenching all the way down.

Surprisingly, this rough road is designed like all the others, with a steep set of switchbacks and even a tunnel carved into the rock fins that run up the mountainside. It's a slow and sketchy descent to Cascas, more nerve-wracking than actually dangerous.

As I reach the bottom of the mountain, an enormous bright blue butterfly flutters by my helmet. Each lovely wing is bordered in a black outline. Magic.

We meet Sam and Erica again in Huanchaco, and together explore the ruins of Chan Chan and the local beachfront lined with traditional hand-made reed boats, before carrying on together to Canyon del Pato. Motorcycle friends suggest it as one of the most incredible rides in Peru, and I'm excited to see why it's so popular.

At Trujillo, we stock up on groceries and water, including food that needs refrigeration, a rare treat. Our friends generously make room in their cooler and truck for the extra supplies which enable us to take a slower pace and enjoy the canyon.

Our caravan moves south toward Chimbote, turning east just before we enter town. The road leads into the mountains, passing through a verdant river valley that narrows while the hills on both sides of the valley lift up around us. Eventually we are surrounded by rising walls, and the tarmac disappears. The languid Rio Santa leads into the mouth of the canyon.

We stop to camp on a level spot below the roadbed for the night, barely 10 miles into the canyon, but perfectly placed for an incredible day tomorrow. As the sun lowers in the west, it casts its orange glow over the walls above us and pierces the still relatively wide canyon, blanketing everything in warm light.

In the morning, we see the same effect, but in reverse, as the sun rises over the mountains to shine into our canyon, again igniting the canyon walls with its light. We pack up and make our way east. This will be a slow road.

The wide roadbed is, I've been told, located where a set of train tracks used to be. Trains carried materials out of the mountains to the coast until 1970 when an earthquake damaged the tracks badly enough for them to be abandoned.

The rail-bed was converted to a gravel road, wide in many places.

Yet, much of the road is still very narrow, and we often find ourselves getting up close and personal views into the deep narrow gorge which drops through a rock crevasse to the river below the left side of the road. Thirty-five single-lane rock tunnels bore through the mountains to create the route.

From where we left the highway at Chimbote, to the next services, it's roughly 120 miles. It takes us all day. This isn't due to the difficulty of the road conditions, it's due to how hard it is to keep moving instead of stopping to take more photos. I'm a forest and beach girl myself, but this might be one of the most beautiful places I've ever seen.

From our camp, the road narrowed, little by little. The canyon walls followed suit, closing in on us more with every mile. While there were still a few shrubs along the road and riversides at the start, less than 10 miles into the canyon they are gone. All that is left is rock and soil. Except for the blue sky above, we are completely surrounded by earth.

The beige of the gravel road disappears against the emerging display of colors going on around us. The river narrows and snuggles itself into the slender floor of the canyon, hiding under ledges and rocks as it runs. Hovering over the water's edge are enormous rock outcroppings and boulders.

I begin to notice dozens of unique layers of soil in the canyon walls and the mountains beyond. It's subtle at first, but as the miles wear on, the striations become more vivid. It's like one of the sand art bottles you make as a child - small handfuls of colored sand, poured in one at a time, making wafer-thin cross-sections of color you can observe through the bottle. Layers of soil eroding away from the mountains are creating the most beautiful sand art I've ever seen, in every shade imaginable – slate, rust, beige, gold, peach, and lavender.

We duck in and out of tunnels, finding most filled with a stagnant lingering dusty haze from the occasional traffic. Twice we meet someone coming from the other direction while in the middle of a one-lane tunnel. At one point, I have to paddle backwards through the soft dust on the tunnel floor to remedy our two-vehicle traffic jam. Some tunnels are long enough, or curve enough, to cause me to lose sight of one or both entrances, engulfing me in complete darkness except for the cloudy glow from my headlight. A few tunnels have windows cut into the side that overlook the river below, creating sidelights that allow soft, radiant shafts of light to filter into the tunnel.

We cross over a bridge to the other side of the river and pass a small settlement before the road curves southeast. The valley widens again, if only temporarily, before reaching the hydro-electric dam and a worker settlement nearby. Mountains stand guard on either side of the canyon, the Cordillera Negra to my right and the Cordillera Blanca to my left, mirroring each other perfectly. I feel like I'm riding down the cleavage of the Andes.

We pass the dam, and carry on to Caraz where we stop for cash and fuel. The land grows green again, and the familiar patchwork quilt of small square farms start to blanket the valley. Clouds cover the mountain peaks above keep me wondering just how high they go.

Our travel companions have scouted a place for us to camp tonight, just outside the entrance to Huascaran National Park, above the village of Yungay. They go on ahead while we stop for supplies. Although we don't have plans to carry on together past here, we have another evening of speaking English with friends to look forward to tonight.

We ride up from Yungay, climbing toward the Llanganuco Lakes and turn off the road into a meadow, high above the village and valley. Having only a pinned location to aim for, the GPS isn't much help as we use trial and error to find one of several tracks that will lead us to our campsite near a lodge. But eventually we see our friend's truck.

Clouds descend, sealing out the view of the peaks, and making the cool evening feel even cooler. We camp on the edge of a lodge's property not far from the main buildings and set up our tent right away to take advantage of the remaining daylight. A pile of adobe bricks nearby offers me a worktable and level spot for my stove as I make dinner.

As I chop vegetables to make a pasta, two pests, unlike any I have ever had before, arrive to see what I'm up to. Long white dreadlocks and perked ears appear beside my right shoulder, nearly causing me to drop my pan. Two aggressively snoopy alpacas stick their faces into my pot. I wave my arms and lunge toward them, calling out "Shoo!", which offers a temporary reprieve. But the male lays his ears back and sets his jaw at me, apparently not taking no for an answer. Laughter emerges from the camper a few dozen yards away as Sam and Erica watch the show.

My stubborn streak holds out, and I pick up a piece of lumber leaning against the pile of bricks and raise it at the male. This must be a clear enough message because he turns and trots away. I was only planning to bluff, until he comes at me again, so I swat him squarely across his rump. He grunts and trots off, giving up for now.

The short grass under our feet makes for a soft camping surface. That and the cool night combine for good sleeping. Brian doesn't feel well the next day, so we decide to take a day off. I hike to the small dried depression where Lake Keushu used to be and scout around the ruins of stone dwellings located on either side of the lake bed. Dense clouds hover overhead, which at first I think are low until I recall we are camped at 11,000 feet.

The morning starts out misty, but by early afternoon the clouds lift and burn off in a few places. The sky above me changes minute by minute. After returning from my walk to the lake, I tinker at camp until a shaft of light beams down on me like a spotlight. I look up at the break in cloud cover and catch a glimpse of a goliath peak that has been unmasked.

Unbeknownst to us, there are a half dozen peaks within five miles of our camp, each over 19,000 feet and one just across the road towers above us at more than 22,000 feet. The swirling sky shifts to reveal glimpses of three enormous peaks, each covered in giant swaths of glacial snowpack. Powder blows off the peaks in a trail of white spray.

The owner of the lodge has three Rhodesian Ridgebacks on the property, and they stop by to collect rubs now and then. This place is a paradise, even from my cheap seat on the ridge. That is, until I look more closely at the dozens of small holes all over the ground near the tent. I'd seen them earlier, but small as they are, hadn't thought much of them. The owner, who happens by at the end of my walk, asks me if I've seen the tarantulas, to which I reply with an audible gasp.

"Tarantulas?" I say, hoping I heard him wrong.

"Yeah. There's one now." He points at a small fast-moving gray blur on the ground, mixed into the tufted grass. I hadn't seen anything move before he pointed, but now I can't miss it. He squats down, gets out his pocketknife to use as a pointer, and shows me the spider. It's only perhaps two inches across, and a subtle, flannel gray color. But it's unmistakably a tarantula, fuzzy and with the same body shape and proportions of its giant south Texas cousins. It's almost cute.

He goes on to say he's surprised I haven't seen them in the tent since we are camped in the middle of a nest of them. Oh. My. God. In another time, it might have been my worst nightmare. But now I only make a mental note to be more careful about keeping the tent zipped shut.

After two nights at camp, we ride into Huascaran National Park and east into the Andes between the high peaks I spied the day before. The sky is more clear today, but clouds still linger around the mountain tops and shield them from view.

Only a couple of miles from the lodge, we enter a crevice between two giant mountains where a roadside stream has been blocked to form the two long and slender lakes, the Llanganuco Lakes. Each is filled with glacial runoff, a silted, milky turquoise color that is beautiful.

Sam and Erica turn off at the Laguna 69 trail. When this area was first being mapped, explorers were finding more and more small lakes each day and couldn't keep up with naming each, so they opted for numbers. I hear this one is a particularly gorgeous hike. I wish we had more time to stop and do things like that along the route, but I don't feel like I'm missing out when I'm in the midst of such incredible scenery.

Just after they turn off, we arrive at the base of a set of switchbacks that disappears into the clouds above. Most of the traffic stops here and turns back, and the condition of the road from here shows that. After making a few turns, the road gets rougher and the gravel grows in diameter, becoming rocks.

So far, the road has been damp, due in part to the light mist falling on and off since we arrived two days before. But it doesn't seem to be a problem. The grade isn't bad at first, just steep and steady. My attention is completely directed at the view - slender turquoise lakes shrinking into the distance and overhanging drifts of snow on the ridges and peaks around us.

Our road has, in a way, hit a dead-end at the end of the slender valley. That is, until some ambitious person decided to climb the wall ahead of him with a series of zigzags that stair-step their way to the top. Some tiers are so steeply perched above the one below that I expect the edge to wash out at any moment and dump me on the layer beneath.

It's spring here in the Andes, in October, and the snow is melting. What I thought was rain water on the road, is now starting to become more intense, and a slender stream runs lengthwise down the road, following the switchbacks down to the valley floor. It wouldn't be so bad, except that the runoff that drains onto the road has eroded a narrow trench into the length of it, dividing it in half and making it difficult to maneuver around corners and obstacles. I'm riding up a narrow rocky trough. My bike starts to act up, sputtering in between gear changes, and hesitating. We stop at one point, and Brian adjusts my idle to compensate for the change in altitude. It buys me time.

I count a dozen corners, which means a dozen tiers, and the top isn't anywhere in sight. We keep moving forward, slowly, enjoying the view all the way up. Betty sputters again and we stop to adjust her once more, using all there is left of the adjustment screw.

Chartreuse colored tufts of grass cover the steep mountain sides, and scrubby bushes grows here and there, each covered in small lavender flowers. The earth is a dark gray, including the stones on the road. Colors combine in a subdued palette that's perfect under the overcast sky. White mountain peaks are camouflaged against the clouds and disappear in the photographs I take. The road isn't much more than a single lane wide, and thankfully there is no traffic. I've counted more than twenty switchbacks, and still can't see the top.

The running water on the road gets bothersome. My bike's sputtering and hesitating aren't helping. At one point, my wheels settle into a soft rut made by the runoff and I can't seem to give my bike enough gas to get it out of it without it dying. Brian gives me a hand, warding off a frustrating moment. Within a few turns the water lessens as we ride above the entry point of the glacial melt. My bike sputters and coughs its way up the road, struggling in the thin air.

As we make one final right turn, I see the road level out in front of me and spot an overlook on the right. I pull up and park, grateful to have made the top. I walk over to the edge, and look down. We've climbed twenty-nine tiers to get here. This is Portachuelo Pass.

The lakes below are now tiny, and the road only a thread in the bottom of the valley. My watch says we are at 15,589 feet, give or take. No wonder Betty is struggling. We take a few minutes for photos, and get back on our bikes to ride through the rock cut in the saddle of the peak behind us, and down the other side. The back side of the mountain has a much subtler slope, and descends to large landings before moving down to the next tier.

The sky opens up for a few minutes, but it doesn't amount to much. It's slow going on this side too, but just as beautiful. We descend to Yanama where Brian had planned to stop for the night, but it's early afternoon and we haven't covered many miles, so we carry on.

Of the two routes to Chacas, the next village that is likely to have lodging and fuel, we choose the one that is supposed to be less rough and steep. Our choice proves to be a decent road until we hit a couple of steep sections between San Felipe and Socos where the road is covered with large rock. We come to a valley where the road turns to follow the path of a river. I can see immediately that we are lucky to be here when we are. Deep dried ruts in the road reveal it must be a nightmare to ride when it's wet. One upward glance at the cloudy sky makes me turn my throttle a little further.

The day wears on very slowly. An hour after dark we arrive at the village of Chacas and ride into the central square. There isn't a single sign for a hostel or place to camp. I stop and ask a woman on the plaza if she can direct me to a place to spend the night and she points to a carved wooden door nearby.

Several knocks later, I'm greeted by an elderly woman who waves me inside. She speaks only Quechua, the local native language, and goes to get her granddaughter to help. As I listen to their conversation I find the language mildly familiar. Heather reminds me sometime later that it was used as part of the basis of a dialect in the original Star Wars movie.

She has rooms. We can bring the bikes through the front door and park them on the tile floor in the small central courtyard of the hostel. It's a cool night in the mountains.

In the morning, I enjoy a stroll around the plaza to admire the elaborately carved wooden doors and balconies on all the facades. Chacas is known for beautiful carving and wood workmanship. When asking about fuel, I'm told there is no gas station in town but that a couple blocks off the plaza is a small garage owned by Luis who will sell us fuel. We buy a few liters each, enough to get us down the mountain.

Chacas is perched at 11,000 feet, and we start climbing up from town as we make our way to the nearly mile-long Punto Olimpico Tunnel somewhere high above. Until 2013, the highway climbed over the top of the mountain but was known to be dangerous and susceptible to closure in bad weather, so the government built a tunnel, the highest in the world, in hopes the road could be better maintained in winter. We pass another turquoise lake on the climb up as glaciers descend from the rugged mountain tops. I'm in awe of how beautiful this part of the world is, and I'm so glad Pete suggested the route.

At the entrance to the tunnel, Brian tries to scout the old road which rides above the tunnel, but it's closed. I count twenty-nine switchbacks down to the valley floor, mirroring our climb the day before. Each of those layers provides stunning views. I'm hypnotized for nearly an hour as we descend.

We pass through Carhuaz, stopping only for a short break before carrying on to Huaraz for the night. It's a popular town with cyclists and backpackers, the jumping off point for a lot of Andean tours. Jim and his two bicyclist companions, happen to be in town. Knowing how many calories they must burn cycling in this altitude, I invite them to dinner and plan a big carb-intensive meal of pasta and garlic bread.

It's strange to play hostess at a hostel, but fun, and it's wonderful to catch up with Jim. We both left the top of the continent at the same time and have come more than a third of the way south while keeping the same pace. I'm in awe of the physical strength of cyclists.

Our route leads south from Huaraz and west to the coast, and to Lima. To be honest, I'm dreading this a little. While crossing paths with dozens of motorcyclists on this trip, Lima is the one place that they all talk about as having the worst drivers and traffic anywhere in the Americas. La Paz may have the steepest streets, and Mexico City may have 20 million residents, but Lima is, according to consensus, the worst place to ride a motorcycle in the Americas.

One night in Huacho is all we have between the Andes to prepare for the traffic of Lima. Brian plots a route and leads the way south on the Pan-American Highway. He's decided to stay at a hostel recommended by friends, right in the heart of the city.

Traffic on the Pan-Am is heavy enough, with all the trucks and aggressive drivers, but I can immediately tell the difference as we get closer to Lima. With thirty miles to go, traffic is already thick and fast. The highway widens from one lane each way to two lanes, to three lanes, and eventually to four. We push on toward the city, all the while the number of trucks increases. Most of the time I feel like I'm riding 60 mph inside a roofless shipping container, with semi-trailers boxing me in on all four sides.

I work hard to keep up with Brian. We don't have communication headsets, which hasn't presented a problem except in cities. But this sort of situation is my worst nightmare. All I can do is stay as alert as possible and track him like a falcon following every dart and dive of my prey. Traffic slows a little as it condenses on the northern edge of the city. Double trailers are common in Latin America, and sit at the top of the motorized food chain, followed by single trailer trucks, then buses and cargo vans, smaller trucks, cars, and lastly, motorcycles. They don't watch out for each other, and no one watches out for us. Drivers switch lanes on a whim and anyone around them is left to fend for themselves.

While this is normal in Latin America, it's exponentially worse here than anything I've experienced so far. The highway has grown to 7-8 lanes moving in each direction. Or has it? Trucks aren't staying in lanes anyway, not that they are clearly marked. We are crammed as tightly as we can be, side to side, and if anything happens, there isn't a safe place for me to get out of the flow of crushing traffic. I keep my throttle steady, stay close with Brian and react as quickly as possible to the changes around me. I shift lanes often, dodging trucks and cars. I say silent prayers. My heart races for more than half an hour from the northern edge of Lima, around the eastern side of the city and past several exits, until finally, we turn off the Pan-Am and dive into the sprawl. I'm grateful to be off the road.

We stop for a much-needed break before making our way into the heart of Miraflores to the hostel. We ride up onto the wide sidewalk and through the front door, to the courtyard. I don't think I've ever been so happy to arrive anywhere. When I pull off my helmet, I notice how black my face is, especially around my nose and mouth. I can't imagine how much exhaust I ate on that highway.

This part of Lima is packed with tourists and all the ancillary businesses that demands. There are cafes, bars, souvenir shops and plenty of American brands that I haven't missed. We spend a few days getting caught up on supplies, blog posts and relaxation. I also have some business to attend to.

My attorney emailed from home to say that my former employers' settlement offer will expire within the next two days. Because we are headed into a stretch of road that will leave us without internet for a few days, I decide to make up my mind here in Lima. That way I have internet and a notary on hand.

One afternoon I wander over to the city park across the road from our hostel. Strangely, the entire park is filled with cats. At first, I see just a few, curled up with a human on a bench or leaned against a tree, and they appear to be pets. Later I notice more of them, sleeping under shrubs and between plants in the flower beds, or hiding timidly in shadows. I find out later that this park is known as a place where locals abandon their unwanted cats.

At first, it makes me incredibly sad, but then I watch the interaction between the people and the animals. Dozens of people come here at all hours of the day, most bringing food, obviously searching out the company of the cats. And the cats curl up with people to their mutual benefit. I'd, of course, much rather see the cats in loving homes, but for the most part, they could do worse.

I work on a few administrative details, like blogs and some minor projects. I email friends and family, and even Skype home. Molly has message from Maine, which makes my day. She's considering planning a motorcycle trip and has asked if I would be interested in tagging along. I'm over the moon.

I pay some bills online and research some "must sees" for the road ahead. Finally, I can stall no longer, and make time to decide what I'm going to do with the settlement offer. We plan to leave the city the day after tomorrow. I have to decide now.

Forcing myself to mull it all over effort, and I realize I've moved on from my old life more than I'd known. It's hard to think about the people I used to work for with any sort of positivity. I'm glad to be free from them. I don't have any interest in fighting them or going over the long story of how we got here through a protracted legal battle. I don't have the money or the energy for the fight. These last thoughts reveal the truth to me even as they occur.

Much as I'd love to discuss all this in front of a judge to find some sort of justice, I'd really rather just be done with it. I decide to close that chapter of my life.

We ride south to Ica and spend a night in the touristy oasis town of Huacachina, where I hike up a sand dune to watch the sunset. After a couple of days riding we drift away from the coast and move to the inland plateau.

Just before the town of Nazca we stop to climb a roadside tower and view a few of the famous figures in the crusted desert surface. It's amazing that several hundred of these have survived for two millennia.

After Nazca, the highway climbs several sets of rolling hills, working its way toward the higher altitudes of the Andes. It will take us three days to cross to Cusco. On a high plateau above Nazca we stop to watch a herd of guanacos, tall and slender camelids, cross the highway. I make a mental note to watch for them on the road. I would guess they can be just as dangerous as a deer on the highway back home.

We spend a night in Puquio where our bikes are kept in a small gated yard with young chickens and rabbits. At first I think they make adorable pets, but then remember they are more likely food for the family who offers us a room to rent.

After Puquio, we move on to Abancay, and the rust-colored landscape reminds me of Arizona. Peru packs every kind of terrain into its borders. The heights and depths of each mountain crossing becomes more exaggerated. Each vista is more gorgeous than the last.

The road winds in series of curves, leading us over a ridge, before leading us around a bend and down into the next valley, repeated over again and again, dozens of times each day. This roller coaster movement, of lots of small ups and downs, only slightly masks the overall climb we've made from the coast.

On distant hillsides, I see circular walls built with piles of stones, varying in size from perhaps 20 feet across to 60 feet or more. Sheep lazily graze as we pass, and I wonder if the stone circles are makeshift pens for them. This land reminds me of the Scottish Highlands, rocky and rugged and dotted with small lakes, with cropped vegetation that seems to intentionally not grow tall enough to be beaten back by the occasional strong winds. There are no trees on the hills, only the short grass and the rocks, which are used to make everything we see – houses, sheds for animals, fences.

As we top one hill and cross into the gray-green valley below, I see what I think is another herd of sheep, albeit this one looks multi-colored, scattered across the floor and sides of the wide glen. But as we get closer I see it's an enormous herd of llamas, several hundred of them. Similar to cattle back home, many of the animals have tags in their ears to mark their ownership. But unlike the plastic tags we use, these are made of brightly-colored tassels of yarn. I stop for a photo and a woman dressed in a traditional woolen skirt, colorful knit socks and a felt Fedora climbs up to the road to see what I 'm doing. I wave at her but she only stares back.

It's chilly up here. We are riding at 13,000 feet on the altiplano. It starts to sprinkle. Later the tiny raindrops turn to snow and sleet that bounces off my tank bag ricocheting under my helmet, hitting me in the chin. It stings. Brian pulls over and gets his rain suit out. He suggests I not linger in the rain but keep moving, and he will catch up. If I see a village with a decent looking café, I'm supposed to stop.

Knowing he stopped for a bathroom break as well as to gear up, I ride off. I only need to go a few miles down the road, before I crest a hill and arrive at the tiny village of Quillaccasa. Surprisingly, I see two small signs on low huts advertising restaurants. A truck is parked in front of the first, and as tiny as the building is, I assume one customer would probably fill it up, so I move on to the second and park on the shoulder of the road, not five feet from the path of passing trucks.

Brian takes ages. I wait with my bike for a while, glad that the snow has stopped momentarily, but finally decide to go inside and make sure the place is actually open. I duck under the dark open doorway of the whitewashed stucco hut and let my eyes adjust to the darkness.

An older couple are sitting and eating plates of hot rice and stewed meat with vegetables. The mountain air is cold which causes the plates to roil with steam. The woman confirms that her café is open. I ask if she has hot tea and café con leche, and she says she does. I order one of each. She goes to the kitchen while I walk outside to see if Brian is here yet. Several men are gathered around my bike. I smile and nod, and say hello. They return my greeting and then step back to murmur amongst themselves.

Finally, Brian comes over the hill and pulls up behind me. The look on his face says that this wasn't exactly his idea of a restaurant, but he takes his helmet off and follows me inside anyway. Our hostess has brought out two pieces of llama hide to put on the plastic chair seats, to make us more comfortable. As is our ritual, we arrange our chairs so that we can watch over our bikes, this time through a five-foot-high doorway. It rains for a few minutes and then quits. The sun peeks out as a small crowd gathers around our bikes. Boys and girls walk up to look at them, and then lean into the doorway to see who the riders might be.

Three young girls, maybe 6 to 8 years in age, come as far into the doorway as is possible without actually setting foot on the dirt floor of the restaurant. I say hello in Spanish and start up a conversation. They smile at Brian. He is likely a foot or two taller than most men they see. They ask where we are from, and ask me to teach them a few words of English. Brian offers them some of the packaged cookies we bought from a glass case in the restaurant to go with our hot drinks. They come in, shyly, one by one, take a cookie, say thanks, and return to the doorway.

The informal young leader of the group is named Jocelyn. Two more girls arrive and a small boy. We have by now eaten or given out all our cookies, so I walk over to the case to buy another package for our new visitors. The kids linger while we finish our drinks and get ready to go.

While I know this place doesn't have electricity or running water, I'm in need of a restroom before we go and ask the woman if she has a toilet that I may use. My thimble-sized bladder won't make it far down the road, so it's worth a try. She takes me through the small room I recognize as her kitchen, if only by the fact that this is where a small propane stove she used to heat our drinks is sitting. She pries a jagged sheet of corrugated tin from the doorway and shoos a few chickens outside. The corner of the door is missing, allowing them to come and go as they please. I follow her around a corner through a walled open air courtyard to a small stucco shack which is the resident outhouse. For a moment, I rethink my request, but it would be rude to leave now. I go inside, noticing there is no door, and squat over the 12-inch hole dug in the center of the room. It's as good a bathroom as any.

Jocelyn is outgoing and friendly, and first hugs Brian's legs and then mine as we walk out of the low doorway toward the road. I lift her high into the air and put her down again.

"Una mas!" she exclaims as I put her back down, obviously enjoying the move I use on my nephews. She giggles and smiles. As we walk to the bikes, I ask some of the adults if it would be okay to take a photo of the crowd of children. The men nod, but opt not to be in the photo and move away from the bikes. The children wave and smile for my snapshot.

As we put our gear on and start our bikes, they call out their goodbyes, in English and Spanish. I call out "Adios!" as we go.

We don't go far before dropping into a canyon, working our way down the switchbacks to a river below. The river leads us for a seemingly long ride to the far end of a deep valley. Somewhere above it is the city of Abancay.

The wind picks up, as our canyon-valley intersects with two other valleys, having run down the length of each at full speed with nothing to stop it. We climb curvy roads to the town itself where slow traffic stops and starts. The city streets are steep, straining both my clutch and my brakes. We have 50 miles of twisty roads ahead which will take a couple of hours, so we skip lunch and keep moving.

I'm learning a lesson on this trip, to make time for rest and to refuel myself and my bike, figuratively and literally. Brian is constantly frustrated with my slow pace, and rightfully so. But like many adventure riders, he started out with a constant drive to cover a lot of miles each day, at the expense of breaks and experiences. I'm more of a traveler than a motorcyclist, and would rather wander. After months on the road, we've found a fairly happy medium somewhere between us. I know many other riders move much more quickly than we are, but I also know what they're missing by doing so. I'm not sure they can possibly enjoy the trip as much as I am.

We ride switchbacks and keep climbing until we're over the top of the next mountain and dropping down the other side. Through clouds I make out a snow-covered peak when the twisting road points just the right way. There's a gorgeous valley below, lush and green, and covered with the ever-present quilt squares of small farms. Storm clouds hover overhead. I will be happy to reach our camp spot and set up before the rain comes. We push on, stopping only momentarily for food for our supper.

In the morning, we pack up and head for Cusco. The road isn't bad, but there's construction underway at the river's edge in the next valley, which slows our progress. By early afternoon, we round a bend and see the outskirts of Cusco stretched out before us. I was here a few years ago, but am still surprised how large Cusco is, and how it spans across the valley, spilling up the sides.

We ride to the Plaza des Armas and try to locate a hostel Pete suggested. Bikers are always quick to recommend good places with off-street parking. It takes some wandering on my part, while Brian stays with the bikes, to find the hostel we're looking for. They have rooms, but they only have space for one of our motorcycles in the common room. The clerk on duty walks me down the street to a parking garage that has open space. We have landed at Machu Picchu base camp.

Over the next couple of days, we explore the city, the ruins at Sacsayhuaman (which gringos refer to as "sexy woman") and several cafes and shops around the main square. Peruvian women tend market stalls all over the narrow cobblestoned streets. I buy mittens and caps to send to home to family. Christmas is still a couple of months away, but it will likely take that long for the packages to get to South Dakota. I buy colorful knit socks and send them home to myself so I can enjoy them some cold winter in the future.

Part of every motorcyclist's journey through this part of the world should include a visit to Norton Rat's, the bar founded by a moto-nomad on the main plaza years ago. It's been on my list for a while, but now seems a melancholy pilgrimage, since the owner passed away in a motorcycle accident last year. We go there and meet up with riders we've met virtually or in person over the past few months for drinks. I find a place for my sticker on a door.

I meet Andrew, another English rider, and an American who now lives in Huancayo and offers motorcycle tours. He asks about where we've ridden so far. When I say my favorite road was in the Cordillera Blanca, except that my bike struggled a bit, he offers a tip to use the petcock valve in addition to the mixture screw to stretch the bike's tolerance as far as I can in the thin air. I'll have to remember that.

Brian gets sick again. I snoop online and find that some internal parasites can cause his symptoms on a three-week schedule, which fits his recent routine. Julio, from Ecuador, wrote Brian to say he had come to a similar conclusion and suggested the de-worming pills we bought in Ecuador, but neither of us has worked up the nerve to take them yet. Brian might be housing the 6th generation of his wormy tenants by now. I could be too.

We meet up with friends, stock up on supplies and make plans to visit Machu Picchu. Aguas Calientes, a small village built to serve tourists at the base of Machu Picchu's mountain, is where all tours begin. There are two ways to get there. We can ride our bikes to the spur road at Santa Teresa, park the bikes at the hydroelectric dam, leaving them unattended, and hike into Aguas Calientes. Alternately, we can leave the bikes safely stored in the parking garage and take a train from Cusco to A.C. Having to abandon the bikes, doesn't appeal to either of us. After some discussion, I book train tickets.

Aguas Calientes is a tourist trap. There's no other way to describe it. Hostels and bars stand shoulder to shoulder with tacky souvenir shops and tour offices. But it's nice to see local businesses thriving, feeding an economy that desperately needs it. We spend the night in a hostel and meet up with Californian friends, Toby and Chloe, and then tuck in early. We're up at 4:30am to catch the first bus up the mountain, which departs at 5:30am. As we walk up to the bus stop, I'm happy to see there's no one ahead of us.

It's half an hour's ride to the top, mostly switchbacks, and it's still dark as we arrive. Dozens of people ran or walked up the stairs to climb the 1000 feet from the village to Machu Picchu itself. They huff, puff, sweat and stink all around us in line. Finally, the park opens and we cross into sacred ground. Remembering my way from a visit a few years ago, I turn left and climb a few stairs, wanting to come out to the point above the ruins. Blankets of mist hover over the entire site, but slowly start to dissolve as the sun finally rises high enough over the surrounding mountains to reach it.

After climbing up to a grassy field built on top of the giant stone terraces, we make our way to the point, like the bow of a ship, perched high above the ruins which offers a stunning overhead view of Machu Picchu. Below me people mill about the complex of buildings like rats in a maze.

Four years ago, I hadn't realized that you could hike to Machu Picchu via the Inca Trail. Nor did I know you could climb Huayna Picchu, the knobby peak on the far side of the complex, for an even rarer view of the ruins. I'd wished that someday I could come back, and now here I am. But although my injured leg has healed well, I don't trust it enough to tolerate four days of the Inca Trail or to climb the steep stone steps to Huayna Picchu.

I lead us around the port side of the ship, to the trail leading to Inca Bridge. From here we can see deep down into the valley worn wide by the Urubamba as it snakes its way around three sides of this mountain.

Wisps of wandering clouds drift between me and the objects of my observation. I can make out the hydroelectric plant and the walking trail leading to Aguas Calientes. After booking our train tickets, we found out that a landslide on that route has blocked the road. We've gotten lucky with our choice.

The trail clings to the edge of the steep mountainside and leads back toward an enormous vertical rock face, several hundred feet high. The rock looks perfect for big wall climbing, and even better for keeping your enemies out of your fortress.

What I thought was already a fairly narrow walkway whittles itself down to a slender thread, wide enough only for one person. Wide rock outcroppings stop altogether as the path arrives at the edge of a several-hundred-foot-wide rock wall. Barely wide enough for a foothold, a narrow ledge stretches out across the expanse of the stone face.

Centuries ago, that ledge might have been the only way in and out of Machu Picchu. As my eyes follow the narrow shelf across the rock face, I spy a gap in the ledge, perhaps twenty feet across, where a wooden bridge has been placed to span the missing section. It could be removed at any point to block the path completely. Ingenious.

Wispy strands of mist dissolve as we walk back to the ruins and enjoy a panoramic view from above before climbing down into the complex itself. Llamas graze on the terraces. While wandering through the stone walls, I look up and see a group of hikers starting up Huayna Picchu, and am a little envious of their unique adventure.

Later, instead of taking the bus down to A.C., we opt to take the stairs. As we meet dozens of upward-bound people, nearly all of them ask how much further it is to the top.

After making our way back to Cusco, I prepare for the last stretch of Peru. We are nearing Bolivia. I catch up on blog posts and get a couple of weeks' worth scheduled in case I can't find internet down the road, although so far it hasn't been a problem.

I plot a route through Pisac, to stop and see the ruins, before riding south to Puno and then on to the border. Children's Halloween costumes hang in the doorways of a few local shops, reminding me that it's the holiday back home. Pisac is spectacular, with its terraced hillsides and stone buildings on the summit, overlooking another settlement of the Sacred Valley. Remnants of the city's water system are still active and a small trough of water runs through the foundation of what remains of one house before making its way to the next. It feels good to spend a day hiking.

In the morning, before I pack my bike for the day's ride, I try to call my dad and best friend, but neither answers. So, I try my grandmother, who answers and sounds happy to hear from me.

"How long is this trip going to last?", she blurts out instead of a normal greeting, making me feel both homesick and slightly guilty for having checked out of reality for so long.

"I hope to ship the bike back to North America in March", I reply, but I really don't know.

Over dinner with Markus and Karin in Cusco a few nights before, I'd said, without really having thought about it, that it's getting time for me to go home. This brief conversation with my grandmother puts the thought in front of me again. I'm getting tired and the idea of home sounds really good to me, even though, technically, I don't have one.

My leg is stiff from the previous day's hiking, so Brian pushes my bike out from under the hotel awning as I ride it through the gate to the edge of the street to wait for him. I climb off and check my gear, while one of the local drunks who had been attempting to talk to Brian gives it another shot. Brian has enough trouble with Spanish when it's spoken clearly. I'm sure this guy's slurred version of Spanish isn't helping at all.

After seeing Brian's blank look, the man walks over to me and asks if I speak Spanish. I say that I do. He asks if we went up to the ruins and what we think of them. His drinking buddy has wandered up to hear my answer, but is too wobbly to stand so takes a seat at a small table belonging to the hotel. They are obviously proud of their village and country, and its history. I tell them that this was my second visit to his beautiful pueblo, and that we are very impressed.

First Drunk beams proudly and walks closer to shake my hand. Feeling it wasn't enough, he leans in to give me a smelly hug and a sour kiss on my cheek while I hold my breath. It's very sweet of him. Inspired by his partner, Second Drunk stands in anticipation of his hug and kiss. I don't want to be rude, so I oblige him. They wish us safe travels and buen suerte (good luck) in the journey ahead.

We ride up the street and round the bend toward the main road, passing a collectivo that honks while the driver calls out to me. I can't hear what he says as I pass. The small amount of traffic grinds to a halt at the entrance to the bridge that crosses the Urubamba and leads to the main highway. I'm not sure, but this looks like a protest of some sort. Trucks are parked bumper to bumper on the bridge, blocking our exit from town.

A man stops to tell me that there is another bridge we can use a little further up the road, so I ride ahead. Maybe 200-300 feet further I catch a glimpse of a narrow walking bridge between two houses, but don't think much of it and keep riding, looking for a car bridge. But there isn't one. It dawns on me that the man was suggesting we use the walking bridge to cross over, so we turn around and go look at it. A woman confirms that locals use the bridge for tuk tuks. Brian can't hear what's being said, so I nod my head toward the walking bridge and shrug my shoulders inquisitively. He responds with a shrug and a nod, suggesting it's worth a try.

I ride off the road and bump roughly up onto the wooden bridge, grateful for its low railings which I hope will keep me from plunging into the murky brown Urubamba below. I slowly ride over the arch toward the far bank, catching sight of a rock at the other end which is intended to block carros from using the bridge. It's tight, but I'm able to nudge my way around it only bumping my pannier slightly. I ride up the slope to the road, park and walk back to take a photo of Brian on the bridge. A frustrated carro driver honks to hurry us up so he can cross the other way.

The highway leads from Pisac to Puno, crossing through Santa Rosa and Juliaca in the process. At Santa Rosa, I stop for a bathroom break. Just the act of taking my riding pants down and walking to and from the bike leaves me out of breath and I feel a slight pain in my chest. My watch confirms that we are at just over 12,000 feet. No wonder I'm huffing and puffing. Riding a motorcycle for months on end hasn't kept me in good shape.

My mind wanders as I ride. I'm disappointed to leave Peru, it's been such an incredibly beautiful country. I'd hoped to make it to Arequipa, a city in the south, and to Colca Canyon to see the Condors. But it's getting late in the year and we still have so far to go before Ushuaia. There are always more things I want to see than I have time for.

Juliaca, the next town we traverse, is so far, the biggest shithole I've seen in South America. I hate to say that about a city, but after comparing stories with other travelers, I confirm that we all agree, it's positively apocalyptic. It may be the dirtiest and most bombed-out looking city I've ever seen.

The wind picks up as we ride the last 30 miles to Puno. Small wooden and plaster shrines dot the edges of the highway, as they have all over Peru. But today is different. Each of the shrines is decorated with fresh flowers, fluttering in the increasing breeze. Locals are paying respects to loved ones lost because today is All Saints Day, and tomorrow is El Dia de Los Muertos.

The road follows the western edge of Lake Titicaca, the highest navigable lake in the world. Somewhere off shore is a small floating village set upon a traditional construction of reeds which I'm told has evolved from cultural display into sad tourist trap.

At Puno, we find a backstreet hotel, with a wide enough front door for the bikes to squeeze through, park in the lobby, and settle in for the night. The next morning, Brian has a terrible migraine and can't even tolerate the glow from my laptop, much less riding to Bolivia today. I pull the shades closed and wander the neighborhood in search of bottled water. While it could be something he ate, I'm guessing his illness is more likely caused by the altitude and dehydration. I feel it too.

On our way to the Bolivian border the next day we encounter a protest road block, but easily ride around it on the grassy plain next to the road. Getting out of Peru proves simple, and we make a border guard friend in the process. He lets me sit at his desk and take a picture while he stamps my paperwork out of the country.

Just as we ride through the barrier to the Bolivian offices, I see the Aduana official closing the office door as he leaves for lunch. Damn. Who knows how long that will take.

There's not much of a line at the Migracion office so I get in line and buy my visa for Bolivia, which is good for five years. It's taken me nearly a year and a half to get here, so I can't imagine coming back in the next five. While I wait in line for my turn, a young woman comes over and asks if I'm traveling on one of the motorcycles parked on the road. I say that I am.

"How long have you been traveling?" she inquires.

"Sixteen months so far."

"Wow. That's incredible." She pauses before asking, "How much longer will you be on the road?"

"I'm not sure. We're headed for Ushuaia which will probably take another couple of months, before riding north to Buenos Aires to ship our bikes back to the United States. So maybe another 3-4 months." It sounds more like question than answer, even to me.

One of a group of travelers in line just ahead of me has been eavesdropping. He tells his companions what he overheard. They all turn to eye me, with mixed reviews. The men look impressed and maybe a little wistful, perhaps dreaming of an adventure like this for themselves. The women look slightly appalled, a far cry from the several thumbs up that I was given by passing cars on the highway the past few days.

After waiting a couple of hours in the warm sun, we finally see the Aduana official return from lunch and follow him inside to process our bikes into yet another new country.

19 BOLIVIA

Depart, depart for distant cities, keep on living your other life…
-Adela Zamudio

The ride from the border to Copacabana takes less than an hour. We ride through town to the hillside lodge and are lucky enough to get a room.

We take a couple days off to take a boat to the Island of the Sun, just off shore, and spend the better part of the day walking along the spine of the island. While I'm enjoying both the warm sun and the view of the deep sapphire lake a Bolivian woman in traditional dress, complete with derby and woolen skirt, minds a small herd of sheep on a hillside.

In the distance, I see the snow-covered peaks that are Bolivia's Andes. Somewhere in those mountains is a beautiful village I've wanted to see, recommended by travelers we met in Ecuador. But alas, we've taken too long to come south and snow is already there, making the road impassable. As it is, the rainy season could come to Bolivia any day now. That actually doesn't sound so bad, as dry as it is here, but it would be devastating to my dream of riding on the salar (salt flat) in the south of the country. We have to stay ahead of the rains.

The highway from Copacabana to La Paz requires a ferry crossing at San Pedro de Tiquina. Brian told me stories of how rickety the wooden barges were when he was here before and we arrive to find they're only more decrepit now. Wide gaps between the deck boards could easily swallow a bike tire or a leg. Brian helps me find a less precarious place to park my bike and we carefully hopscotch our way across the deck to get a photo.

A small pickup is parked on the front of the barge, and we are the only other customers for the 15-minute crossing. A family pours out of the truck to better enjoy the novelty of the trip, and their two sons walk over to look at my bike.

I smile and say hello. The youngest, perhaps five years old, seems interested in my motorcycle but is shy. His mother asks where we're from and is surprised by my answer. It's out of most peoples' realm of thinking that we've ridden this far.

She sees her little one admiring my bike and smiles at me. I ask her if he would like to sit on it and she nods. She helps him astride while I hold it steady and her husband snaps a few photos. Expecting him to be excited, I'm surprised to see the small boy seize up with fear instead. But after his mother puts him safely back on the deck of the barge, and he knows he has survived his big adventure, he smiles.

As we ride to La Paz, I'm engrossed in the landscape ahead of us, the mountains growing much larger as we near them. Our route carries us to the outskirts of La Paz and through the hectic chaos that is El Alto. La Paz is the highest capital city in the world at 12,000 feet, and is intimidatingly large with just over 2.5 million people. The city itself spills across and over a bowl-like depression in the altiplano surrounded by snow-capped peaks.

In an effort to avoid its infamous traffic, Brian routes us around the edge of the city to the small village of Jupapina where a fellow rider is camping. Just a few miles south of El Alto, Brian turns into a gas station to fill up, our first time in Bolivia. We park and shut off the bikes as the attendant walks over to help us. I ask her to fill up both bikes and start to dig for money to pay. She hesitates and walks over to talk to someone in a small office. She returns a couple of minutes later to tell me that they cannot sell us fuel.

Having not yet fully learned the new version of Spanish used in Bolivia, I struggle to understand why. She explains the fuel will cost me three times the "local" price because we have international license plates and that the government requires forms to be completed for us to purchase fuel. She thinks this will put me off, but it doesn't. I ask her to proceed, but it really boils down to a lot of work that she isn't willing to do.

She hesitates and just stands there. I instruct her again to fill up both bikes and bring me the paperwork. This feels like a game of chicken. She waits for me to give up and go, but instead I let my hair out of its messy ponytail, loosen my jacket and tinker with my cell phone. I'm not going anywhere until I get fuel, and she knows it. It's an off-the-beaten-path station and there are no other clients at the moment, so she doesn't really have any excuse not to help us. Finally, she does, begrudgingly.

Her triplicate-copy form, with old school carbon inserts, requires my passport number and signature. I complete it and pay, and we leave. Little do I know that this will be the easiest it ever gets for me to buy fuel in this country.

Our friend, Andrew's, recommendation for the campground turns out to be fantastic. This small oasis, perched on the edge of Jupapina on the precipice of a canyon, has a lovely open air kitchen, immaculate and modern shower house, and a relaxing palapa overlooking the gorge. Space for tents is relegated to a grassy terrace just below the rest of the camp. The view of the rough red canyon walls and jagged peak, with its rooster comb profile, is spectacular.

La Paz is one of the few cities I've been most excited to see, mostly because of the incredible descriptions of its sheer overwhelming-ness provided by other travelers. Not only is this enormous bowl of land filled with more than two million people, a chaotic assemblage of hasty constructions and winding terraced dead-end alleys, it's brimming with the stew of mixed cultures of worldwide travelers and colorful Bolivianos. Add to that, its altiplano location above the entrance to the infamous Road of Death, and I'm filled with nervous excitement.

Up to this point, I've tried to control my fear of both perceived degrees of difficulty of various roads (ie. grade, length, corners, switchbacks, etc.), and of the surface material of said roads. But gravel, of course, has taken over as my Chief Nemesis since my accident.

The Death Road is much talked about, and is a "must do" for anyone travelling through La Paz. It's been on my top ten list since leaving home, right up there with Machu Picchu and Copper Canyon, but now that I'm here, I'm having second thoughts. I'm not sure I'm a skilled enough rider for the road, and I certainly don't want to find out in person that I'm not. I stew in my own private first-world-problem pool of fear and anxiety. I replay the internal dialogue I had with myself before boarding a single-engine plane, piloted by a pimply teen to traverse the Southern Alps of New Zealand to Milford Sound. I'd rather die doing this than from choking on a microwaved hot dog late at night, all alone in an apartment back in South Dakota.

Andrew's already ridden the road and says, from the perspective of a well-traveled rider, that it's not as impressive as he thought it would be. He reports that since the road was closed to traffic a year ago, and replaced with a new concrete highway on the other side of the gorge, it's fairly safe and quiet. There are even guardrails now on the most exposed cliff edges.

For the first few days we catch up with friends and settle into a comfortable stay at camp. The full Swiss contingent, Markus and Karin, and Michael and Simone, are camping at a Swiss hostel just up the road, and rave about finally getting a decent fondue. Californian friends, Toby and Chloe, and their sweet dog, Tia, arrive at our campground and settle in too.

I walk into the village to visit the butcher, produce market and grocery in order to make the most of the campground's kitchen, a luxury after months of cooking on a backpacker stove. We hatch plans for a bbq one night to celebrate life, something we do regularly when we hang out with other overlanders. It takes me thirty-nine minutes to hard boil eggs at this extreme altitude, requiring me to keep refilling the pot so it doesn't boil dry. But my American-style potato salad is worth the trouble.

With a nervous stomach, I follow Andrew and Brian out one morning, bound for the Road of Death, all the while hoping it won't be the cause of mine. It's a gorgeous day. Andrew leads us through the Valley of the Moon, and into the heart of La Paz. He winds his way through the main thoroughfares, between high-rises and up steep side streets, working his way past the maze of the city to the eastern edge where we will exit toward the Yungas Road.

As we climb, stifling traffic and nearly vertical narrow streets give way to a wide, open stretch of highway and eventually dissolve into mountain slopes covered with tufts of grass. The road carries us past power line towers, graffiti-covered rock walls, and a few small reservoirs. The air cools as we climb, enough to chill me. We pass a couple of vans parked at the crest of the ridge and watch them unload two dozen mountains bikes and riders so they can begin a long descent to the village of Coroico below, via the Road of Death.

The highway crests the climb through a saddle in the ridge between mountains at La Cumbre Pass and begins its sweeping descent to the North Yungas below. We round a few bends, emerging into the highest part of the valley, and are offered a jaw-dropping view from the side of the highway. Our route begins here at 15,260 feet and will descend more than 11,000 feet over the next 32 miles to 3,900 feet at the village of Coroico on the other end. The cold I'm feeling won't last long when I ride from snow-edged roads on top to steamy jungle trails below.

The sheer size of the landscape here is incredible. Jagged charcoal-colored mountains pierce the soft clouds overhead, and then fall sharply to drop out of sight in the mist below. The road laces a loosely switch-backed path through the valley below, while clinging to the mountainside, for ten miles. Andrew leads the way.

Several miles ahead we stop at a roadblock and confirm for officials that we are not carrying drugs. We get stopped again a few miles further ahead at a similar checkpoint, and are told we need to purchase permits to descend the road for $3 USD each. None of us has recovered sufficiently from the cold of the snow-fringed pass yet, so we decide to duck into one of the small shacks on the side of the road for a hot drink.

After a short break, we carry on down the highway until Andrew recognizes the turnoff and pulls off the tarmac onto an unmarked dirt road. We wind along for a few minutes and stop to ooh and aah over the long brown slash that the road cuts in a continuous descent along the length of the distant dark green ridgeline. The road is wide and comfortable here, and isn't what I expected from "the world's most dangerous road". We make a couple more turns and finally see a sign, confirming that we are indeed on the Camino de la Muerte.

We've already gone from barren mountain pass above, to a lower altitude where plants sprang up over the last half dozen miles. Not far past the entrance sign, the road shrinks to a single narrow lane, turns sharply east and gets down to business. The Earth falls away below my left hand as I round the bend and ride onto a thin ledge suspended over a deep chasm below.

Although I'm sure the presence of a westbound bus in my eastbound path would change my perspective, at the moment I'm simply in awe of the view. I feel relatively safe on the road with the entire width of the single-lane road to myself. That is, if you don't count the occasional swarm of mountain bikers we encounter.

I'm amazed how quickly everything changed in just an hour. It must be 30-40F degrees warmer here, and we've already shed more than 5000 feet of altitude. Sun shines across the valley onto our narrow ledge, drying the exposed parts of road from dirt to dust. But in the shadowy corners, the road is slick from the spring water constantly running off the wall above the road. Where water cascades, vines and plants have grown unchecked, covering everything.

There are no switchbacks, we simply descend in a long line, rounding bends at the contours of the ridgeline. At outside corners, we park our bikes and walk back to get better perspective for dramatic photos. The edge really does drop straight into the abyss.

The further we carry on and descend, the warmer and drier the day becomes. My nerves disappeared miles back, and I'm thoroughly enjoying the ride down, while careful not to get complacent.

At the bottom, we turn onto a cobblestoned road which climbs up to the village of Coroico. We stop for lunch and put our stickers on a window of the café. The road out descends in a cloud of fesh fesh as we aim for the new highway for our return to La Paz.

I'm lost in daydreams and vistas on the climb up from the jungle floor to the high pass above. I catch glimpses of the Death Road as our route mirrors its line on the opposite side of the valley. Brian and Andrew ride ahead and are stopped at the overlook on top as I arrive. When I pull in, Brian rides out the other end, leaving Andrew to fill me in. It's Friday afternoon and Brian wants to pick up his policy at the insurance agency before they close for the weekend, so he's decided to blast ahead. We will meet him at the agency.

Andrew leads me back to La Paz and down steep hills to the center of downtown which are already choking with Friday evening traffic. We turn onto the street where Brian's bike should be, but find he's already gone, so we continue up a steep one-way street to round the block and turn for home. As Andrew reaches the end of the block and turns around the corner, my bike sputters and stalls. It's all I can do to hold it upright on the harsh grade.

I try to restart Betty, but she's not having it. I shouldn't be out of fuel, but maybe my tank is low enough to starve my bike at this steep angle. I reach down and turn the petcock onto reserve. She finally fires up. Cars pile up and honk behind me before I finally get moving again. I reach the top of the hill and turn left onto the level terrace expecting to see Andrew. But he isn't here.

I know this general area, having walked through the neighborhood in search of the insurance agency a few days before, and take the next left, aiming for the main boulevard below. Still no Andrew. While I feel safe, I'm worried about finding my way through the meandering streets of this enormous city and out to our camp fifteen miles away, especially with no help and no map. Brian has my GPS.

I pull over and turn on my cell phone, locate Pocket Earth, and put my phone in the mountain bike bracket on my handlebars. It isn't perfect, but it will do. It's hard to navigate by the small screen as I ride through the dark city streets aiming for Jupapina, but I move in the general direction and plan to dial in my route after I get out of the downtown chaos. I make steady progress until my bike sputters and dies once more, luckily, across the street from a gas station.

Pushing my bike in, I ask the attendant to fill it up, but get the usual response about not being able to sell to foreigners. A nearby police officer eavesdrops as I explain that I have no choice. My bike is out of fuel and I can't leave until I get some. But it's like talking to a brick wall and the attendant does nothing. I can't decide whether to scream or cry.

Finally, the officer walks over and instructs the young man to give me enough fuel to get me where I need to go, which the attendant deems is two liters. Hours after dark, and hours after I last saw Brian, I roll into camp, tired and pissed off at Bolivia's fuel policy. Brian's here, but Andrew's still out looking for me.

After arguing with a station attendant in Jupapina and getting asked to leave, we find fuel at another place up the road. I realize this isn't personal, but it's frustrating that it's so difficult to buy gasoline here. We've heard similar stories from other riders, but I think it's worse for us because we have two bikes to fill, meaning twice the paperwork which is even less appealing to gas station workers. I don't know if it's the combination of homesickness and altitude, or if it really is the difficulty in buying fuel, but I'm getting fed up with things being this hard.

We ride south to Oruro and spend the night, only to find the highway blocked by a protest in the morning. We spend an hour following locals through back alleys and over a pedestrian bridge to try and get around them, but find that there are layers of blockades and we have yet another in front of us.

Finding myself out of patience, but thankfully not manners, I park and walk over to a man at the front of the protest, a large crowd blocks the road. I say that I have "much respect" for their cause, but wonder if we may be allowed to go around because we are simply travelers trying to continue on our journey. He ponders for a moment, then directs the others to help move the large rocks and tires they use as a blockade. I thank him and wish them well. I walk back to my bike and carry on toward Uyuni.

We stop in Challapata for water and a bite and then head south on the highway, only to watch it dissolve into a sandy construction project a few miles south of town. I'm slow and frustrated. Brian gives up on it and suggests it might be easier for me to go back to Challapata and take another road to Uyuni, via Potosi, so we do.

As much as I wanted to meander through the country, I'm ready to move on to another. Any other. This one is too much work. I know I'm being a baby, but I don't care. I'm tired, frustrated and getting depressed, and I have no idea what, if anything, will make me feel better. We've come so far, but still have so far to go. I don't feel like I have the energy for the road I have left in front of me.

Brian's pissed at my slow pace, and I'm pissed at him for any number of reasons, or no reason at all. Right or wrong, I associate my mood with the country I'm in, and want to change both as soon as possible, with or without Brian.

My crisis thinking slows a little as I start to enjoy the beautiful ride to Potosi, through more John Wayne scenery. Enormous high plateaus and red canyons soften my mood. Wild herds of llama graze in clusters spread out over miles of prairie.

We make a turn at Ventilla and stop for a short break, shutting off our bikes and stretching our legs. I reach into my tank bag for a banana, my normal stash for quick energy. Between two mud and tin houses, a Bolivian woman paces back and forth comforting her teething little boy on her hip. She's dressed in traditional clothing – skirt, loafers and woolen derby. He's dressed in only a thin shirt and diaper at 12,000 feet. I catch her watching me, wave to her and am surprised when she waves back. I'd done it, more or less, to distract the little one from his crying, and find that it worked.

On a whim, I hold up the banana and wave it to the little boy to see if he would like to have it. He and his mother exchange a glance, and she starts toward me. I smile and hand it to her. She passes it to her little one, who opens it with small practiced hands. That's all it takes for me to fall in love with Bolivia again.

Opting for the chance to enjoy a unique environment up close, we camp one night on the Salar de Uyuni. Brian has to use a punch to drill tent holes into the salty crust to anchor the tent. It's a good thing he does, since a chilly wind kicks in as the sun sets.

We debated about attempting the Laguna Route from Uyuni into northern Chile, but don't have the fuel range or water carrying capacity for the rugged crossing on our own. The Swiss offered us a chance to tag along, but we decided to go west instead.

The following morning, we rise early to take a few of the unique perspective photos you can create on the salar, but the sun isn't high enough so we decide to pack up and get moving. Although we had planned to go back to Uyuni for fuel and water, we decide to make our way across the salt plain, finding that it makes for better riding than the sand roads in this part of the country.

We haven't planned this at all, and don't have much fuel or water. We don't have any information on the border crossing or cash, and don't know if there will be a bank along the way. We're headed for a border totally unprepared, and don't know if there are any services there. So much for our experience serving us well. You'd think we'd be better at this by now.

From our camp on the salt flat near the Salt Hotel and Dakar sign, we ride west across the salar, finding dark, well-worn tracks in its surface. It's nearly fifty miles to the other side where we climb up onto a dirt pier near Tanil Vinto and adjust to the rutted, sandy washboard of road.

We spend a long day bouncing and rattling along on roads that have been pounded to bits by the salt mine trucks. It's agonizing and tiresome. But the flat surface of the salt flat has given way to rolling sandy hills and widely spaced rows of volcanoes in the distance, making the view more interesting. We've crossed into a desert.

We stop in tiny San Juan for water, but find all the tiendas abandoned for the lunch hour, so carry on without it, stupidly ignoring our hard-earned knowledge and going against my instincts. I silently begrudge Brian for his rush to continue, even though I'm equally to blame.

The road ahead is more of a series of sandy tracks through the flats, interspersed with bits of gravel road. Since we left the highway at Uyuni, there really hasn't been much more than a gray path left by previous traffic for us to follow. But it's easy enough to see.

I drop my bike in the sand a couple of times until we finally reach a surface of packed flat trails that crosses between two volcanoes. They look new, as though recently burst through the Earth's crust, pushing up colorful layers of sand and silt in the process which trickle like sand-art down their shoulders. Two dozen pink flamingoes stand in a shallow lake near one.

Today has had more cross-country riding than I'd expected, and we've ticked off more than sixty miles on trails since bouncing up out of the salt flat. We've encountered occasional Landcruisers filled with tourists, out for a joy ride, reminding me that as deserted as a place seems, it's usually only momentary.

Just before 6:00pm I finally spot a cloud of dust from a passing truck in the distance, across an enormous sandy valley, indicating the main highway which will take us to Avaroa and the border. I hope it's still open.

20 CHILE

...play with the light of the Universe.

-Pablo Neruda

We made it in the nick of time. Never have I been so happy to arrive at a backwater border town. The officers in Avaroa were pleasant as they processed us out of Bolivia and opened the gate for us to ride ahead to Ollague, a couple of miles up the road through no man's land.

A large dog sleeps on the floor of the Aduana office as I walk up to a closed window to request entry. An officer slides it back, but doesn't make eye contact with me, watching a soccer game on a small TV instead, while I explain why I'm bothering him.

A few minutes' work and a quick search of our panniers for fruit and meat is all it takes for us to enter Chile and ride freely into the small railroad depot town to find a place to stay. We land in a comfortable room at an unmarked inn and arrive just in time for dinner and a cold beer. They'll accept our U.S. dollars and even sell us fuel from canisters since there isn't a gas station in town. I feel like we've hit the lottery.

We have only one more country to cross into before Ushuaia, but over 3000 miles left go. We're just halfway down the continent.

The road from Ollague to Calama is beautiful, running through a wide red valley between multi-colored volcanoes. We ride into the Atacama Desert to meet friends who chose the Laguna route from Uyuni. Brian spends a day using precious water in San Pedro to scrub the corrosive layer of Uyuni salt from our bikes.

From there we ride to the coast at Antofagasta and past the Mano del Desierto as we cross the giant desert plains of windswept Chile. We cross south of the Tropic of Capricorn where I nearly pass up a photo because I'm too frustrated with the gusty wind to bother. It's good practice for Patagonia, where Brian and others have said the wind is worse than anywhere else on earth. I don't look forward to it.

Brian appreciates landmarks more than I do, collecting the northernmost this, or the southernmost that, and the highest or lowest whatevers. I vaguely remember crossing the Tropic of Cancer, but definitely remember crossing the Equator.

Every so often we see shrines along the highway, some surrounded with mountains of full bottles of water, reflecting the bright sun. Others offer shaded picnic tables, like rest areas, for travelers to use. I ask a friend from Santiago who says a Chileno woman died of thirst in this desert and these are gifts offered in her memory.

Our road leads us back to the coast, and a night in Taltal where we splurge for a room. Ten adorable puppies are living under an abandoned car in the back yard, each with very different coloring and fur texture. I spot their mother sunning herself in an empty lot surrounded by three males who each match a few of the pups.

Highway 5 teases me with stretches of coastline before ducking inland again. I spend days admiring the varied terrain of this whisper-thin, but oh-so-long country. Crazy to think that Chile is twice as long as the United States. Unlike our normal 150-200 mile days, in this fairly barren place we cover 1000 miles in three days, straight south.

We take a detour to Vicuña to sample fresh pisco at a distillery and go stargazing for a night. Chileno skies are among the clearest in the world because of the lack of light pollution and the consistently clear weather. Countries from all over the world come here to build giant research telescopes. There are half a dozen observatories within a twenty mile radius of the village, some of which offer tours, so I sign us up for the only night we are in town.

Ever since I was a little girl, I've been interested in the night sky and all its occupants. I remember my mother showing me the big dipper, which she called "the plough", and me always struggling to find its little sibling. In the summers of my youth, my late grandfather's brother, brother-in-law and an old cowboy friend took their grandkids and various cousins (including me) on trailrides each summer. All day we would ride horses in the forest, retracing some of the steps of the Custer Expedition, and at night we would sit around a campfire telling ghost stories, or wander off into the dark to gaze up at the immense Milky Way. My great uncle, Oakley, taught me the name of the giant "W", Cassiopeia and pointed out the Seven Sisters.

After a bumpy shuttle ride up a dusty red dirt road at dusk, we are deposited in a parking lot between two school buses. Cerro Mamalluca is operated by the town, and is open to the public, much of which appears to be here tonight.

Approximately fifteen of us gather at the appointed meeting place and are guided through the grounds over the course of two hours. Our guide narrates as he tracks down various targets and then allows us each a turn to look through the lens, which opens an entirely new world to me. The up close view of the surface of the moon is breathtaking, a marbled mixture of pastel gray and ghostly white terrain. For the first time in my life I see the live version of the Sea of Tranquility.

Luis shows us Mars and the Orion Nebula. He shows us a twin star, which looks like the headlights of a car driving through the universe. He shows us the Oort cloud, something I've never really paid attention to before, but now wonder how I could have missed.

Our guide says that over the centuries many constellations have gone through various names, each given by a different civilization. Orion was known as a deer in ancient Sanskrit and as a bison to the Lakota. In passing, Luis mentions the Butterfly Cluster. I make a mental note to look it up.

Butterflies seem to be the theme of my trip and are popping up, bother literally and figuratively nearly every day. Each one reminds me of my mother. While he tells us stories about red dwarf stars, black holes and nebula, I feel the cliché smallness and fleetingness of my life. It's a reminder that I'm very lucky to experience this journey, and to not take a single moment for granted.

While for many years it hurt to think of my mother, now thinking of her always brings me joy. I imagine her with me on this trip, soaking up every happy moment right alongside me. Maybe she's the butterfly, having morphed into another form of herself. Or maybe we are both butterflies, in different stages of our beings. During my online late-night tinkering after the visit to the observatory, I stumble across a quote from Rabindranath Tagore – "The butterfly counts not months but moments, and has time enough." The words bring me peace. I'm grateful for each of the moments I shared with her.

The further south we ride, the greener the land gets. First come the desert-fringe oases of croplands and vineyards. Then come trees and grasslands, followed by an explosion of farms, fields, and orchards once we start to see more rivers. This part of Chile is the fruit and wine region of the nation.

We stop for fuel one day along the Pan-American Highway at a Copec station, one of the nationally known brands, and carry on south. About half an hour from the station we reach a long stretch of highway with a slightly uphill grade stretching out before me. I roll slightly onto my throttle to maintain my speed in the climb and find my bike stutters and starts. I roll off it and think for a moment and try again, but it does it again. Brian, with his fancy fuel-injected bike, pulls away from me up ahead.

I maintain as much speed as I can until I top the low rise and slowly descend onto the next wide stretch of highway. My bike seems to run okay except when I'm trying to climb even the slightest grade. Luckily, along the coast there isn't much altitude change on the highway. I'm guessing it's bad fuel, but will defer to Brian's expertise.

In Valparaiso, I'm enamored with the spectacular street art that decorates nearly every building, fence and wall. Graffiti has been taken to a masterful level in this lovely rundown seaport. We spend a nice Thanksgiving with Sam and Erica enjoying sushi before riding the vertical streetcars and strolling neighborhoods.

On a whim I price tickets to Easter Island one morning before we depart for Santiago. Shockingly, it's only $550 each, so I quickly book two tickets for the next week as a Christmas surprise for Brian. I know he wouldn't splurge like that for himself, but I also know how much he wants to go there.

Brian rides ahead of me, pedaling quickly up the grassy hill and out of view. I take my sweet time, enjoying the warm sea air and the view of waves lashing the coast. Wild horses grazing just off the path ignore me, as I coast by, conserving energy for the climb ahead.

Our no-frills week on Easter Island has been better than I'd hoped. I had no idea this place was so beautiful. Campsites are cheaper than they are in many places on the mainland, and bringing food from Santiago to cook in the campsite kitchen has saved us money. There've been a few things worth splurging for, like fresh passion fruit juice and renting mountain bikes today to ride along the coast. We splurged on a rental car the day before to loop the island. Seeing the giant Moai heads backlit by a lavender and lemon yellow sunrise at Aho Tongariki was one of the most breath-taking things I've ever seen.

I reach the hill and lose most of my momentum in an instant, not having achieved enough speed to reach the top. A stray dog pops up out of the grass, scaring me momentarily, and then trots happily along beside me up the trail while I get off and walk my bike up the steepest part. Brian's stopped not far ahead at a sign and waits for me to catch up.

We've reached the first cave, a black lava tube formed when the island was freshly born and cooling, and go inside to explore. It's not a large one, but it's dark and I'm glad to have my flashlight and new guard dog for company. What a perfect place for pirates to hide their loot, which was the cave's original use, especially since this is one of the most remote places in the world.

Ten minutes more pedaling brings us to what we've really come for, the banana caves. Our companion leads the way down carved lava steps and into the cavern. Collapsed parts of the roof serve as skylights and catch basins, offering just enough sun and water for the banana trees growing inside the cave. I wander into various rooms of the lava channel and enjoy the shade before we proceed to the next Moai platform at Ahu Akivi. We stop at the quarry at Puna Pau and then head back to camp. By the end of the day my camera must be exhausted, but surprisingly, I'm not.

Brian and I walk into Hanga Roa for dinner at a nice restaurant overlooking the ocean. It's our last night on the island, so we treat ourselves to fresh fish and a bottle of wine. Afterwards, we walk to Ahu Tahai, a platform of five Moai just north of the village, perched on a cliff above the sea. It's where we saw our first giant head statues, backlit by an incredible sunset. We're hoping to catch it one more time before we fly back to the mainland tomorrow.

A crowd gathers on the grassy hillside, as it does every night, and stray dogs wander aimlessly between couples collecting debris from impromptu picnics and pats from willing tourists. We sit on flat rocks and enjoy the view having arrived just in time to admire the cloud-speckled dusky heavens. Within fifteen minutes the sun sinks the last finger-width of sky to the horizon and disappears under the water, leaving a bright orange glow in its wake, followed quickly by a darkening evening.

As per usual after my half of a bottle of wine, nature calls to me. I pick up the pace on Brian's leisurely stroll back toward the village, needing to find a restroom or a tall shrub. Being a motorcyclist this long has helped me to lower my standards.

Brian stops and starts, dragging behind me. I assume it's for one more photo and wait for a moment before starting to walk again. But he grabs my hand, bringing me to a stop and turning me to face him.

A man of few words, Brian still is never one to hesitate if he has something to stay. But he just stares at me for a moment. He looks pale. I ask, "What's wrong, babe?"

"Nothing's wrong," he replies, still staring.

Now I'm getting nervous. Something's up. My heart races and my head starts spinning.

"It's only that I was thinking," he continues, but then pauses, "Will you marry me?"

"Really?" I ask, having been completely caught off guard. "Yes, of course."

I must be living some women's fantasy. I know I'm living mine.

In Santiago, we spend a couple of weeks, one before and one after our stint on Easter Island, exploring the grand city and spending time with friends Roberto and Daniela who I met on the side of an interstate when they traveled by motorcycle from Chile to the United States. They're incredibly kind to put us up, help us with the bike, and store them while we're away.

Roberto guides us to the top of El Cerro in central Santiago to enjoy the view of the very metropolitan and modern city, and treats us to mote con huesillos, a type of softened grain served with peaches and juice. Daniela accompanies us on a walking tour of the city which visits the incredible farmers' markets and enormous city cemetery. We enjoy our time with the immensely.

Nearly every day for a week Brian works on the motorcycles in Roberto's yard, getting them prepped for the hard road ahead. Between them, the bikes need new tires, sprockets, chains, spark plugs, brake pads and filters, as well as fuel tank cleanings after the bad batch of gas from a station north of Valparaiso. We're intentionally buying parts and tires while here in Chile. Chile is a much easier place to get parts, rather than Argentina where strict customs regulations and taxes make things cost two to three times as much.

Markus and Karin have recently discovered this problem. They rode south from Bolivia into Argentina and haven't had access to Chile's cheaper and more plentiful motorcycle shops. We're headed over the mountains to Mendoza soon so they ask us to bring along some parts for one of their bikes. Toby and Chloe need a filter for their truck too. I've become a parts mule, motivated by promises of steak dinners and Malbec.

Roberto accompanies us on his bike us as far as the northern outskirts of Santiago where we stop to say our goodbyes before carrying on to Uspallata Pass and the border into Argentina. There's a world of difference between the Andean mountain roads of rural Peru and the concrete highway we ride today with its smooth surface, wide shoulders and modern illuminated tunnels. It takes a full day to ride from Santiago to Mendoza even though it's only 120 miles as a bird flies, but more than double that on twisting roads.

We cross out of the Chileno border and ride into the widest no man's land yet, roughly eight miles of the barren, rocky spine of the Andes.

21 ARGENTINA (AND CHILE)

The forest, the sky itself, is like an explosion of a thousand colors…
-Rafael Obligado

After somehow missing the Argentinian border offices, we double back and get our paperwork to make it legal. Towering just to the north of the road is the highest peak in South America at 21,500 feet, the snow-capped giant, Aconcagua, which is brilliantly lit by the sun as we ride by.

One of my habits when entering a new country is to pay attention to road signs, and try to decipher them. They differ greatly between countries, even though they're all in Spanish. A bright blue sign catches my eye not more than a mile into Argentina. It takes me a moment to understand its meaning, and it causes me to bristle. An outline of two large ragged-edged islands and the Argentinian name, Las Malvinas, is what caught my eye. The sign says, "The Malvinas (aka Falkland Islands) are, and always will be, Argentina". I hope no one gives us a hard time because Brian is from England.

Toby and Chloe have landed at a nice campground on the outskirts of Mendoza, and are thoroughly happy, fresh from their route through northern Argentina. It's wonderful to see them, and we settle into a decadent couple of weeks enjoying daily rituals of asado (grilled meat) with a couple of large bottles of beer and a couple of bottles of wine at our campsite.

Months before reaching Argentina I read online about two shortages that I needed to consider, one personal and one business. There was a lot of chatter on a Pan-American Traveler page on Facebook about the shortage of food and supplies in Argentinian grocery stores, including, according to panicked women, tampons. The dramatic chatter of female travelers amuses me, but such a shortage is a reality. Thank goodness for Diva Cups.

The other had to do with money. Similar to the situation in Venezuela, a black market exists for currency in Argentina. The best way to take advantage of it is to have U.S. dollars, preferably in big bills, to trade for a better rate for "blue" pesos than the standard peso exchange rates. Thankfully, we knew this months ago and were able to get American money from ATMs in Bolivia and stock up in advance. Toby has already been to the sketchy money-exchange neighborhood in Mendoza and knows the ropes, so he takes us under his wing. He drives a hard bargain and isn't afraid to shop around, helping Brian and I make a good deal.

We've been debating about when and where to ship the bikes from after Ushuaia. There's a few different options, but nothing stands out so far. A lot of riders opt for Buenos Aires, and since we're heading that way, it seems like a good choice.

At this pace, we should be in Ushuaia within a month, which I find both exciting and scary. As much as homesickness had been stalking me, it's dissipating, and I'm not sure I'm ready to go back to reality. Especially since that will mean a full-time job and bigger expenses. Perhaps as a way to prolong the end, we start thinking about riding further north than Buenos Aires, and make plans to aim for Florianopolis in southern Brazil. That means another visa for me, my third of the trip, while Brian hasn't needed any.

We take a taxi to the Brazilian Consulate one morning in hopes of filing for my visa before the Christmas holiday. The cab driver makes polite conversation, asking where we're from. Without thinking, I reply that I'm from the United States and that Brian is from England. The man clams up instantly and glares at Brian through the rearview mirror, obviously holding a grudge for the Falklands War. It's uncomfortable all the rest of the way.

At the consulate, a stroke of luck offers me the chance to get my visa the same day, instead of having the normal 7-day wait. The man in charge of the office is leaving for Christmas at the end of the day, but will expedite my application if I can complete everything by lunchtime. Brian and I sprint around the city in search of places that offer passport photos and internet access to complete the online application, and then to the bank where I need to pay the visa fee. It's a hurried scramble, but worth it.

Not having spoiled ourselves enough with our carnivorous and alcohol-laced eating habits, our foursome splurges at Christmas for a wine tour of three local vineyards complete with a three-course gourmet lunch and samples of wines. Dozens of vineyards bask in the sun on the flat terrain surrounding Mendoza. All the while, the snowy Andes linger in the west, providing an indescribable backdrop to everything.

Just before the end of December, we hit the road again, pushing southward to Siete Lagos where we meet up with our friend, Pete, to celebrate New Year's. My first taste of Ruta 40 is better than expected, because most of the 700 miles we ride in this two or three day stretch is paved. The bad parts are further south, where the insane wind will make them even more miserable and dangerous.

The alpine lake region around Junin de los Andes and Villa la Angostura is lovely. Influences brought by refugees from war-torn Germany in the 1930s show in everything from architecture to restaurant menus. Pete treats Brian and I to a parrilla dinner for our engagement, and we ring in the new year with Argentina's famous outdoor asado and lovely red wine, and a new friend at his hostel.

After a couple of days, we ride north, retracing our route to Junin, and cross the Andes, back into Chile, near the volcano, Lanin. We bypass touristy Villarrica and go on to Coñaripe and camp across the road from Calafquén Lake.

A luxury that I'm not afforded in South Dakota, but that much of the world enjoys, is an abundance of hot springs and the pools built to take advantage of them. Just a short hitchhike from our camp, we take a day to enjoy this rare treat at the base of the goliath volcano, Villarrica, and visit a thermal spa with twenty-one pools built above a hot spring, my new idea of heaven.

We stop for a night in Valdivia and walk along the brackish riverfront to watch enormous sealions begging at the fish market. There's a German beer plant here, which I assume means the influx of Germans in the last century didn't stop at Argentina.

We ride on to Osorno where Brian shops around town for one last set of tires on my bike before the Carretera Austral and the final push to Ushuaia. For a small town, it has a surprisingly large number of shops that carry motorcycle parts. But the few we stop don't have much on hand in the way of tires. The Dakar Race is on up north and the entire continent's tires are being funneled there to supply the event. At one shop I am reminded of the subtle differences between the various versions of Spanish I have encountered. When I ask for a llanta, which in some places has meant tire, the clerk shows us photos of actual motorcycle rims, thinking we want to order one for my bike. When I explain that we want the outside part of the wheel, she teaches me the new word I need to use around here, pneumatico.

Everything south of us is considered Patagonia, home of the wild wind, both in Chile and Argentina. Although the wind hasn't picked up for us on this side of the Andes, not far east of us on the other side of the mountains, winds are already challenging some of our friends.

At Puerto Varas we walk along the lake and gaze at the giant volcano Osorno across the water, and enjoy tacos from a food truck.

I window shop for tents in this backpacker town, knowing that ours might not have enough life left in it to survive Patagonia. The zippers have been failing for a month and could quit altogether any day now.

We take a ferry from Puerto Montt to the island of Chiloe and camp for a couple of days near Ancud. We ride out to a beach on the western shore and take a Zodiac to three small islands to see penguins, a trip which finishes off my camera, my fourth of the trip, with a deluge of rain.

Chiloe is gorgeous, if a little rain-soaked, oozing with fishing village charm. Brightly painted houses nestled along the shore defy the gray weather. We warm up with curanto, a meat and fish stew, in a café before riding to the far end of the island to find the marker at the end of the Pan-Am Highway. At Castro, we catch a ferry to Chaiten where we set up our tent in the backyard of a small house for the night. Tomorrow we'll set off on the Carretera Austral, one of the most remote roads in the world.

The Carretera Austral, which means southern highway, was started in the 1970s under Pinochet. The nearly 800-mile-long road was built to connect the remote villages of southern Chile with the rest of the country. They were previously only accessed by boat. By now, we are nearly as far south as Seattle is north from the equator, which might explain the similarly drizzly weather. It feels like the coastal mountain ranges and jet streams are conspiring to drown us.

There are more villages than I expected along this road, and lots more people. I'm amazed at the steady stream of cyclists, motorcyclists, hikers, backpackers and hitchhikers coming down the road. Their presence might have something to do with the shortage of fresh food in the handful of stores we find. It's easy enough to find pasta and canned tomato sauce in this part of the world, but produce bins are reduced to a handful of limp carrots and a few small onions. I'm glad I thought to buy things on Chiloe before we boarded the ferry. We will at least have some veggies for the first couple of days.

We ride south from Chaiten, alongside Corcovado National Park, through thick rainforest, past fjords and glaciers, which drain into countless streams and rivers. We camp at Puyuhuapi and again at a turnoff to Queulat National Park where we spend a day hiking to see the stunning hanging glacier. Even from the other side of the small lake, I'm mesmerized by the bright blue ice of the glacier and the slender waterfalls created by its melt.

Back at camp we meet another rider, Erin, who recently continued her journey to Ushuaia after having taken a year off while her bike sat in Peru. She started her journey with her boyfriend, but they split up along the way. She's come back to finish the trip on her own. I'm impressed.

The landscape is stunning. The gravel highway snakes its way south over low hills, across rivers and along the coast lacing together a handful of communities. Even though we entered Patagonia hundreds of miles north of here, the close nestling of the road against the coastal mountains seems to protect us from wind, if there is any.

At Coyhaique, I find a larger grocery store and make good use of it before we make our way to Rio Tranquilo on the shores of Lago General Carrera, an enormous turquoise alpine lake famous for its shoreline caves. On the way, we pass the jagged black mountaintop rock formation of Cerro Castillo and encounter spectacular views at every turn.

After riding over rolling hills across a stretch of grassland meadow, the road returns to the shelter of the trees. At the last of the open stretch, we pass a dozen or more cyclists pedaling along the shoulder of the road, at which point Brian pulls over. Mr. Observant spotted our friend Jim from Minnesota again.

We camp together at Rio Tranquilo for the night and are only mildly surprised when Markus and Karin show up too. This is what happens when there is only one road south through a country. Another motorcycle couple arrives, Thomas and Tina from Germany.

The group of us enjoys our newfound cyclist brethren the

following day at shared meals and a short visit to the rodeo going on in Rio Tranquilo. Brian and I, and Markus and Karin take a boat to tour the famous marble caves on the western edge of the lake, and are spellbound by the cathedral like domes worn into the marble mountain by the turquoise waters of the lake. The four of us head for Cochrane and plan to camp together for a day or two. On the way, Brian spots Sam and Erica's camper on the edge of the Rio Baker so we pull over for a brief hello. I'm not surprised by so many people we know taking this road, but I am surprised that we're keeping the same pace.

From Cochrane, I take a day-tour to Caleta Tortel, a lovely seaside village whose buildings are strung together by a series of long wooden boardwalks. It's enchanting. When I get back, I find that Michael and Simone have arrived in their Defender. We are still 1000 miles from Ushuaia.

Brian and I choose to ride along the stunning peak-fringed southern shore of the great turquoise lake, Lago General Carrera, on our way to Chile Chico and the border to Argentina. The Swiss opt for the equally stunning Paso Roballos route.

The rough road along the lake provides incredible views and traverses the Andes. It's a gorgeous long day. At the border between Chile Chico and Perito Moreno I find I've forgotten to use some of the food I had in a pannier, and have to throw it out. It makes me sick to think of tossing two lovely avocados, crisp apples and some fresh cheese, so I ask a border guard if she can take them home rather than letting them go to waste. She smiles and says she will.

We rejoin Ruta 40, this time on long gravel sections fully exposed to the strong crosswinds. I'm grateful for Brian's knowledge of this part of the journey, as he makes sure to stop at Bajo Caracoles for fuel, something that, if missed, causes other riders to run out of fuel on this long, empty stretch of road.

At Gobernador Gregores, we fuel up just before the station announces they've run out. As I go inside to pay, I see a familiar face, Juan from Mexico, a fellow Stahlratte passenger. We haven't seen each other since Colombia. As we share our last six months' travel experiences, Michael and Simone arrive along with Sam and Erica. This is getting almost ridiculous. It feels like a private party road trip nearly every day.

We camp and grill together in the municipal park before going our separate ways the next morning. Brian and I ride to Puerto San Julian where the afternoon winds force us to take shelter in a cabin by mid-afternoon.

The morning after, we get an early start, encouraged by a blog I read the night before explaining how the Patagonian wind works. It's largely influenced by the warming of the earth created by the sun each day. Gentle morning breezes continue growing throughout the day until reaching their peak in late afternoon. Winds usually die off late in the evening, around 7:00pm this time of year.

After only three days of riding in strong winds, I install an app on my phone which forecasts wind speeds for the next few days so I can prepare myself for how bad each day will be. At least it generally comes from the same direction all day, and other than having to adjust for the change in the direction of the road riding into it, I get used to the angle of lean I have to use to stay upright against the crosswind.

My helmet and glasses push hard against the left-side of my face as we ride south. My tires wear down twice as fast on the left half of my tire as I lean roughly 20 degrees into the wind. My neck and back hurt from constant battering and having to ride at the awkward angles in compensation for the wind.

We reach Rio Gallegos and spend the night in a hotel, sure that our tent wouldn't survive the current gale. The next morning, we wake to even stronger winds than the day before, and a worse forecast for the day ahead. I ask Brian if we can hold off a day and reach for Tierra del Fuego tomorrow instead. I wash my face in the bathroom and spot a strange new mole on the side of my nose which makes me worry until I figure out it's actually a small sore caused by a tiny paint chip on my sunglasses, which have been pushed hard into my face for several days.

I'm intrigued by the small differences in my body that the journey has made. I have a thin dark tan line that reveals the gap between my riding jacket and my summer gloves. My cheeks are freckled and the bridge of my nose is brown, but my sunglasses and full-face helmet have robbed me of an overall glow. My hands are less graceful looking than they used to be and my shoulders are a little bigger. I haven't been sick in while, and overall I feel healthier than was back at home.

We decide to get out, and opt to wander through town to a grocery store and buy a few things to tide us over for the day and for the road ahead. On my way back through the lobby to the room I stop to admire the framed handwritten poems in the lobby and find one decorated with delicate painted butterflies around its edges.

The next day, I brace myself for the day's hammering and ride out, bound for the border crossing back into Chile and the ferry to Tierra del Fuego. We are 350 miles from Ushuaia.

This wind is crazy. The mid-day ferry rocks and rolls its way across the Strait of Magellan before depositing us in front of a café just in time for a warm drink. Afterward, we gear up and ride to Cerro Sombrero and try to find fuel before setting out across the island toward Ushuaia. But the station attendant has gone out, leaving a sign that says he will be back soon. There are already other vehicles waiting in line. We wait for a few minutes, but the wind is getting even stronger so we debate about pushing on without fuel.

The attendant returns just in time. We fill up and head out of town riding west a couple of miles before rejoining the main highway and turning south. As soon as we turn the corner and get blasted broadside by the wind, I feel more than my usual amount of uneasiness. Not far ahead the pavement ends and then we'll be swimming along in gravel with a 60-80mph, gusty crosswind, not exactly my favorite conditions.

I pull over at an enclosed bus stop and ask Brian what he thinks.

If he thinks we should carry on, we will. I trust him and I know we don't have any choice. There will always be wind here. It's just that it feels stronger and gustier at the moment.

Brian agrees, it's bad. We decide to go back to a café in Cerro Sombrero and wait a couple of hours for the wind to die down as it usually does in the late evening. By 7:00pm the wind drops from 70 mph to 30 mph and feels much more manageable. We start out again, hoping to reach San Sebastian near the border tonight. We've crossed from Argentina today and have to cross back into Argentina on the other side of Tierra del Fuego to get to Ushuaia. The island belongs half to Argentina and half to Chile.

The darker it gets, the more the wind drops, a conundrum for a rider. Both gravel and darkness present hazards. Sometime after 9:00pm Brian pulls into the yard of the only farmhouse we've seen to ask if we can camp nearby, but no one answers. We ride across the gravel road and onto a dirt trail. We round a small knoll and set up our tent out of the wind and view of the road.

In the morning, we break camp early, make the border in good time, ride past Rio Grande and stop for fuel and lunch at Tolhuin. The north half of the island was open grasslands, but the south half is covered in sparse patches of low cedar trees, damaged and deformed over time by the strong winds.

The forest thickens and closes in on our route as we round a lake. As if creating one final hurdle for us to prove our worth, the land rises up in a last mountainous display before plunging into the Drake Passage. We climb and climb before crossing through a narrow pass to ride down the other side through the last forested valley before Ushuaia.

As we get closer to the city, I try to gauge where to turn my camera on, while saving the miniscule amount of battery I have left.

A million helmet thoughts flood my mind:

- I'm freezing.
- I can't believe I'm going to make it.

- I'm going to have the biggest celebration drink ever and toast my mother. Then maybe I'll have another to toast my parents for giving me life and allowing me to experience this journey.
- And maybe still another to toast Brian, and our future.
- I'm so glad I didn't have another wreck before I got here. Well, hold that thought. I still have 5000 miles to ride before I get home.

That last thought keeps me from getting ridiculously giddy, adding an anti-climactic feeling to my arrival. This isn't really a finish line. It's just the point where I stop going south for the first time in eighteen months. It's like diving to the deep end of the pool. I'm reaching to touch the drain, but still have to hold my breath until I get back to the surface.

Brian leads us around a softly-arched right curve. As we round the bend the road straightens. Up ahead I see the recognizable turret towers that guard the entrance to the city.

I can't believe it. I made it.

We spend the next two weeks reveling in our faux-finish line crossing with friends. Markus and Karin arrive, as well as Erin, the girl we met on the Carretera Austral. Several other riders come and go from our hostel just off the main street, including a lovely Australian couple and their sweet dog who rides in a crate on top of one of their bikes.

Brian and I ride out to the official end of the road at Bahia Lapataia. We celebrate his birthday with motorcycle friends, a year after having done similarly in Mazatlan.

A mutual Facebook friend suggests we try to connect with Steph Jeavons who is in town only another couple of days before boarding a sailboat for Antarctica. That's a trip I'd hoped to make too, but a search of last minute deals turns up nothing in my meager price range. Steph is attempting to ride her small motorcycle on each of the seven continents during her round-the-world ride, and is headed to the most remote one in just a few days. We have beers with her and the sailboat captain, and dinner with the owners and crew on the Icebird before they sail.

Markus and Karin, and Brian and I ride out to meet Jim from Minnesota as he pedals his way through the gates to Ushuaia, his finish line. Brian received a message from Jim the night before and has a rough idea of when he should arrive. The four of us make a welcome banner for him to ride through, put welcome gifts on his bunkbed at our hostel, and make plans for a celebratory dinner.

After waiting half an hour, Brian gets impatient and rides ahead to see how far Jim is from town. He meets him ten miles out, but Jim's making good time thanks to that last mountain range. Brian comes riding back a while later, beeping his horn to tell us to get ready. Karin and I stretch the banner while the guys document the whole thing on cameras.

Watching Jim pedal and push to the finish line brings me to tears. Whatever emotions I didn't feel for my own arrival at this beautiful seaside town, I certainly feel for him. He's worked so hard for this, pedaling every mile of two continents in the endeavor. I'm overwhelmed with happiness and pride for him, and run over to give him a hug as we all cheer. This is how crossing a finish line should feel.

After nearly two weeks of rest, recuperation and celebration with friends, we finally retrace the dead-end route, this time from Ushuaia back to Rio Grande and across the border into the Chilean half of Tierra del Fuego. Instead of turning north to take the ferry we arrived on, we opt to ride west to Porvenir to see the western side of the island and take a ferry to Punta Arenas, Chile.

We decide against stopping to see the Emperor penguin colony, something I regret later, in hopes of catching the last ferry of the day. When we arrive at Porvenir, the boat is still due to arrive from its crossing of the Strait of Magellan. I sit in a small bakery and sip a hot chocolate made from melted dark chocolate pieces and fresh hot milk. The gift shop sells sheepskins, something I've been wanting for my bike seat, so I buy one.

The boat loading goes quickly, and Brian and I use as many wedges and straps as possible to tie the bikes down to the deck before taking the stairs to the passenger deck for the crossing. All the benches, seats and tables look filled, but we finally find a small place to settle as the ship rounds the last bend in the harbor and nears the breakwater. The steel-gray sea looks rough today, but there are no other ships on the water to survey for reference.

The further we clear land, the more the ship starts to pitch and roll. Brian and I had planned to get something to eat, but as I stand in line at the deli counter I reconsider. I have to hold on to a fixed barstool and lean heavily from left to right as the ship moves, trying to keep time with her. After a long wait, I carry our two drinks and sandwiches back to the table, grateful for cups with lids.

We look out the large window of the deck which overlooks the bow, and watch the horizon plunge below the rail, and then return for millisecond before disappearing high above the window as the ship noses down the face of a wave. The process repeats itself over and over while mixing in twisting side action as well. I've never been a person who gets seasick, but that may change today.

After what seems like hours, we finally arrive safely at Punta Arenas. After the ship is secured, we are allowed to return to our bikes. Expecting to see Betty as seasick as I nearly was, I'm pleasantly surprised to find her upright and no worse for the wear.

In Punta Arenas, we take advantage of the Zona Franca (duty-free zone) and buy more bike parts while we still can in this tiny oasis of southern Chile. We cross paths with a few other friends, including Mat and Pam, and check out the world's southernmost brewery.

We ride north to Puerto Natales, bucking the ever-present Patagonian wind across low coastal tundra, as early in the day as we can, before they peak. There's a package waiting at a DHL office for me. I have more mule-work to do. Two French riders are a day's ride from here, in Argentina, and one needs clutch plates. Mat and Pam asked a few days before if I would be willing to pick up the parts and carry them into Argentina for him, which would save him a sizeable expense in duty and fees. I look forward to meeting two other riders and hearing about the section of Ruta 40 that they rode.

Our friend, Pete, recently messaged to say that he came off his motorcycle on a section of Ruta 40 near Tres Lagos. That part is under construction and isn't covered yet with gravel. When it rains even the slightest bit, the clay sticks to tires. Pete's wheel caked up with mud so badly that it damaged his brake line, and caused him to wreck. The same thing happened to one of the French men we're going to meet.

While there are still so many places I hope to see before the end of the trip, the last "must see" for me is Torres del Paine National Park. We plan to ride a 150-mile loop from Puerto Natales into the park and camp, return to Puerto Natales for fuel, and then ride across the border to Argentina and start making our way north. The only problem is that horrible wind.

Walking around town is bad enough, and the battering winds we hear outside our room all night nearly put me off the idea altogether. The gravel roads into and through the park aren't bad, but the 90 mph wind gusts are too dangerous. I check my trusty new app and see that in the next four days there is a single 36-hour lull in the winds during which they die down to 30 mph sustained and gusts to only 40-50 mph, nearly wind-free by local standards. We decide to make a run for it.

Getting on the road early, with freshly charged camera batteries, we ride out on dusty roads. I stop for a photo every few miles before crossing through the park's southern entrance and making my way to the visitor center. The unique peaks of Torres del Paine, including Los Hornos, are stunningly beautiful.

We don't really know what to do with only 36 hours but we're going to try and make the most of them. A volunteer suggests we ride out to see Glacier Grey and take the boat to the glacier face.

The road from the visitor center leads north. A dead-end spur road leads into the rugged southern mountains, over Rio Grey and all the way to Hotel Glacier Grey. We stop at the hotel to buy tickets for the tour and have lunch before catching a ride to the walking trail to the lake.

While most lake and river water in this part of the world is colored a beautiful milky turquoise color, the water of this lake is named aptly, even if not for its color. The dark grey water is drab and sad, but carries us just as well as the prettier stuff does. Our small boat pounds and bumps across the windswept surface of the lake until it reaches the bright blue face of Glacier Grey itself on the other end. Once stopped, we leave the safety of the enclosed cabin and make our way to the top deck for the stunning view and a glass of whiskey chilled with fresh glacier ice.

I'm amazed by the texture of the ice, and its crystal clarity. The glacier face is bright blue in places and nearly blue-black in others, with miraculous shapes and textures worn into the face by the wind and water. Deep crevasses disappear into ice caves and round eyelets decorate the ice wall.

I see a couple watching something on a cliff nearby and look up to catch sight of two giant black and white birds settling into a nest on a ledge high above the water. They are Andean condors. After all this time on the continent, it's the first time I'm sure I've seen some. While I've seen birds off in the distance and wondered, these are only forty feet from me and are absolutely stunning.

From Puerto Natales, we cross back into Argentina and make our way north to El Calafate to deliver the parts to the French bikers and stock up on more dollar blue pesos. A day trip to Perito Moreno Glacier, complete with crampon-equipped ice trekking and more glacier-chilled whiskey, makes an incredible memory. After the close-up experience, I find the sheer scale of the glacier is easier to appreciate from the observation decks across the narrow channel of the lake.

Continuing north, we ride a couple of hours along the eastern edges of the glacial lakes. The wind and lack of sun make for chilly riding. At La Leona, we stop for a warm drink and find we have stumbled upon a hideout of Butch Cassidy and the Sundance Kid, and enjoy reading the stories of them on posters on the walls of the café.

In El Chalten I attempt to have my tent zippers repaired by a local woman who repairs gear in a small abandoned camper. We opt to dwell indoors for a day or two. As nasty as the howling winds are, I'm grateful for the stronger shelter. We hike out of town to get a closer look at Mount Fitzroy, which is incredible. Patagonia amazes me with its spectacular landscapes.

I can't tell at first, but I think my bike steering is acting up. As much as I've had to lean the bike into the wind as we rode south, and again now in the other direction, it feels like I've worn flat spots in my steering head bearing.

After riding more long stretches of Ruta 40 and making our way to the east coast, we keep plugging along, always moving north. We have days to ride before getting out of the Patagonia wind again.

Our Swiss friends post photos on Facebook showing killer whales beaching themselves on the north shore of Peninsula Valdes during their seal hunt. It's a rare sight, and only happens when the seal population, lunar calendar and whale hunting migration patterns align. They've been very lucky. Sam and Erica write to say they're headed that way because, according to something they read online, the stars will only be aligned for a couple more days. They invite us to come along.

Rudely, we break plans with an Argentinian biker who invited us to stay for a couple of days, and instead ride hard in hopes of catching one of nature's most spectacular hunting displays. I really don't want to see a seal pup being eaten, so I'm torn. But my absence or presence won't change the outcome, and this is one of the only places in the world where killer whales use a self-endangering beaching technique to hunt. It's a once-in-a-lifetime opportunity.

At Puerto Pirámides we park our bikes and hop into Sam and Erica's truck, and blast across Peninsula Valdes to the north shore. There's only a few hours each day where the light, wind and feeding times might align correctly, and we don't have much time left today.

On the next to the last day of this lunar cycle, we arrive at the beach and rush down to the sandy overlook to observe from above. Fifty other people are already here. Sweet pups bask in the sun, in duos and trios, while their mothers sleep not far away. Adults laze about on the beach while a few younger adults and pups alternate between napping and swimming, testing their independence. It's a gorgeous day. There isn't a killer whale in sight. Hours of waiting never produce one, but I still enjoy watching the seals. It was a lovely afternoon with friends anyway.

Our friends invite us to camp with them at a remote beach on the southern side of the peninsula with another couple. They are both in self-contained trucks, luxury in comparison with our means of travel. Sam takes us back to our bikes and offers to carry our gear and supplies out to the camp. We buy water and wine, and enough food to last for a couple of days. They've described this rugged plateau as worthy of enjoying for several nights.

After loading up, we follow the truck out of the village and turn onto a road that leads across the peninsula flatlands. It's an awful road. Sam says the severely washboarded gravel, followed by a deep sand path in the dunes, will only last for three miles. In actuality, it's nine. As I bounce and jostle my way along every inch of it, I look more and more forward to a glass of freshly purchased box wine and a day at camp tomorrow. Brian's taillight disappears into the darkness, leaving me semi-alone in a dusty cloud. When I finally reach the turn off the main road and onto the sandy trail, I find I've developed a sudden fondness for sand in comparison with the bumps, even if it's slow going.

Somewhere up ahead, I see the truck waiting and keeping watch over us. Brian is parked next to it, and even though he thinks I can't hear him, his voice is carried on the wind as I ride up. He's complaining loudly to the others about how ridiculously slow I am.

We reach camp well into the starless night and set about pitching our tent in the light cast by the trucks, which park perpendicularly in an attempt to provide us a windbreak. After a few minutes, we go inside the larger of the two trucks to meet Betty and John and have cocktails. Betty has a roast in the oven of their rig, making me envious of the luxury of truck camping, and treats us to a delicious dinner and great conversation. A strong breeze blows outside, not that these travelers would ever notice.

In the morning, I wake to find my sleeping bag, along with everything else in the tent, covered with a fine layer of sand, sifted through the skylight screen above. While I appreciate their trying, Sam and Erica's efforts to build a windbreak haven't had much effect. Both trucks have such high ground clearance that the wind blows freely under them, and smack dab into our tent.

No matter. It's a beautiful sunny day.

A few of us hike around the high ledge of the peninsula and wander. The wind died down during the night, but starts to pick up again in the middle of the day. On the way back to camp, I climb up a short knoll for a better view and blow out one of my flip flops in the process. I hobble back to camp on one, trying not to cut my feet on the shell fragments baked upright into the crusty ground.

Betty puts out the remnants of last night's dinner for sandwiches for lunch. The wind is annoying and gritty so we pass on al fresco and gather around the table in the large truck and share travel stories. Each of the couples ranks their favorites from our individual Pan-American journeys and some of the unique moments we've experienced.

The truck feels too warm to me, so I go sit on the floor by the open back door to get some air. I can see Betty and John's full-size bathroom and shower from my seat and admire it with a tinge of envy. A renewed wave of heat washes over me. I feel a little dizzy, so I decide to step outside and take a moment to catch my breath.

Outside I find the wind has picked up from strong breeze to intimidating gusts. I walk around the back of the truck toward our tent and stretch my legs. My back hurts, probably stiff from last night's horribly bumpy stretch of road. Strangely, even while the wind chills me, I break out in a sweat. Ten minutes does nothing to help. I don't feel well.

John comes out to check on me and I tell him so, but that it will probably pass. I decide to go lay down. It's early afternoon but I'm exhausted and feel like sleeping.

A couple of hours later the sun sets, leaving me in the glow of the lights cast from the truck window. I drifted off to sleep and wake to laughter coming from the window above. Another hour goes by and Brian comes to check on me. I've been in the tent for four hours, thankfully sleeping a bit. I'm feeling worse by the hour, and can't think of anything that will help. It feels like a stomach bug, or food poisoning. He goes back to the truck.

Half an hour passes and finally, it's official. I'm going to be sick. I unzip the tent and crawl out, racing barefooted for the shrubs in the distance that I've been using as a bathroom for the past 24 hours. I'm not sure what to do first, but instinct kicks in and I lunge forward throwing up violently into a bush, withdraw to reload, and heave again. I drop to my knees and wipe my watery eyes on my shirt sleeve. There's a strong wind blowing, but I can still hear laughter coming from the truck. I'm freezing and start to shake.

As I stand to do a self-assessment, another wave hits me, but this one lower. I quickly drop my pants and back into the same bush as a wave of cramping diarrhea hits me. Thankfully, I usually have tissues stashed in my pocket. I use them to clean myself up as well as is possible before tucking them under a rock so they don't scuttle off into the wilderness on the wind.

I stagger back toward the tent and walk over to my bike. My usual stash of wet wipes and plastic bags comes in handy. I walk back to the bush to retrieve my tissues just as another wave hits me. I literally don't know which end it will come out of this time, and try to prepare for either disgusting scenario.

After I try to do some damage control, I walk back to the tent and crawl inside, leaving my supplies and flashlight handy for the inevitable next round. I lay down and drift into a miserable, shivering sleep. The worst part is that to get to a hotel for rest and a shower, I'm going to have to ride an hour through the sandy dunes and up the horrible road back to the highway, and then ride another hour or two to the nearest town, all while feeling horribly weak and sick.

Sometime after midnight, Brian crawls into the tent to go to bed without saying a word. He smells of alcohol. Unknowingly, I've tossed and turned my way in front of the door while I slept and have to scoot out of the way so he can get into his bag. As I wiggle around, I decide I'd better make another run for it. I struggle through the night, making multiple trips into the dark until my last one sometime just before dawn.

I finish hunkering down in the bushes and start walking back to the tent as exhaustion and depressions take over. In our hurry to get here we didn't make time for showers, and I haven't had one in two days. I feel utterly disgusting. I'm filthy. I'm exhausted. I'm embarrassed. I'm sick, and I don't want to be around the others. I just want to take a hot shower and crawl into a bed, not my sleeping bag. I collapse in the shelter of a shrub, somewhere between my toilet bush and my tent, and start to cry.

We arrive late in the afternoon on a Thursday and park in front of the unassuming stucco building covered in hand-painted bike-related signs, and ring the bell. After a couple of minutes, I ring it again, and then one last time. But no one answers. We start to check the GPS for nearby places to stay while I put my helmet on to go. Just then I see an older woman standing up the street a few doors who waves to me and points to the door of La Posta. I have ear plugs in, so it's silent and surreal. I point at myself as if to ask if she's waving to me. She nods. I look at the door of the La Posta and work to get my helmet and earplugs stowed just as a spunky, bald Latino man opens the door and steps out.

Jorge stretches out his arms and welcomes me with a hug and cheek kisses, and greets Brian with a warm and friendly handshake. He introduces himself and then nods at Blanca, his mother, who was the woman waving to me. I feel rude for having arrived unannounced, but explain that we just wanted to stop and say hello. I had no idea what to expect, but it probably wasn't this. I have the feeling we just arrived at Jorge's home rather than a hostel or motorcycle clubhouse.

We chat for a few minutes about where we rode from and where we are going. I ask Jorge for a recommendation of where to stay for the night. "Here, of course," he says with waving arms and energetic Spanish flourish.

I say we don't want to impose, and I feel like we are, but he insists. Blanca opens the gate and before we know it we are whisked inside the courtyard of the La Posta and Jorge's home. They are one and the same.

La Posta del Viajero en Moto is Jorge's incarnation of an oasis for people traveling by motorcycle through Azul, Argentina. Literally hundreds, and more likely thousands of riders have passed through here and been welcomed by Jorge and his family.

Although I'm quick to adapt, it takes me a few minutes to adjust to what is happening. Jorge shows us a well-worn and sun-starved spot on the lawn under a weeping willow where two riders camped for eleven days. They left yesterday and the spot is being passed on to us. We park the bikes, set up the tent, and gratefully accept this as our landing place for the night without even discussing it together.

Jorge stands and chats with Brian after we get our gear into the tent, while I admire the paradise we've been invited into. Just behind my bike, next to the tent, is the back of the La Posta building which we had been parked in front of just minutes before. This side is covered with murals, one is of Jorge's doing of John Lennon and the Beatles. On the other side of the willow from us is a small pond, and it overflows with ducks and other birds, including three pink flamingoes. A freshly-stuccoed wall across the yard awaits Jorge's planned painting of Marilyn Monroe.

I wander inside the shop where a bike is stored. Metal working and carpentry are obviously in progress as tools are strewn about the concrete floor. A sort of great room, and kitchen adjacent to it, is filled with a ramshackle collection of chairs and two long tables. Jorge says we should think of the place as our home. We can use the kitchen, the bathroom on the back of the shop, and whatever else we may need. He's a rider and has traveled to other countries by motorcycle too. He is kind and genuine.

I'm struck by the number of signatures on the surfaces of the La Posta, as it appears a sort of guest book has sprung forth in ink on the walls, doors and ceilings of every room. Jorge points out some of the older ones, nearly 20 years old. Many of the autographs come in the form of art, and there are lots of names we recognize, some are of people we know. There are stickers, and flags, photos and license plates, bike parts and riding gear...all left as a piece of each rider to say "I was here".

This place, and Jorge, are legends. It's amazing just to sit and soak in the atmosphere and to think about all the memories and history it has witnessed. I read a few of the guestbook entries and see that everyone who comes here feels just the same – warmly welcomed into a brotherhood of riders. We don't actually meet any other travelers on our way through, as most people who come here do not. But because the oasis preserves memories and names we feel like we have met many of them already. The common link that connects all of us is Jorge.

He has had riders from all over the world stay and has some incredible memories. He shares a few stories with us. He asks me to translate for Brian as he tells us a few.

In 2003 a rider from the UK, Simon Milward, stayed with Jorge during his Millenium Ride that raised funds for international medical aid. Jorge and Simon became fast friends and Jorge shared with Simon his lifelong dream of riding his bike on the Falkland Islands (Las Malvinas). I can't imagine how difficult an undertaking that would have been given the bad blood between Argentina and Britain. But somehow Simon managed to pull it off, and the two were set to ride to Punta Arenas to catch a boat to the Falklands after Simon finished his ride. But sadly, Simon was killed in an accident in Africa and they never took that trip.

This place is incredible. What Jorge has given to motorcycle travelers is something of a living time capsule, a crossroads, a virtual meeting point and message board. You don't actually cross paths with other riders, but you see who has come before and can leave a kind word or message of inspiration for those who follow, or to Jorge in thanks.

We settle in for the night, make pasta in the kitchen, and have hot showers. Jorge suggests that we stay again tomorrow night since he has an asado every Friday night. We gratefully accept.

In the morning, Brian snoops around admiring the graffiti and decides he will paint his logo on the wall. I decide to pencil in a bison and an American flag in one of the few blank spots I can find. Thanks to two German riders we met in Ushuaia there are leftover paints to use on the great room table.

The next morning, I ask Jorge about a nearby laundry. It's time to wash my clothes in a machine, because sink washing can only hold me for so long. He checks with his wife, Monica, and she offers to wash my laundry for me in her machine. She washes, dries and folds it all. I tell her it's the first really clean clothes I've had in three weeks, and I'm so very grateful.

That night Jorge's friends and a few riding buddies turn up after 9:00pm for the asado. Jorge disappears out front, presumably to get the fire going, while we make new friends. They're friendly and funny, a dozen everyday working men.

We make pleasant conversation, chatting about our travels and their lives in Azul. When asked, Brian's hesitant for me to tell them he's from England simply so that no one feels uncomfortable. He's still mindful of the reaction he got from the cab driver in Mendoza at Christmastime. But I think this feels like an atmosphere of honesty and take a chance. No one even misses a beat.

One of Jorge's friends, Santiago, suggests that Brian and I go out front with our cameras, and it takes me a moment to understand he means for us to walk out onto the street in front of the shop. We grab our cameras, not knowing what's coming, and step into the dark. Jorge stands next to a flagpole, which I barely noticed the day before, working with two pieces of fabric and a rope. In a moment, he starts to raise two flags, our flags, ironed and pristine American and British flags. I'm moved by it, perhaps even moreso by the sight of Brian's flag than of my own.

Some of Jorge's neighbors, and many of his friends here tonight, are old enough to have lived through the Falklands War, and no doubt could still carry hard feelings toward the United Kingdom. Having the flag of the old enemy flying overhead, even on a backstreet in a small town, is risky. But Jorge raises it proudly to welcome Brian.

That long and difficult history between England and Argentina doesn't belong at La Posta, Jorge explains. Jorge and Santiago each mirror the same sentiment to me in different conversations – we are all the same, flesh and blood. When it comes down to it, so many things do not matter, like politics, material things, and so forth. They both say something like "if you have a good heart, you are my friend". That is the unwritten motto of the brotherhood of riders, I think to myself, and am reminded of a Lakota phrase – mitakuye oyasin – which loosely means we are all related.

We spend hours sharing beers, stories and some of the best asado we've had yet. Jorge's friends are right, he is a master griller. At the end of the evening in a momentary lull in the conversation, I step outside to look up at our flags, and the white of stars and stripes glowing softly in the moonlight. Then I look in through the window at the comradery of these men. Brian, my favorite Englishman, sitting among a room full of Argentinians who are teasing him like he is one of their own. I know already, this is going to be one of my favorite memories from this trip.

In Buenos Aires, we contact Dakar Motos to make arrangements to ship our bikes back to North America. I can't believe it's almost time to go home.

We've been researching online for the past several weeks, and weighing our options. We can ship via air or sea, to any number of ports between Mexico and Canada, to get close enough to home and ride the rest of the way. In the end, we decide to fly the bikes to

Vancouver and take a leisurely route through British Columbia and Alberta before riding home to South Dakota. The arrangements will take about a month, so we decide to make the most of it and ride to a few neighboring countries.

We catch up with a dozen friends from the road before we go. Everyone seems to be shipping or flying their vehicles and bikes off the continent from here. We enjoy a week with Pete at a small hostel with a big courtyard. He's still in travel mode, wandering and dreaming of his next destination. No timeline. No agenda. I'm happy for him.

Just four months before, I was homesick and it took effort to keep going each day, not that it lasted for long. But now here I am on the other side, of both Ushuaia and my mood, longing for more time on the road. The grass is always greener.

We spend a day or two scouring the city for bike parts, finding there is a motorcycle district in this city too. Brian works on the bikes, replacing his chain and my tires, and tries to figure out if there's a fix for my notched steering head bearing. The ratchet-y feeling is getting worse, making it awkward to steer.

I spend time catching up on journals, editing photos, and writing blog posts, and schedule them to post over the next six weeks, buying me time to go off grid. One day I get an email and find out I've been added to the esteemed list of Jupiter's Travelers, part of the Ted Simon Foundation. I'm honored.

We explore the beautiful narrow streets and wide boulevards of Buenos Aires, enjoying the modern European feel of the city. We watch tango dancers in a nightclub and meet up with friends almost every night for wine and asado.

On afternoon, we visit the Plaza de Mayo to watch one of the Thursday night vigils that have been held here for nearly 40 years. I've heard stories about the "lost children" of Argentina but haven't openly asked what happened. Something like 30,000 children went missing in the 1970s and 80s and were never heard from again, part of the "Dirty War" when the government cleansed itself of the children of any opposition. I'm told most of the citizens of Argentina still believe the government propaganda that "it never happened".

Those who were affected were too afraid of the government to speak out in public for fear of disappearing themselves. But as a way of silently honoring their lost loved ones, the heartbroken mothers of the missing children started to hold silent vigils in the Plaza de Mayo every Thursday evening. Several of the original founding mothers also "disappeared" in the beginning, but others filled their ranks and the silent protests carried on. It's sobering to watch. These women have gathered each week for forty years.

As we ride north of the city, hoping to make Colon and camp for the night, my mind wanders to anywhere but the road before me. The details of the trip home are shaping up. Brian reached out to his friend, Al, in Victoria, Canada to make plans for us to ride to Vancouver Island before going home. We've tried to contact Allan, who crossed into Mexico with us too, but so far haven't heard from him.

Deep helmet thoughts today…

- I'm feeling bittersweet about going home, excited to see friends and family, but nervous about returning to the real world. I don't have a job or a home to go back to and will need to find both in short order. I can already feel the pressure of the enclosing walls of responsibility. This trip has changed my priorities. I see things more clearly at the moment, and don't want to lose my new viewpoint. I worry that going home will change me back, but I don't want my old life. I've burned through a lot of savings, and need to be a grown up for a while.
- What will my life be like now, after this amazing trip? What will I create for myself? How will I adjust to coming off the road?
- I wonder if my life is something like the evolution of a butterfly. Am I moving on to the next stage?

- I think of the movie, The Matrix, and feel a little like Neo, having awakened from the superficial existence of the matrix. I don't want to return.
- If, on average, a person takes two weeks' vacation each year, I've spent fifty years of vacations on this trip. Wow.

22 PARAGUAY

Gratitude is the least of virtues; ingratitude is the worst of vices.
-Paraguayan proverb

Encarnacion is nothing like I expected, not that I had anything in mind. It sprawls along the riverfront in the manner of an oceanfront city. We find a clean hostel near the center of town with a concrete courtyard for the bikes. It's a holiday and nearly everything is closed.

Nearing the Tropics again makes for hot humid days, rain-filled afternoons and insect-filled nights. For a moment, I wish I hadn't sent my anti-malarial pills home, but then remember that Dengue fever could still get me, so I wouldn't have been out of danger anyway.

We plan to ride to the Jesuit Missions for a day of wandering through the ruins, but when I try to start my bike the morning after our arrival, Betty refuses. The evening before covered her in a colossal downpour, for hours on end, and apparently, she is still pouting about it. Brian gives it a try, but it's no use. He has to take her apart and give her a new spark plug to sweet talk her into coming out of her coma.

We are only delayed for a few hours, and ride to the missions afterward. The remains of lovely stone carvings are impressive now, making me wonder how beautiful the churches must have been when they were first built. As we wander the complex of ruins, the blazing sun beats down, causing me want to run for shade.

After a couple of days, we make our way to Asuncion. The city feels different to me. But different from what, I cannot say. It's got an undercurrent of oppression. As with most cities, poverty is more visible here. And while there are some tourists, it doesn't seem very tourist-oriented. Military boats patrol the river.

It's only a few weeks until we plan to deliver our bikes to Dakar Motos, so we want to cross Paraguay fairly quickly and carry on to Iguazu and eventually to the lovely beaches of Florianopolis in Brazil. We only stay in the capitol for a couple of days before making our way east across the country.

Dark clouds hover overhead and darker clouds lurk in the distance as we make our way out of Asuncion, bound for Colonel Oviedo and a campsite. A German man named Walter offers tours in Citroen 2CVs and has rooms and camp spaces for rent.

The GPS leads us through the meandering streets in the outskirts of the city and, finally, we break free, riding out onto the lush open grasslands of Paraguay just as it starts to rain. Flashes of lightning streak horizontally across the distant sky.

Water droplets run off my visor but don't obstruct my view. But the inside fogs up, making it difficult to see. It's a lovely warm rain, as long as it stays light.

But the further we ride, the heavier the downpour gets. At first, it's not worrisome, but somewhere between Ypacarai and Caacupe water starts to stand on the roads causing me to worry about hydroplaning. We slow down, but carry on. Only having 120 miles to ride today makes me want to push through and get this over with.

Plains give way to hills which carry us up to a high grassy plateau just beneath the storm cloud. Having eroded land on the way downhill, rivers of muddy runoff water from side roads empty onto the highway, crossing it with wide vermillion stripes. The water is nearly a foot-deep in places.

I feel water seep into my pants at the crotch and run down my legs into my boots until it's up over my ankles. Wiping my left hand across my visor isn't keeping up with the deluge, so I slow down further. Surprisingly, I'm doing well, and feeling good, focused on maintaining my speed and watching for obstacles.

Out of the corner of my right eye I see a bright flash as a horizontal streak of lightning rips across the sky right next to me, disappearing up ahead. The bolt explodes in a flash of white, blinding me for a split second. Alright, now I'm scared. That was too close for comfort.

There's no place to take cover though and we have to keep going. Brian leads us over the next ridge, through the blackest part of the storm and into the abyss. As I top the hill and start down the other side though, I can see a bit of light in the distance. We're getting through it. We carry on for another 45 minutes before reaching Coronel Oviedo and turning off the highway to find Walter's place. A soft rain still falls.

It's easy enough to find. Walter greets us at the front door and runs to open the gate to his yard so we can ride through and get out of the rain. We park our bikes under an open-air shelter and step off the bikes for the first time since leaving Asuncion. The 120 miles has taken us nearly four hours.

I ask Brian to hold my camera and video me taking off my boots. I can feel water standing well above my ankles, and want to document this reverse effect of waterproof boots to look back at someday. But having forgotten the mechanics of displacement, the end result isn't as impressive as I had hoped. My toes are pruny and gray, not surprising after their three-hour soak. That was the wettest riding I've ever done.

Walter is incredibly friendly, and helps tend to our basic needs and questions. We opt for a room in the house as a treat after the drenching of the day.

Walter's wife is Guarani, a native of this land, and he speaks a little of the language, along with his native German and the German-tilted Spanish he has acquired over his 30 years in this country. He came to Paraguay to teach auto mechanics at a local university, and liked it so much he never left.

While our gear and boots hang on lines to dry, Walter takes us on a tour of his place. His shop and knowledge bank are well-stocked, a bonus for travelers in need, and he and Brian bond over tools and their shared love of automobiles and mechanic-ing. Walter shows us a couple of his 2CV cars which he has taken on tours all over South America. They look like good fun, and a lot of work.

We enjoy cocktails with Walter in the evening and share stories of our travels, using Spanish as our common language. Brian's Spanish is getting better all the time and he understands a lot of what Walter says. He only asks me to translate when he wants me to tell Walter something.

Three hens wander in and out of the open-air shelter which serves as both garage and lounge. A giant grapefruit drops with a bang onto the tin roof, making me jump. My boots and pants leak drops of water from the line onto the floor.

Just north of Ciudad del Este is the smaller town of Hernandarias, home to the Itaipu dam. Brian and I secure and abandon our bikes in the sauna-like heat to board an air-conditioned bus to tour the dam.

I'm tired today, and a little withdrawn. As the guide offers insight, I don't bother translating anything. The views speak for themselves. It's a dam, no disrespect intended. There's not much more I really need to know at the moment. I will read about it online later.

We got an email from a friend in Canada who says that Allan, the friend who crossed into Mexico with us, died of cancer not long ago. No wonder we hadn't heard from him. I'd been looking forward to seeing him and thanking him for the role he played in me overcoming my fear as I crossed into a new land. I'm crushed.

Brian wonders aloud if Allan knew he had cancer for a while and if he had it when he crossed into Mexico with us. That hadn't occurred to me. What I had thought was Allan's celebratory post-retirement solo ride across Canada may have actually been him making a long last journey because he knew he hadn't much time.

It reinforces one of the beliefs that led me to take this trip to begin with – life is short. We shouldn't wait to do things "someday". We should make the most of every moment and every day while we can. That doesn't mean taking an enormous trip like this, it just means living in the moment and not taking time for granted.

23 BRAZIL

Between the beginning and the end, there is always a middle.
-Brazilian proverb

Crossing into Brazil is a breeze. They no longer require vehicle import permits, so it amounts to a 10-minute wait and a passport stamp.

A local ambassador from Horizons Unlimited, Rod, has agreed to meet Brian and I and direct us to a hostel not far over the border from Paraguay. We plan to stay a couple of days to visit Iguazu falls before riding east to the coast and turning south toward Uruguay. We stop at what we think will be a hostel, only to find out that the hostel has moved. Rod arrives just in time to guide us to Manga Hostel instead, which belongs to his friend Joel, a lively Brazilian who makes us feel instantly at home.

Joel and his fiancé, Gisele, help us into an empty room and return to the kitchen to keep brewing their culinary magic. Joel is an incredible cook, which I get to observe firsthand a couple of nights during our stay. He treats guests to incredible homemade Brazilian cuisine. He also takes us to a traditional Brazilian restaurant on a side street somewhere in Foz where most of the locals apparently go for lunch. Joel says it's popular because most of the food is like things a Brazilian grandmother would make. We carry our plates of fresh roasted meats and home-cooked vegetables out to a table under the shade of a giant Jacaranda tree.

One morning I walk out from the hostel to go and buy some fresh bread at a local bakery. I get a strange look from the woman at the counter when I ask for bread, which I think is pronounced "pow" in Portuguese, but must not be. When I get back and tell Joel he laughs at my pronunciation and says I'm actually saying a dirty word instead. He advises me to correct my pronunciation of "coco" too so that I will be sure to get coconut flavored things instead of something vulgar.

Brazilians are passionate and vibrant people in everything they do, and that includes motorcycling. Its people are connected, and divided, by hundreds of motorcycle clubs all over the country. But, as in other countries, there are many very different ways to motorcycle.

Rod is an adventure rider, like us, and often helps fellow adventure riders traveling through this part of the country. He and his fiancée, Mariane, invite us to join them for dinner a couple of nights and treat us to cooked pinions (giant pine nuts). And when Brian has a problem with his bike, Rod helps him find parts and tools to make the repair.

While Brian spends two days working on his bike, I work on planning the details of our next couple of weeks. From here we will ride to the coast, across the southern stretch of Brasil through Curitiba and then south to Florianopolis. I'm hopeful we can catch up with another rider we met for only a few minutes in Valparaiso. Besides, a couple of days at the beach sounds nice.

We will follow the coast south and cross into Uruguay where perhaps in Montevideo we can catch up with Pete one last time before leaving the continent. Uruguay will be our home for a few days while we stock up on U.S. dollars to pay for our bike shipping.

Not once, but twice, we make a pilgrimage to one last UNESCO site, the beautiful and incredible falls at Iguazu. Viewing platforms on both the Brazilian side and, thanks to a long slender arm of land, Argentinian side offer stunning views. I leave off my heavy riding gear for the short, humid ride from the hostel, through the city and out to the edge of the deep gorge of the Iguazu River.

On the day of our first visit, the Brazil side visitor center is swarming with people. A bus carries us to the trail that runs along the top of one side of the gorge. We have 15-20 minutes of walking from our drop off point to the face of the great falls. All along the way we catch sight of many sections of waterfalls across the river on the Argentinian side. Some are narrow and some are wide. Boats filled with people drift into the mist on the river below to get a closer look.

Because this isn't the rainy season, the volume of water is, by comparison to peak season, fairly light. But it's still an amazing amount of water, and the added bonus is that the water is clear, free from the silted runoff that occurs during heavy rains.

Coatimundis, long-snouted cousins of raccoons, wander along the trail, undisturbed by people, and try to break into garbage cans for midday snacks. Butterflies of every size and shape imaginable flutter by, between dangling jungle vines and tall trees. I watch one rest on the rail of the path, and it looks exactly like the tree bark of the tree across from it. Another, while resting with closed wings, looks exactly like a dried brown leaf from another tree nearby.

At a wide part of the path, a family stops to enjoy the cloud of butterflies rising from the forest. A little boy holds out his hand to show his mother the pretty yellow and black butterfly that landed on his finger.

I keep hoping to see one of those incredible bright blue and black Peruvian butterflies that I still dream about. Maybe I will get lucky and one of those will rest on me. I can't help but think of the message a friend sent me a while ago about butterflies being the spirits of loved ones lost, and smile to myself.

My mother has been my guardian angel on this trip. If one of those blue beauties lands on me, I will know it's a sign from her. That's silly, I correct myself. It would take more than that, something more personal and clear.

We carry on along the rim of the gorge to the next overlook, this one not as crowded. A butterfly whose coloring resembles a piece of pink and black granite lands gently on my arm. I stand still while it takes its rest and can't imagine a more peaceful experience.

Further ahead I can see the face of the largest stretch of the massive falls themselves. It's incredible. Brian walks ahead, working his way toward the waterfall for better photos. I linger in my own world for a moment.

Mist blankets everything in a layer of moisture, one microscopic drop at a time. Another butterfly alights on my arm, uncurling its tongue to drink from one of the tiny droplets of mist on my skin.

Its wings are decorated in concentric rings of black and white with a splash of red, my high school colors. What a strange and unique color pattern. I've never seen anything like it before. Surprisingly, in the center of each, plain as day, as though it was handwritten, is the number "88", the year I graduated from high school. Not that it would mean anything to anyone else, it certainly means something to me. I smile to myself.

We ride across the most southern part of Brazil to Curitiba and then to the coastal resort of Florianopolis where we meet up with Johnny, a fellow Jupiter's Traveler and rider originally from Mississipi. We enjoy a couple of leisurely days in his good company before carrying on along the coast.

For a couple of days we make our way leisurely toward our final new country of the journey, stopping in coastal towns for the night along the way. I'm amazed how many motorcyclists there are in Brazil.

24 URUGUAY (AND ARGENTINA)

In a corner of this land with the colors of earth, I adore this pale moon…

-Delmira Agustini

The last thirty miles of riding from Rio Grande, Brazil to the border with Uruguay take us across miles of farmland. We aren't far inland and I occasionally catch a glimpse of what I think is the ocean, but later realize is a tidal basin at the far end of a long pasture filled with cattle. There haven't been any fuel stops or towns along the way, so halfway to the border we opt to double back and fill up at Quinta just in case. I was already on reserve, making me regret not having filled up before we left town this morning. I think the longer we've been on the road, the more careless we get. Or maybe it's just that we've relaxed.

Even though it's nearly winter here, the weather is mild and warm. We run into the occasional rain shower, but have enjoyed sunny calm days while riding across southern Brazil.

Up ahead I see what looks like some form of roadkill, and it's in my lane. A quick check of the road and my mirrors doesn't reveal any cars, so I cross into the oncoming lane to go around it. It's big, and looks like it might be a dog or a calf. But as I get closer, I can see it's neither of those. It's a capybara.

And it's not alone. For the next ten miles I have to weave my way around dozens of them as they pass through various stages of decay on the warm road. Just a few miles before the border, I pull over to watch a family of these giant hairy rodents, each weighing perhaps 100-120 pounds or more, sunning themselves on a muddy island in the center of a canal running alongside the road.

After stopping for a photo in Chuy and passing up a couple of places for fuel and lunch, we cross into Uruguay, only to find there aren't any services on the other side of the border. Brian pulls over for us to chat and we decide to double back, but then see how long the line is now and give up the idea.

The highway into Uruguay is in great condition and lined on both sides with rows of tall trees. At one point it widens dramatically, and it takes me a moment to realize that there's a small airplane runway embedded into this section of the road. Cars pass me on both sides as they sprint from the border toward Punta del Este.

Not more than twenty miles ahead we find our turnoff which leads into the beach town of Punta del Diablo. An assortment of lovely cabins and colorful beach homes lines both sides of the sand roads in the village, but most of them look abandoned for the season. We see a sign for an ATM and pull in to get some local currency, but it's closed, as is the shop housing it. In fact, the more I look around, the more I see we may be in a bind today. There aren't any places to buy fuel, or to get cash, much less to stay, from what I can tell.

I stop to ask a passing car about where to find a bank and fuel. They suggest we go back to the highway and backtrack to the national park just up the road and see if it's still open, but they think it may be too late in the season. We may need to go another fifty miles into the country before finding what we need. Half an hour later we find ourselves doubling back to the highway for a second time after confirming that the national park was shut down as well. A quick check of the GPS doesn't reveal anything for services, so we turn west toward Castillo.

Meandering through the small town for a few blocks reveals a baby blue stucco building with a small line of people waiting at an ATM. We have found our first bank. Brian goes first while I wait with the bikes. It's a relief to find an ATM, both for money we need for meals and lodging, and so I can start making daily raids on my savings account. My ATM card allows me to withdraw $300 per day, which I will need to do every day for a week or more to get enough money to get my bike and myself back to North America. If I can pay with U.S. dollars I will save $600-$800 in expense with the black market dollar blue advantage in Argentina.

A few minutes later Brian returns with a deer-in-the-headlights look on his face. I ask what's wrong. He's in shock, and tells me that the ATM didn't give him any money, and worse still, it ate his card. Oh, no. Now what?! Brian has another ATM card but, understandably, is afraid of trying it now. I've just finished doing the math and know we barely have enough days to get our money stocked up before sprinting back to Buenos Aires to deliver our bikes to the shipper. I could withdraw enough for us both and loan Brian the money if we had 2-3 weeks in Uruguay, but we don't have any breathing room in our schedule for that.

I'm nervous about trying it now, but have no choice. It's evening and our bikes are nearly out of fuel, we haven't eaten yet today and we need a place to stay. I pluck up some courage and go get in line. Thankfully, my card works and I get the maximum amount of Uruguayan pesos allowed by my card limit, and, more importantly, I get my card back. It's enough to fill our bikes, buy dinner and pay for a ridiculously expensive room at a hostel a few blocks away. We're tired and need to make a plan. I decide to take a quick photo of the bank in case Brian needs the name or address of it later. As I finish, a police officer comes running from across the street and yells at me for taking the photo. I try to explain what happened but he doesn't care, so I put my camera away.

I suggest we come back to the bank first thing Monday morning, the day after tomorrow, and try to get Brian's card. In the meantime, I can get enough cash to keep us afloat and start stocking up on cash for him with a credit card I have. The fees will hurt, but not as much as paying full price for shipping his bike. Brian doesn't want to wait that long and instead wants us to push on to a larger town. We will find another bank and stick to our schedule.

After an unsettled night, we ride on to Rocha, aiming for its central plaza. A large brick bank has an ATM which we nervously eye while taking off our gear. My debit card works but doesn't allow me to get my full daily limit. I stash the fresh pesos in my pocket before trying to get dollars with my credit card. It doesn't work, and while I'm offered no explanation, at least I get it back.

Brian tries his card and doesn't get any cash either. When he goes to cancel the transaction the machine won't release his card. He tries another button, but the machine goes back to its welcome page, effectively telling him to move along. Shit.

He's not taking it well, and I don't blame him. Not only is he unable to stockpile cash to pay for his bike shipping, which means he will pay several hundred dollars more, he can't get cash for his travel expenses. He's thousands of miles away from his banks and mailing address in England and has only one bankcard left. I feel awful for him. But I also know that I can cover us both until we get back to North America.

This time he agrees that we will come back in the morning and try to get his card returned. In the meantime, we ride to the coast at La Paloma and find a cheap room in a hostel for the night. I go for a walk on the beach and hunt for seashells while a strong wind uncovers them for me.

There's a small market in town where I buy supplies to make us a nice pasta dinner. Brian surfs online and tries to contact his bank while I reach out to my credit card company and am told my card has been cancelled because of suspicious activity. Banking and credit card transactions aren't going very well for either of us in Uruguay.

In the morning, we return to Rocha and wait for the bank to open. When it does, I lead us in, past an armed guard and back to the customer service desk, as we are eyed suspiciously by everyone in the building. Our heavy riding gear is intimidating looking.

The woman at the desk shows us a small stack of cards that was retrieved from the machine this morning and Brian sees his in the pile. For a moment I'm afraid he will try to snatch it out of her hand, but he restrains himself. I try to explain our desperate situation and ask her politely to verify his identity with his passport and return the card to him. I explain it's his property and we won't leave without it, but it doesn't do any good. She cuts the card in half in front of him and tucks it back into her desk drawer. Well, then. That's that.

After making our way up the coast to Punta del Este and eventually to Montevideo, we meet up with Pete in a hostel in the center of the city. It's nice to finally have someone to talk to again. Brian isn't much for conversation these days, not that I can blame him. It's wonderful to catch up and wander the city with Pete and to share a few meals and beverages in the communal kitchen. I make daily pilgrimages to an ATM just up the street for my allowance, still whittling away at my savings. Pete takes us to a lovely market for lunch one day and then shows us a gorgeous bookstore on a promenade near the capitol building. Montevideo is beautiful.

Brian works online and comes up with the idea of wiring money from his bank account to himself at a local Western Union or Moneygram office. After a small scale test goes well, he sends a large sum which takes care of his stockpiling all at once. Thank goodness.

We make one last stop in Uruguay, now having gotten over some of our bitterness toward the country after sorting our money situation out. The UNESCO town of Colonia del Sacramento and its colonial buildings, cobblestoned streets and abandoned bullfighting ring make for good exploring. Afterward, we make our way deep into the country to find a way across the enormous Rio de la Plata back to Argentina.

Converting our money to blue pesos goes well. Dakar Motos gives us easy-to-follow instructions for arranging payment, completing paperwork and delivering our bikes to the airport cargo office for their flight back north. Air Canada requires a few specific things be done before they will accept the bikes, and we spend a couple of days preparing them. It feels strange to leave Betty at the airport and take a taxi back to our hostel, the first time I haven't been with her in nearly two years. I'm already looking forward to getting her back in Vancouver.

Several of our overlanding friends are in Buenos Aires, most enjoying a vehicle-free holiday while waiting for their overseas flights back home. We meet for dinner and drinks a few times, and enjoy watching couples dance the tango in a small neighborhood plaza one evening. It's the perfect way to enjoy our last days in South America.

Finally, one morning in the middle of May, we catch a taxi to the airport, burdened with several bags of heavy motorcycle gear and luggage. Our trip will be broken up into a few flights, the first of which lands us in Atlanta for a three-hour layover.

After a nearly two years away from home, the United States feels a little strange. I'm instantly struck by what I perceive as shallowness, self-indulgence and arrogance from every direction. People are rude and impatient. Newsstands are covered with models pushing the latest materialistic trends, Kardashian drama and celebrity gossip. I love my country, but not much has changed in two years. Except maybe me.

The second flight takes us to Seattle, where we enjoy a ten-hour layover by wandering the city center. We have lunch at a café in Pike Place Market, pose for a photo in front of the gum wall and visit Chihuly Garden and Glass. At the airport that night we catch sight of Nicolas Cage waiting for the same flight as us.

25 CANADA

There are a thousand ways to kneel and kiss the ground; there are a thousand ways to go home again.

-Rumi

What a small world. The receiving agent at the Air Canada desk helping us with our shipping documents is from Peru. While we wait for the two pallets carrying our bikes to be brought to the loading dock, we chat about our experience in his beautiful country.

As the forklift operator passes by the office with my bike, Brian and I follow him out to the warm sun of the dock and set to work pulling the crates apart and unwrapping our things. Brian reattaches the windshield, mirrors and other parts he dismantled for shipping. I cut an assortment of tie-down straps and unwrap our helmets.

After two hours work, Brian has both the bikes running. We put our gear on and ride out of the cargo area of the airport toward a nearby fuel station. At our hotel a couple of miles away we spend another hour reloading and packing our bikes before heading for the ferry to Vancouver Island. Packing is a little easier without having a tent or camp stoves to carry. We couldn't ship our stoves home on the bikes, so had to leave them in Argentina. And as my tent was on its last legs, we left it at a hostel for someone to scavenge.

We enjoy a quick lunch on the deck outside the ferry terminal while soaking up the atmosphere of the Pacific northwest. Tall evergreens are a novelty for me these days. The ferry loads quickly and offers a beautifully smooth sailing across the Salish Sea before ducking between islands on its way to deliver us at the terminal at Swartz Bay.

Brian met Al a few years ago when he was riding to Alaska and he and his wife, Lucie, generously welcome us into their lovely home for a few nights and give us the royal tour of Victoria. The men spend a couple of days getting the bikes serviced and even tackle replacing my steering head bearing.

We spend a lovely day riding a loop route north from Victoria to Duncan before turning southwest to have lunch in Port Renfrew. Shannon, the solo female rider we befriended in Nicaragua lives in Victoria, and she comes along for the day too. It's a beautiful ride around the southern part of the island, and a nice way to test out how good my bike feels with its new steering.

On the way back to Victoria, I lead the back half of our pack around a slow-moving car. As I pass it, I pour on some throttle at the entrance to a long stretch of woods just as a dark mass trots out and crosses the road in front of me. I'm not sure at first because it looks so thin, but when I get close I see it's a big black bear, still lean from winter. The first bear I've seen on the trip.

I'm getting anxious. The closer we get to South Dakota, the faster I want to go. And yet, part of me doesn't want the trip to end, so I try hard not to rush these last few weeks. There isn't any deadline for me, except that my driver's license is due to expire in June, and I'd prefer to renew it before, saving some extra work. Brian's not in any hurry, but then he isn't heading to his home like I am.

We make our way across southern British Columbia, spending a night in a provincial park and another in Castelgar, before making our way over the Continental Divide in Kootenay National Park. Nevil, the rider we greeted at the end of his round-the-world ride at Cape Spear, Newfoundland has invited us to stay with his family.

Nevil, his lovely wife, Michelle, and their daughter, are incredibly kind and friendly. They have a beautiful guest room that is enjoyed by motorcyclists on a fairly regular basis. As Nevil and Michelle are also from England, I become a minority when it comes to the English stories, but I enjoy them thoroughly in spite of that.

They spoil us with curry dinners, hard ciders and good conversation. Being an adventure rider who has crossed the expanse of Asia, Nevil has the best travel stories. I find even as I near the finish line of this trip that I'm already planting seeds for another big adventure somewhere in the future. His tails of riding across Mongolia stoke that fire.

Luckily, we've stumbled through here at the perfect time. Nevil and his riding friends have been making films of their travels and rides, and Nevil is holding a small film festival the coming weekend to showcase some of their creations. It's fantastic fun. The local riding community around Canmore is an incredible group of people.

But eventually my itchy feet get the better of me and we pack up and head for home. It's hard to be this close to the proverbial finish line and not want to get across it.

The Going-to-the-Sun Road isn't open yet, but our route will take us across the edge of Glacier National Park on our way south. I've been hoping to take Brian over Beartooth Pass on the way back to South Dakota, which is a stunning road in its own right. It opened for the season just a few days ago making it a possibility.

We make our way south from Canmore, and stop to meet a friend, John, at our last Tim Horton's stop of the trip. Afterwards, we ride south along the Cowboy Trail through green valleys on the eastern slopes of the Rockies.

At Lundbreck I hear a buzzing sound and swear we must be passing a sawmill. I turn to see where it is but can't find it. After making a turn onto our next road, Brian pulls into a small gas station and shuts off his bike. I think we must be right next door to sawmill because the buzzing is getting loud. As I shut off my bike and its engine noise ceases, I jump a little at the new louder and clearer version of the buzzing sound. It isn't a sawmill, it's a bee. And it's inside my helmet.

To be fair, it isn't really a normal bee. It's an enormous bumblebee. I'd seen several flying along the roadside, each large enough to make a mess of any windshield, and tried to avoid them, but must not have done a good job of it.

I quickly undo my chinstrap and tear off my helmet, hoping to get him loose before he stings me. As I hold my helmet with my right hand, I use my left to brush through my hair and clear him out. But I can't find him. I turn over my helmet assuming I will find him still inside it, but he isn't there either. Oh, well. Maybe I didn't see him escape.

As I hang my helmet on my bars, I hear the sound again, but this time it isn't in my ear and doesn't make me jump as badly. I look closely at my helmet and follow both the sound and vibration of the buzzing to its source. There he is, wedged between my helmet peak, my visor and my helmet exterior. I must have ridden right up behind him and scooped him up into my path with such a force that it pushed him through a narrow gap into my visor hinge. He sounds good and angry.

Brian gets a screwdriver and sets to work removing the single plastic screw that holds my visor and peak in place and finally loosens it enough for him to fly out. But his poor leg is stuck in the screw hole, so I have to reach down and give him a tug to free him. When he finally tears loose, he is off in an instant, like an angry drunken zeppelin pilot.

26 AMERICA

Twenty years from now you will be more disappointed by the things that you didn't do than by the ones you did do. So throw off the bowlines. Sail away from the safe harbor. Catch the tradewinds in your sails. Explore. Dream. Discover.

-Mark Twain

Just before the border crossing at Chief Mountain, we pull over at a scenic overlook and get our papers in order. Brian is his usual level of nervous for a crossing, and I find that I'm surprisingly a little nervous too. Maybe it's just excitement. I'm going home for the first time in two years. And I'm bringing my incredible adventure to a close. There's only one word for it – bittersweet. I take a quick photo and find when I stow my camera and go to start my bike, I'm a little choked up.

Brian goes first, gets processed in fairly quickly and rides past the guard gate to a parking area off to the side. I ride up and hand my passport to the border guard. I think to myself that I may get some normal questions - Where have you been? How long have you been gone?, etc. - and may have to reply with some abnormal answers. I imagine a scenario where I briefly explain my trip and the guard says "welcome home" at the end of it. A lump forms in my throat. If he says that or anything like it, I will probably cry.

Lucky for us both, he doesn't. I stop for a photo of the border and the first American flag I've ridden under in a very long time. It's good to be home.

Early June must be bug hatching season in northern Montana, and this year's crop must be a record-breaker. I have to stop and wash my visor a few times today, but the changing altitude and roads means it won't last long.

We make our way south to Great Falls and then through Lewis and Clark National Forest to White Sulphur Springs and on to Livingston before turning toward Red Lodge. It's a fun, western town, that's the perfect place to spend a night before making our way up the mountain to Beartooth Pass in the morning.

A series of enormous switchbacks carries us up and over the mountains on the very edge of Montana to the Wyoming border high above. I stop to feed the chipmunks at a scenic overlook and get some cute photos of them nosing right up to my camera lens. It's a gorgeous sunny day, which makes the fields of deeply packed snow glare blindingly. While the road surface is dry, I can clearly see the recent path created by a snowplow. Walls of snow nearly ten feet high line both sides of the highway. Two ice climbers practice their craft on a cliff edge as we pass.

At the Top of the World Café we stop for a hot cocoa and to watch more chipmunks before descending the scenic Chief Joseph Highway into Cody for a late lunch. Strangers buy our meal when they ask where we rode from and are surprised by our story.

We ride to Worland and through a section of construction into Ten Sleep. I'm reminded of the old joke that we have two seasons in this part of the world, winter and construction.

The highway runs through a scenic red and gold canyon as it leads east from Ten Sleep and then climbs up and over the Bighorn

Mountains. Storm clouds cluster overhead. I pull over and get my tank bag cover out and zip up. We're going to get wet.

First come the little gentle drops of rain, followed by a light round of sleet. The higher we climb, and the closer to the storm clouds we get, the heavier the rain becomes, but it's manageable. The road gently winds its way through mountaintop meadows that seem to chain together in a neverending series of vistas. When I first crest the range and round a bend, I spy a faint rainbow up ahead in the meadow. Falling back to a habit from childhood, I look to see where it ends, and find that it arches perfectly to land fittingly on the road in front of me. The rainbow stays just ahead of me for the next six miles, always landing on the road.

The closer we get to my "neck of the woods", the harder it is to slow down or even think about stopping for a night, but there's no way we can cover the distance in a single day. Besides, we have a date in Buffalo, Wyoming tonight.

Luke, a rider from Montana, contacted me late last year when he was beginning his journey by motorcycle to South America. Brian and I hoped to cross paths with him in southern Argentina or even Ushuaia, but it didn't work out. He's returned to his home and job in Montana and has offered to drive down to Buffalo to have dinner with us, which sounds great.

It's wonderful to hear Luke's stories of South American riding. We find we had many of the same experiences. He treats us to dinner, and then sets up his tent next to ours at a campground nearby. In the morning, it's all I can do to focus on packing up and saying our goodbyes. After all, I'm going home today.

I'm filled with a mixture of emotions. My Type A personality is overjoyed at putting a bow on this trip, if nothing else, for making it home in one titanium-filled piece. But that's tempered with an equal dose of dread at what the transition will be like. Many friends and fellow travelers that we know have had a rough time of it, and we know very well there will be a lot of adjustments to make.

Helmet thoughts:

- The Black Hills look smaller, and somehow larger, than when I last saw them so many months ago. They look good, green and healthy. It's comforting to see places I know and love. Places where I spent time and created memories.
- I spy Devils Tower off in the distance and am again, as always, reminded of the Spielberg movie, Close Encounters.
- Why do I so often have two feelings about many things? I'm happy and excited to see family and friends, and sad to think of not being on the road. I already miss my road family, all the friends we have enjoyed so much over the past two years.
- For a split second I wonder if I know where my house key is, thinking I will need it to get back home. But then I remember. That home is gone. And I will have to make another for myself. I sigh a momentary sigh of sadness at the loss of my former happy life, before exhaling it and inhaling the optimism that fills my hope for whatever new life I make for myself.
- Rocky Raccoon by the Beatles lingers on my mind as we ride. "Now somewhere in the Black Mountain Hills of Dakota…"
- I can't wait to hike Bear Butte and Harney Peak. I can't wait to go for a drive through the Badlands, and ride Iron Mountain Road and Needles Highway.
- Am I wearing wings? I feel like I'm floating today.
- Achoo! Oh, yeah. Forgot about the sweet clover.
- Seriously?! How can a 200mile ride feel like it's taking forever?

I've reached out to a friend who offered me a job when I was in Newfoundland and now have one waiting for me whenever I want it, which will likely be a couple of months from now. My dad's girlfriend has offered us a place to stay with them for a few days when we get back. My friend, Jen, has agreed to take us in for longer, allowing us a lovely guest room in her home, until we get incomes and plans in place for the longer term.

I haven't even begun to think about any of the bigger picture. I'm still very much living in the moment, a skill I've refined during my journey, and will worry about the details later. For now, I'm just excited by the chance to see my family and friends and the thought of having a hot shower, getting a good night's sleep and washing some clothes.

The half-day ride from Buffalo to Sturgis seems to take a lifetime, and isn't helped by my stopping for photos at the state line and a few road signs along the way. We turn off the interstate and ride up Sturgis' Main Street before carrying on to Piedmont.

We park the bikes under the shade of a pine tree and stretch our legs. Dad and Fran welcome us with a round of hugs and cold beers, just my kind of greeting. After catching up for half an hour, Brian and I retrieve some gear from the bike and go settle into the guest room to change into more comfortable clothes and take a breath.

As is often my habit, I stand in front of him with my arms outstretched, my way of asking for a hug. He obliges me, as usual, pulling me into his warm, strong embrace. I whisper, "Thank you."

"For what?"

"For getting me home safely and for taking me on the adventure of a lifetime." I relax further into him and breathe deeply. "Where to next?

ACKNOWLEDGMENTS

I owe an eternity of gratitude to whatever force in the Universe allowed me to cross paths with some of the most amazing women I could ever hope to find. I love them all.

Grandma, thank you for being my rock, my roots and my wings, my home, and my inspiration, always.

Heather, thank you for being my soul mate, my travel companion, my teacher and guru, and my best friend "Heater" for the past twenty years. I've always aspired to be more like you.

Megan, thank you for your friendship, for doing all the behind-the-scenes work that allowed me to take this trip, for sharing the gift of motherhood with me and for being one of the most incredible people I know.

Jennifer, thank you for being a wonderful friend, for leading me into the world of adventure, for encouraging and supporting me before, during and after my trip, and for giving me a soft place to land.

ABOUT THE AUTHOR

Michelle Lamphere was born and raised in South Dakota. She earned her B.S. in Business Administration and Accounting from Black Hills State University in Spearfish, South Dakota, and began a 20-year career in the hospitality industry, including serving on several local, state, regional and national boards of directors while nursing a severe case of wanderlust through a sprinkling of short vacations each year. She lives and works in South Dakota.

Michelle self-published a book on tips to use while traveling overland in Latin America in September 2015. The blog from her two years on the road can be found at www.SturgisChick.com.

63273307R00177

Made in the USA
Lexington, KY
03 May 2017